THE THEOLOGY OF THE LETTER TO THE GALATIANS

In his letter to the Galatians, Paul sets out an astute vision of what God has done in Christ against the backdrop of a world out of joint, a world engulfed in identity-distorting domination systems. Theologically profound and prophetically challenging, Galatians showcases God's initiative to empower liberation from those systems and their relational toxicity. For Paul, the union of Christ with his followers fosters flourishing forms of relational life that testify to the sovereign power of God over all competing forces. In *The Theology of the Letter to the Galatians*, respected New Testament scholar Bruce W. Longenecker cuts through the complexity of a notoriously opaque text, disentangling and interpreting Paul's discourse to reveal its multifaceted cosmology, its comprehensive coherence, and its penetrating analysis of humanity and the divine. Offering a new interpretation of Galatians, his volume synthesizes the best of four main interpretative alternatives, finding new solutions to scholarly gridlock.

Bruce W. Longenecker is the Melton Chair of Religion at Baylor University. He is the author of *In Stone and Story: Early Christianity in the Roman World*, coeditor (with David Wilhite) of *The Cambridge History of Ancient Christianity*, and editor of *The New Cambridge Companion to St. Paul* and *Greco-Roman Associations, Deities, and Early Christianity*.

"Outstanding! Deeply informed by recent scholarship, Longenecker provides an unmatched corrective lens on Galatians (and Paul) by refusing to fixate on a single interpretative approach (apocalyptic, "within Judaism," etc.) and, instead, by employing them all where appropriate. The result is clear, compelling, even captivating."

Douglas Harink, Professor Emeritus of Theology,
The King's University

"This outstanding companion to Galatians achieves the rare combination of being both accessible to students and stimulating to scholars. Longenecker's nuanced guide to Paul's argument and his rich exploration of Paul's theology brilliantly demonstrate the letter's power to challenge and inspire, in the first century and today."

Teresa Morgan, McDonald Agape Professor of New Testament and
Early Christianity,
Yale Divinity School

"Bruce Longenecker's fine reading of Galatians has the notable and nearly unique merit of staying close to Paul's message without a hint of the anti-Judaism that haunts so many (if not most) readings of Galatians. I applaud a genuine step forward."

Daniel Boyarin, Hermann P. and Sophia Taubman Professor
Emeritus of Talmudic Culture,
University of California, Berkeley

NEW NEW TESTAMENT THEOLOGY

The New New Testament Theology series will provide an up to date analysis of the theology in each book in the New Testament. Volumes will focus primarily on the theological content of the texts, with less emphasis on introductory matters, such as authorship or date, unless discussion of the theology hinges on such matters. Contributions will represent both established positions and original perspectives. Intended for use in upper division undergraduate and graduate courses, the New New Testament Theology series is ideal for classroom use.

GENERAL EDITOR
John Barclay
University of Durham

ASSOCIATE EDITORS
Ben C. Blackwell
Houston Baptist University
John K. Goodrich
Moody Bible Institute, Chicago
Jason Maston
Houston Baptist University

CONSULTANT EDITOR
Beverly Gaventa
Baylor University, Texas

TITLES IN THIS SERIES
The Theology of the Gospel of John Alicia D. Myers
The Theology of the Letter to the Galatians Bruce W. Longenecker

THE THEOLOGY OF THE LETTER TO THE GALATIANS

BRUCE W. LONGENECKER

Baylor University, Texas

Shaftesbury Road, Cambridge CB2 8EA, United Kingdom

One Liberty Plaza, 20th Floor, New York, NY 10006, USA

477 Williamstown Road, Port Melbourne, VIC 3207, Australia

314–321, 3rd Floor, Plot 3, Splendor Forum, Jasola District Centre, New Delhi – 110025, India

103 Penang Road, #05-06/07, Visioncrest Commercial, Singapore 238467

Cambridge University Press is part of Cambridge University Press & Assessment, a department of the University of Cambridge.

We share the University's mission to contribute to society through the pursuit of education, learning and research at the highest international levels of excellence.

www.cambridge.org
Information on this title: www.cambridge.org/9781108836968

DOI: 10.1017/9781108873208

© Cambridge University Press & Assessment 2025

This publication is in copyright. Subject to statutory exception and to the provisions of relevant collective licensing agreements, no reproduction of any part may take place without the written permission of Cambridge University Press & Assessment.

When citing this work, please include a reference to the DOI 10.1017/9781108873208

First published 2025

A catalogue record for this publication is available from the British Library

A Cataloging-in-Publication data record for this book is available from the Library of Congress

ISBN 978-1-108-83696-8 Hardback
ISBN 978-1-108-81948-0 Paperback

Cambridge University Press & Assessment has no responsibility for the persistence or accuracy of URLs for external or third-party internet websites referred to in this publication and does not guarantee that any content on such websites is, or will remain, accurate or appropriate.

For EU product safety concerns, contact us at Calle de José Abascal, 56, 1°, 28003 Madrid, Spain, or email eugpsr@cambridge.org

for Eric Howell and Jenny Howell
who live in ways that honor Paul's Galatian vision

and in honor of Elizabeth Käsemann (1947–1977)
who died in opposition to the grip of
the power of Sin upon the stoicheia *of Argentina*

Contents

PART I READING THE THEOLOGY OF GALATIANS

1 AN INTRODUCTION TO THE STUDY OF
   GALATIANS 3

2 AN OVERVIEW OF THE MESSAGE OF GALATIANS . . . 12

3 THE DISCURSIVE FLOW OF GALATIANS 24

PART II PROBING THE THEOLOGY OF GALATIANS

4 THE PROBLEM IN LAYERED PERSPECTIVE 67

5 THE TORAH IN LAYERED PERSPECTIVE 85

6 PARTICIPATION IN CHRIST AS POWER-VORTEX . . . 100

7 DECENTERING IDENTITY VALUES 114

8 THE SLAVERY OF CHRIST-GIVING LOVE 127

9 THE HOPE OF RIGHTEOUSNESS AND THE
   FAITHFULNESS OF GOD 141

PART III POSITIONING THE THEOLOGY
OF GALATIANS

10 GALATIANS AND THE NEW TESTAMENT 163

11 THE AFTERLIFE OF GALATIANS	176
12 WHAT PAUL MIGHT SAY	204
Appendix: Did Galatians Accomplish Paul's Purpose?	208
Suggestions for Further Reading	213
Bibliography	214
Index of Ancient Literature	241
Index of Authors and Names	249
Subject Index	252

PART I

Reading the Theology of Galatians

What is presented within the covers of this book follows the structure of the volumes in this series.* Part I establishes the context for reading the theology of Galatians. Part II explores the theological discourse of Galatians through selected themes of particular importance. Part III explores some ways that Paul's Galatian discourse pertains to other texts within the New Testament, outlines some ways that Galatians has been interpreted over the centuries, and offers a short prospectus for the contemporary challenge of Galatians.

Chapter 1 in this section introduces the occasion for Paul's writing of the Galatian letter, while Chapter 2 frames the main contours of the message of Galatians. A light overview of the flow of Galatians is offered in Chapter 3.

---

* My thanks to Ben Blackwell, John Barclay, and Jeff Hubbard for their invaluable suggestions for improving the presentation of this book.

CHAPTER 1

An Introduction to the Study of Galatians

Galatians was written when the world's population was probably around 60 million. According to common estimates, only about 1,400 of those people were Christ-followers, dotted around the Mediterranean basin in small groups of roughly two dozen to three dozen people. Some of those groups were based in the Roman province of Galatia, and to them Paul wrote this letter. Laser-focused in its vision, the letter's contents advance at a fast clip, and its discourse is powerfully unrelenting.

At the same time, this letter is anything but straightforward in its theological discourse. It is tremendously rich and densely packed, often ambiguous, sometimes with important aspects of the argument left unarticulated or extremely truncated. This is what makes the study of Galatians so intriguing for people who love the thrill of the chase, in a sense. It is also what makes some aspects of Paul's discourse in Galatians so resistant to simple takeaways. Theologically profound, conceptually complex, and prophetically challenging, the discourse of Galatians makes theological contributions not only with respect to what God has done in Christ but also with respect to what life looks like apart from that divine initiative. To understand the profundity of Paul's presentation of "the solution," we need also to understand the profundity of Paul's presentation of "the problem" that the solution corrects. For Paul, properly aligned relationships in Christ offset the relationality that characterizes "the present evil age" (Gal 1:4) – a toxic relationality in which forms of identity are prioritized over others, in endless cycles of social discord. Subsequent chapters of this book often explore Paul's presentation of the problem (especially Chapters 4 and 5) as much as his presentation of the solution of what God has done in Christ (Chapters 6 through 9).

Before looking in particular at Paul's theological discourse in this letter, it will be helpful to glance at the situation that he seems to be addressing.[1]

THE GOSPEL IN JEOPARDY

Paul's letter to the Christ-followers of Galatia is nestled within a context of his ministry of preaching the "good news," or gospel, in urban centers of the first-century world. It was a world where (as many Jews maintained) "pagan idolatry" was rampant. Where Paul's gospel was welcomed by gentiles, he expected them to abandon their entrenched idolatries and "serve the living and true God, waiting for his Son from heaven, whom God raised from the dead – Jesus, who will rescue us from the coming wrath" (1 Thess 1:9–10).

Paul often entered cities that were devoid of Christ-followers of any kind, since Christ-devotion had not yet arrived within their walls. Paul sometimes stayed in a city just long enough to establish

---

[1] Unless otherwise noted, all translations of Paul's Galatian letter are my own, from the Greek but often in consultation with academic commentaries and translations (in particular, the New Revised Standard Version [NRSV], the New International Version [NIV], the New English Translation [NET], and the Common English Bible [CEB]).

a small cohort of Christ-followers before moving on to another city. In Thessalonica and Philippi, for instance, he stayed perhaps only a few months. He stayed longer in other locations, but even then his residency was not protracted.[2] One way or another, Paul was often on the move again, articulating his message in the next rented workshop while plying his trade. By the time he wrote Romans (about 57 CE), he could say that he had "completed the circuit of preaching Christ's gospel from Jerusalem all the way around to Illyricum" (Rom 15:19, CEB).[3]

In the aftermath of his departure from any given city, small groups of a few dozen people met together to worship Jesus Christ in houses or workshops or apartments. In one sense, they did not have much to nurture their corporate life of Christ-devotion. There were no Christian publishing houses churning out devotional literature, or systematic theologies, or inspirational books of historical fiction. There were no websites to explain and promote devotion to Jesus Christ. There was no "back catalog" of traditional Christ hymns to draw upon and no long-standing reserves of Christian history to reflect upon. Although Christ-groups may often have had recourse to the scriptures of Israel in some fashion, perhaps not all were in that beneficial position. There wasn't even anything identifiably known as "Christianity" at that time (only messianic forms of Judaism that were often distinctive when judged by other ways of practicing Jewish ancestral traditions). All of these things would come later. Whenever Paul left a city to

---

[2] He seems to have stayed in Corinth for about a year and a half and in Ephesus for about two and a half years. For the chronology of Paul's life, four reconstructions are roughly similar and the most convincing: Riesner 1997:3–28, 318–26; Hengel and Schwemer 1997 (esp. xi–xiv); Wedderburn 2004 (esp. 99–103); Dunn 2009 (esp. 497–518).

[3] Illyricum is roughly equivalent to the territory of Bosnia and Croatia today.

move to the next, most Christ-groups would have very few resources to enhance the devotion of their corporate life. They will have had the memory of Paul's theological reflections on the story of Jesus Christ and perhaps (although we have no way of knowing this) a few sayings spoken by Jesus and (with even less certainty) a few selections of scripture that Paul had interpreted in the light of Jesus Christ (although some Christ-groups may have had copies of scripture made for them, or some of their members might also have attended Jewish synagogues, where the scriptures were read and expounded).

These resources are (historically speaking) scant and slender. But Paul had confidence, it seems, that these fledgling Christ-groups would survive and thrive after his departure, even though the time until the Lord's return might well be short (e.g., 1 Thess 4:17; 1 Cor 7:29; Rom 13:11–12). This confidence seems to have been based on little other than his belief that those groups were richly endowed with and empowered by the Holy Spirit – the Spirit of God that would resource and guide these small groups that were already enjoying eschatological blessings, even in the midst of their paltry numbers.

GALATIANS IN CONTEXT

Paul's confidence in the power of the Spirit seems to lie at the heart of the issue that Paul addresses in Galatians. In one of the clearest windows into the Galatian situation (3:1–5), Paul asks, "Does God supply you with the Spirit and accomplish powerful things among you on the basis of your observance of the Torah?" (3:5). Paul is certain that the Spirit has been "supplied" to the Galatians in powerful ways. But the Spirit becomes increasingly important throughout the remainder of the letter, as Paul focuses on the Spirit's role in the ongoing formation of the Galatian Christ-followers.

A strong case can be made that the situation in Galatia is driven by the Galatians' interest in preserving and enhancing the Spirit's presence among them.[4] The Galatians (or at least some of them) seem to have been under the impression that their experience of the Spirit needed to be protected (and perhaps enhanced) by means of observance of the Mosaic Torah – the faithful practice of following the instructions given by God to the ethnic people of Israel. This would ensure their protection from the ways of idolatry, immersing them in the people-group (the Jews) whose ideals of devotion to the one sovereign God often differentiated that group from the "polytheistic" nations all around them. If Christ-followers were called to turn "to God from idols," it would make sense if that rejection of idolatry necessarily involved adopting the ancestral traditions of the only ethnic group known to have rejected polytheistic idolatry: the Jewish people. Christ-devotion and Jewish practices could be seen as interlocking components of what nonidolatrous relationship with God through the Spirit looks like in the aftermath of the death and resurrection of Jesus Christ.

It made sense to (some of) the Galatian Christ-followers. But Paul saw things quite differently. For him, the Galatians' interest in circumcision (and, beyond that, the full observance of the Torah) was not in step with their worship of the one God. Instead, Paul saw it as "turning back" (4:9) into the situation out of which they had already been extracted. Embracing a distortion of the gospel, they were in danger of losing the Spirit altogether. This distortion had been conjured up by teachers who had

---

[4] Cosgrove 1988.

recently arrived in Galatia, intruding on Paul's relationship with the Galatians, who were being "compelled" (6:12) to adopt the teachers' point of view.

Who were these "new teachers" who had been "agitating" the situation (1:7)?[5] We have no information about them and their message apart from what we can glean from Paul's discourse in Galatians. From that, we can surmise that they had linked their case to the figure of Abraham, whose story is told in Genesis, and to the interpretation of passages from the Pentateuch that highlighted the necessity of observing the Torah – the Mosaic covenant between God and the people of Israel. That story and that covenant can easily be interpreted in ways that match the interests of the new teachers. In fact, Abraham was often considered the model par excellence of someone who did exactly what the Galatian gentiles had done – turning away from idolatry and adopting exclusive devotion to the one and only God (see *Jub* 12.1–21; Josephus, *Ant.* 1.155; *Apoc. Abr.* 1–8; Philo, *Virt.* 219).[6] But in turning away from "paganism," Abraham had also embraced certain practices as a consequence, including circumcision for himself and his male descendants. The new teachers were probably adept at interpreting scripture and saw direct lines of applicability from the Genesis account of Abraham to the life of Galatian Christ-followers. They were calling Christ-followers to a consistent form of life in relation to the story of Abraham, the ex-pagan whose obedience included the adoption of circumcision. Along with that, other passages in the Pentateuch make clear that observing the Torah is expected of all who trace their identity to

---

[5] I borrow the term "new teachers" from de Boer 2011.
[6] On the reception of the story of Abraham in Early Judaism, see Calvert-Koyzis 2004.

the blessed, nonidolatrous Abraham – both the specific practice of circumcision (e.g., Gen 17:9–14) and all other instructions spoken by the God of Abraham, Isaac, and Jacob as well (e.g., Lev 18:5; Deut 27:26). Abraham himself is said to have "obeyed my [God's] voice and kept my requirements, my commandments, my statutes, and my instructions" (Gen 26:5).[7] It is little wonder that Paul feels the need to engage with scripture repeatedly in Galatians 3–4. There he offers a novel interpretation of the Abraham story, together with other passages that, instead of supporting the view of the new teachers, are used to support the gospel that he had already proclaimed to the Galatians.[8]

It is possible that the new teachers were not overtly hostile to Paul. They may simply have thought that his gospel was an introductory version of the gospel for pagans, a version that merely needed to be supplemented by further efforts to take Christ-devotion to the next level. But it is also possible (and perhaps probable) that the new teachers sought to diminish Paul's influence by disparaging him and his message, characterizing him as a dangerous maverick beyond the controls of the leadership of the Christ-movement based in Jerusalem. Paul himself seems to imagine them having some animosity toward him (4:16–17), and his claim right at the start of the letter that he is not a "people-pleaser" (1:10) may have countered the way the new

---

[7] On this basis, some texts suggest that Abraham knew and observed the Torah (often understood as the Torah in truncated fashion) even before it was revealed to Moses. See *Jub* 15.1–2; 16.28; Sir 44.19–20; 2 Bar 57.1–3; *CD* 3:2–4; Philo, *Abr.* 275–76.

[8] For reconstructions of the message of the new teachers, see Martyn 1997a:117–26; Hurd 2005; de Boer 2011:50–61; Fredriksen 2017:102–7; deSilva 2018:16–26; Keener 2019:31–36; Bachmann 2021. On the availability of scriptural knowledge among the Galatians, see Abasciano 2007.

teachers depicted him – also explaining his rather aggressive rhetoric toward them (see 5:12 and 6:12–13). Along the way, Paul's discourse includes reframing the legitimacy of Jerusalem-based leaders of the Christ-movement (1:15–20; 2:1–10; 2:11–14; 4:21–31), with whom the new teachers were evidently aligning themselves. The new teachers may even have wanted gentile Christ-followers to adopt Torah observance so the good news of Jesus Christ might be more compelling as the Jerusalem assembly took that news to Jews, not least to Jews in Jerusalem, where the temple of Israel's God was standing.

A few years after Paul left the Galatian Christ-groups, word got back to him that those communities (or at least some of their members) were enamored with the message of the new teachers. Messengers must have left the Galatian communities and traveled for several weeks to reach Paul (whether in the city of Ephesus in, say, 54/55, or, much more likely, in the city of Corinth in 50/51). Upon hearing the news, Paul decided to write and give guidance to the Galatians. In his emotional letter, Paul writes at times as if the Galatians are still considering whether to adopt observance of the Torah at some point in the future (5:2–3; 6:12; perhaps 1:6; 4:21) and at other times as if they have already done so (4:10; perhaps 5:4, 7). These two forms of discourse might suggest that the Galatians had adopted certain practices already (such as the observance of certain Jewish festivals, as in 4:10) but not circumcision itself (as in 5:2–3). Or perhaps members of the Galatian communities were at different stages in their adoption of Torah observance, with some already having gone fully down that road and others lagging behind in certain respects.

Scholars continue to debate matters that are not necessary to determine for the purposes of this book (with its focus on Paul's theological discourse). In what cities were the Galatians resident?[9] How does Paul's account of events in Galatians relate to the origins story recounted in Acts?[10] More can be done to press into these intricacies, but that is not necessary for the purposes of this book. So we move from this brief overview of the Galatian situation to an overview of Paul's message to the Galatians.

---

[9] For recent contrasting arguments, see John 2022 (south Galatia) and Coşkun 2022 (north Galatia). See also Sanders 2015:749-77; deSilva 2018:39-48; Keener 2019:16-22.

[10] See deSilva 2018:33-38.

CHAPTER 2

An Overview of the Message of Galatians

In this letter, Paul seeks to convince Galatian Christ-groups, whose members were (primarily?) gentiles, that their profound experience of the Spirit is not protected by adopting practices of Jewish covenantal identity. Instead, their trust in Jesus Christ continues to be all that they need in order to preserve the blessings of their intimate and nonidolatrous relationship with the God who is exclusively sovereign above all forms of spiritual power. Making a legitimate micro-identity within Christ-groups (i.e., Jewish identity) into a necessary macro-identity of all Christ-followers will only disrupt the blessedness the Galatians have already experienced. There is only one legitimate macro-identity of Christ-followers – that is, being found in Christ, participating in his death and resurrection. Requiring any other form of identity to be necessary (in this case, adopting "the works of the Torah" as a beachhead position against encroaching idolatry) does nothing to enhance the situation; instead, it nullifies the whole thing in a single stroke. To postulate that gentile Jesus-followers must observe the Torah undermines the essential character of trust – a trust that is status-vacant and configured solely in relation to Christ.

Here's why. In co-crucifixion with Christ, the identities of Christ-followers are reanimated by the power of God through the Spirit of the self-giving Christ. In co-crucifixion with Christ, the reign of the cosmic power of Sin over people and people-groups is annulled, breaking the grip of that suprahuman force that props up the self-fascination, the self-infatuation, and ultimately the self-idolatry that promotes a realm of relational chaos – what Paul calls "the present evil age" (1:4). Living by the Spirit puts an end to the caustic self-intoxication and pernicious self-involvement evident in the lives of people individually and people-groups collectively. By the Spirit, patterns of the self-giving Christ take shape in the lives of Christ-followers, who are incorporated into the power-vortex of Jesus Christ's death and resurrection. When Christ-followers die with Christ, they die to their various enslavements under Sin. As Christ comes alive in them, the Spirit empowers new patterns of life – "new creation" (6:15), with Christ-followers enslaving themselves to others in lives of mutual, beneficial flourishing. Those new forms of "Christ-full" relationality testify to what the Galatians most desire: the continuing presence of the Spirit in their midst. As people of trust in Jesus Christ (who was himself the "progeny of Abraham," 3:16), Christ-followers are righteous in the eyes of God, enlivened by the power of the Spirit, and incorporated into Abraham's progeny. As they walk by the Spirit in patterns of Christ-likeness, their corporate and (thereby) their individual lives become the arena in which eschatological power is manifest, in "the hope of righteousness" (5:5) and the manifestation of "the kingdom of God" (5:21).

Paul unpacks this theological vision in thirteen interlocking text units throughout the letter, as follows:

1:1–9	Outlining Stories of God, Authority, and the Galatian Communities
1:10–24	Impressions of Esteem, the Exalted Son of God, and Apostolic Legitimacy

2:1–10	Affirming "the Truth of the Gospel" by Apostolic Agreement
2:11–21	Affirming "the Truth of the Gospel" in Theological Discourse
3:1–9	The Spirit, Trust, Scripture, and the Cross, #1
3:10–14	The Spirit, Trust, Scripture, and the Cross, #2
3:15–29	Abraham's Progeny, the Torah, the Power of Sin, and Christ
4:1–11	Divine Sending and Redemption from the Slavery of the *Stoicheia*
4:12–20	A Theological Inventory of a Relationship
4:21–31	Abraham's Progeny and the Direct Speech of Scripture
5:1–12	Circumcision and the Work of Trust
5:13–6:10	Moral Character, the Spirit, and the Propensity toward Self-Centered Living
6:11–18	Social Reputation, the Cross, and New Creation

THE FOCUS OF THIS INTERPRETATION

In this interpretation of Galatians, I do not subscribe to any single "school of interpretation."[1] The reading that appears within this book overlaps with various interpretations of Paul's theology in general – "traditional" readers, "apocalyptic" readers, "new perspective" readers, and "radical new perspective" readers (more on these later). While there is breadth and diversity within each of these four interpretative approaches, most approaches have also spawned "perfected" readings of Galatians that tend to squeeze out alternatives. In my view, Paul's discourse resists that pressure. Consequently, I do not subscribe to a "perfected" interpretation within any one of these approaches but instead adopt a more

---

[1] Nor do I force my interpretation to conform to arguments I may have made in the past.

nuanced approach. In my view, four aspects of Paul's theological convictions give each of these four interpretative approaches a legitimate foothold (to one degree or another) in the interpretation of Galatians:

1. Paul believed that all individuals are in a calamitous situation before God, due to the erring of (what might be called) "the propensities of the human heart" or "the human condition." Accordingly, my reading frequently aligns with traditional (or Lutheran) readings that place the individual's relationship with God front and center – not least in terms of "the hope of righteousness" (5:5).[2]
2. Paul held that individuals beyond "in Christ" communities are locked within larger systems that form their identities in fundamentally unhealthy ways. These identity-forming systems are what Paul calls the *stoicheia* of the world (4:3, 9). Paul uses this Greek expression as a way of capturing the sense that a person's identity is never solely the product of that person's own determining but is also influenced by overarching forces that shape identity. Those "identity influencers" may not be unhealthy in and of themselves, but they become unhealthy influences (and so they become *stoicheia*) when manipulated by yet another phenomenon that Paul sees at work in the world: "the power of Sin." This is a cosmic force beyond the *stoicheia*, a force that stands hawkishly over identities, relationships, and institutions, having them all firmly in its grasp. This includes people individually as well as whole people-groups. The phrase "all things" that Paul

---

[2] See further Westerholm 2003 and 2013. For a discussion of the use of descriptors for this approach, see Prothro 2016b.

says are "under the power of Sin" (3:22) includes even the *stoicheia* that structure identities. My reading, consequently, often meshes with interpreters of "the apocalyptic Paul," who highlight the situatedness of individuals and people-groups (and even God's good creation) under the influence of suprahuman forces.[3]

3. Paul frequently articulates his discourse in relation to the identities of different people-groups, different ethnicities – probing the character of relationships between people-groups both within Christ-groups and (contrastingly) beyond them. This is not sociology on Paul's part; this is theology applied to the way Christ-followers live in relation to others. This aspect of Paul's agenda is clearly indicated by his description of "Jews by nature" and "gentile sinners" (2:15) and pertains to his vision of diverse Christ-followers supporting each other through the patterned practices derived from Christ's own pattern of life. So, my reading at times intersects with the "new perspective" on Paul, especially in those places where he wrestles with the difficult issues of ethnic differences within the unified body of Christ.[4]

4. Paul's letter to the Galatians should be understood, historically speaking, as situated within the broad spectrum of Jewish discourse about God's grace and God's messiah.[5] We can say

---

[3] See in particular Martyn 1997a and 1997b; de Boer 2011 and 2020.

[4] Early articulations of this appear in Dunn 1993a and 1993b. A much different approach appears in Wright 2021. The foundations for these scholars were laid by Stendahl 1976.

[5] On Paul and grace, see Barclay 2015 (compare undeveloped articulations along similar lines in B. Longenecker 1991:18–19, 31–33). On theological scaffolding for Christ-devotion within Jewish traditions, see Segal 1977; Boyarin 2012; Schäfer 2020.

that it is one particular expression of and within the Judaism of his day. Moreover (and importantly, in light of the use of Paul's letters in some later periods of history), Paul was not in the business of denouncing Jewish identity in general or eradicating Jewish practices from Christ-groups in particular. If a son had been born to him after his "Damascus Road experience," Paul would have circumcised him and taught him to observe the Torah, as well as raising him to worship Jesus the messiah and exalted Lord. The charge that Paul teaches Jews "to reject Moses" and "not to circumcise their children nor to live according to our [Jewish] customs" (Acts 21:21) is shown by the author of Acts to be an incorrect understanding of Paul's gospel (Acts 21:18-26). Paul's own autobiography in 2 Cor 11:22-33 recalls his experience of receiving the thirty-nine lashes of synagogue discipline on five occasions (11:24) – a discipline meted out by Jews upon fellow Jews perceived to need correction within, not ejection from, the synagogue assembly. Especially when we study a text like Galatians, we need to recognize that Paul did not denounce Torah observance for Jewish Christ-followers. I will say more about this in due course. Here it is enough to note my affinity with the so-called radical new perspective interpretation, which has recently articulated this point better than other interpretative approaches (although not without precedent from others within alternative approaches). As Luther upheld, Paul "did not reject circumcision as a damnable thing, neither did he by word or deed enforce the Jews to forsake it."[6]

---

[6] Luther 1953:94. Another interest of the "radical new perspective" is the view that "Paul continued to live a basically Jewish lifestyle" (R. Longenecker 1990:

Of course, precisely because of my eclectic interpretation, the most committed representatives from each camp will find my interpretation disappointing, since at times they will think I don't go far enough down their respective trajectories. In my view, however, while each of these interpretative approaches has at least a foothold within the theological convictions of Galatians (and often more than a foothold), each approach can also over-read the text if it is not held in tension with the others.

FINE-TUNING THE FOCUS

One aspect of Galatians needs to be given further precision in this regard, precisely because it is a locus for creative tension within Paul's theological discourse: the issue of Jewish observance of the Torah within Christ-groups. In point 4 of the previous section I noted that Paul was not intent on denouncing Torah observance for ethnic Jews. Paul did not oppose the presence of Jewish identity within groups of Christ-followers. When Paul says "neither Jew nor Greek" in Gal 3:28, for instance, he is affirming the

> xcviii; see also his 1964:245–63 = 2015:225–42). (Against reading 1 Cor 9:19–23 to the contrary, see Bockmuehl 2000:171.) Those adopting the "radical new perspective" as their sole interpretative lens have more recently preferred to label their approach as the "Paul within Judaism" interpretation (frequently associated with the work of Ehrensperger [2019], Fredriksen [2017], Nanos [2002, 2017], Novenson [2022, 2024], Thiessen [2016, 2023], and Zetterholm [2016, 2020]). This is a somewhat unfortunate term when used to describe a particular way of reading Paul, however, not least since the same conviction (that Paul was "within Judaism") easily characterizes a much wider canvas of interpretations than those who claim the title (see, for instance, B. Longenecker 2010:14, 204–6, 299–300). But if their efforts are successful in invigorating a widespread respect for understanding Paul within his Jewish context, one might echo Paul's words of Phil 1:18: "I'm glad and I'll continue to be glad."

respective places of Jews and Greeks, as Jews and as Greeks, within Christ-groups. Although Jewish identity is not to be universalized within the diversity of Christ-groups, neither is Jewish identity unwanted or an embarrassment within Christ-groups.

The point might gain clarity by considering other forms of ethnic identity in relation to Christ-devotion. There were many ethnic groups in Paul's world. These included, for instance, ethnic Egyptians, ethnic Armenians, ethnic Gauls, and so on. Paul was not opposed to Christ-followers being Egyptians or Armenians or Gauls. He did not want Egyptian Christ-followers to stop being Egyptians, Armenians to stop being Armenians, Gauls to stop being Gauls, and so on. In the same way, he did not expect Jewish Christ-followers to stop being Jewish. In fact, his corporate vision of Christ-groups required their very presence within the Christ-movement. In a later letter, Paul says his "rule in all the assemblies of Christ" is that Jews should continue to observe the Torah (1 Cor 7:17–20). In context he is referring to the practice of circumcision, but we may reasonably presume that the rule applies more generally: Jews ought to continue to be Jews who continue to observe the Torah. In fact, in an even later letter Paul goes out of his way to affirm Jewish presence as necessary to the integrity of what God is doing within Christ-groups (see the discussion of Romans 11 and 14–15 in Chapter 7). Whenever Jews put their trust in Jesus Christ, Paul did not expect them to renounce their observance of the Mosaic Torah.

Paul's discourse in Galatians, then, should not be read as an attempt to eradicate Torah observance from all Christ-groups. His discourse is directed to a separate issue altogether – the question of whether *gentile* Christ-followers should be adopting Torah observance. Paul's answer, of course, is an uncompromising no. Disallowing Torah observance for one sector and allowing it for another is where the creative tension of Paul's discourse often lies. Paul deals with the complexities of his vision by, in effect, differentiating between two levels of identity: a "macro-level" and a "micro-level." In this regard, Torah observance is legitimate for Jews in their micro-level identity in Christ, but Torah observance should never be moved to the macro-level position of being necessary to the identity of Christ-followers before God.

This places significant interpretative constraints on what we should expect to see in Galatians. In Gal 2:19, Paul says that he has "died to the Torah." Paul is not simply speaking of his own experience in this verse but uses himself as emblematic of what Jewish identity in Christ is to look like. So how does dying to the Torah interface with maintaining Jewish identity, even in Christ? Although Paul has died to the Torah, there is nonetheless a sense in which the identity reinforced by the Torah (Jewish identity in distinction to all others) can continue to exist even in Christ, as long as it is not understood to be essential to the identity of those in Christ.

We need, then, to be able to articulate a way in which dying to the Torah is allowed its full, shocking force without simultaneously allowing that statement to preclude Torah observance for ethnic Jews in Christ. The key, I think, is to properly conceptualize the problem that God sets right in Christ. That problem includes two interrelated phenomena: both (1) the power of Sin (which Paul refers to in 2:17 and 3:22) and (2) the so-called *stoicheia* of the world (which Paul refers to in 4:3 and 4:9). As we'll see, by differentiating these phenomena, a path opens up for seeing how Paul can affirm a dying to the Torah while also maintaining the integrity of Christ-groups as comprised of both Jews (who continue to observe the Torah) and non-Jews (who don't).

TERMS OF ENGAGEMENT

Precisely because of the complexities of Paul's discourse in Galatians, there is much more to be said on these matters. Those things will be articulated in the chapters that follow. Here, however, I highlight three terminological choices that characterize my engagement with Galatians.

First, I will regularly translate the Greek word *nomos* as "Torah." Traditionally this word is translated as "law." That is an acceptable translation, of course, but there are some downsides to that translational choice that are avoided by defaulting to "Torah" instead.[7] In Galatians, Paul predominantly uses the word *nomos* to reference "the Mosaic covenant," with its instructions being given as a way of ordering the corporate life of the ethnic people of Israel in distinction from the other nations.[8]

Second, I will regularly translate the Greek word *pistis* as "trust" and its verbal form (*pisteuein*) as "to have trust in." Traditionally these words are translated as "faith" and "to believe." Those are acceptable translations, of course, but there has recently been some pushback against them since "belief" is often heard as prioritizing content ("doctrinal beliefs"), as if Paul just wants Christ-followers to hold certain cognitive "doctrines" – propositions to which they

---

[7] The term "law" often has a "legalistic" resonance. Moreover, that translation too easily opens the door to interpretations where the issue Paul addresses in Galatians is seen as "law-ness" per se, rather than Torah observance.

[8] Paul's use of *nomos* may not reference the Mosaic Torah in a few passages. In 3:21, the second of three occurrences of *nomos* refers to "a collection of instructions" in general. In 4:21, the second of two occurrences of *nomos* is unpacked in relation to the Abraham narrative of Genesis, not the Mosaic covenant; Paul pivots in 4:30 to call this "scripture." In 3:10, Paul's phrase "the book of the Torah" seems to reference the Pentateuch that contains the Torah. Debated in this regard is Paul's mention of the "*nomos* of Christ" in 6:2.

simply give intellectual assent. While there is certainly a content to Paul's gospel, in Paul's world the word *pistis* was primarily a term of relationship, whose nuances are often better captured by words like "trust" (in a trustworthy God) or "loyalty."[9] In Galatians, "trust" usually captures Paul's relational sense quite well.[10]

Third, in this book I use the terms "Judaism," "Jews," and "Jewish." Certain scholars have recently helped us to think of Paul's ethnic people as "Judeans."[11] Just as Egyptians retained their ethnic status no matter where they lived in the Mediterranean basin, or Armenians as people of Armenia no matter where they resided, so too the ethnic people who observed the Torah of Moses retained their ethnic status as "Judeans" no matter how far-flung they were from the Judean homeland. In this light, the best term for the ancestral practices of Paul's ethnic people should be "Judeanism," with that people-group being "Judeans" who live by "Judean" practices. What then of the "Judaism" that Paul speaks of in Gal 1:13–14? There he highlights his days "in Judaism" prior to his encounter with his risen Lord. Not long in existence prior to Paul's day, the word "Judaism" was sometimes used to signal the attempt undertaken by self-selecting Jews to preserve Judean identity by pushing back against the influx of pagan influences among the Judean people (2 Macc 2:21; 8:1; 14:38). Paul's use of the term in 1:13–14 seems to resonate best with that meaning. It references a posture of strident defense adopted by Paul and other Judeans to maintain the

---

[9] See especially Morgan 2015.
[10] One exception is in 1:23, where the word *pistis* refers to "the faith" (= the gospel) that Paul now proclaims.
[11] See especially Esler 2003:63–74; Mason 2007; 2021; Mason and Esler 2017. For discussion, see Law and Halton 2014.

distinctive identity of the Judean covenant people.¹² "Judaism" was, then, a phenomenon within "Judeanism." While I think this is generally correct, I have nonetheless abandoned my initial attempt to stick to these terms within this book, since they seemed at times to require too much clarification along the way, or they got in the way of the discourse. So I have reverted to standard terms that, to a certain extent, are less satisfactory historically even though they are functionally easier to use in a project such as this.

The next chapter offers an overview of the flow of Paul's discourse in Galatians, where trust in Jesus Christ is interpreted in stunning theological complexity and uncompromising focus.

---

¹² See, for instance, Novenson 2014; deSilva 2018:140-41; Keener 2019:78-79.

CHAPTER 3

The Discursive Flow of Galatians

Galatians divides well into thirteen interlocking units of text (as outlined in Chapter 2). Here, we follow the flow of Paul's presentation of how the gospel addresses the situation of the Galatian Christ-groups.

1:1–9: OUTLINING STORIES OF GOD, AUTHORITY, AND THE GALATIAN COMMUNITIES

The opening paragraph of the letter foregrounds the essentials of what might be thought of as two narratives: the narrative of what God has done in Christ and the narrative of Paul's apostleship. In Paul's mind, however, these narratives are inextricably interlocked. In fact, the task of demonstrating this tight narratival interlock lies close to the heart of Paul's theological discourse in Galatians, to the extent that even allocating them as separable narratives runs the risk of misunderstanding their essential character as two components of the same story of God's action in Christ. Paul's adventurous theological discourse and his bold interpretations of scripture in later sections of the letter are licensed by the knowledge that the story of his apostleship is rooted within the larger story of what God has done in Christ.

Paul was eager to demonstrate that his apostleship had nothing to do with "human" commissioning. He was not accountable to important figureheads, nor was he an emissary acting on behalf of a group of people or a community; instead, his apostleship was rooted in a divine commissioning (1:1). Of course, any wild maverick could claim divine commissioning. This is probably why other senders of the letter are listed in 1:2: "all those 'brothers and sisters' [*adelphoi*] who are with me." These people are not coauthors of the letter, but their "presence" in the letter's occasion testifies to the fact that, as he writes the letter, Paul is embedded in a community of Christ-followers who recognize his apostolic authority (probably in Corinth in 50 or 51).

From the start, Paul highlights the power of God, exhibited most evidently in the astounding resurrection of the crucified Jesus Christ by God the Father (1:1). As the resurrected one, Jesus Christ is also identified explicitly in terms of his self-giving on the cross (1:4). This characteristic, the offering of himself, will become a key feature in the moral discourse of Galatians. This self-giving of Jesus Christ was "according to the will of our God and Father" for the purpose of delivering "us from this present evil age" (1:4). The present age is said to be evil not simply because of "our sins" (which Paul clearly references, 1:4) but because life in this age is formed by a "suprahuman" dimension of existence that ensures that sinfulness will arise within and among all people. This is not articulated at this point in the letter, but it is something that Paul will elaborate further in Galatians.

The first thing Paul says directly to the Galatians is "grace to you and peace from God our Father and the Lord Jesus Christ" (1:3). Although his tone will soon change to one that chastises the Galatians, he nonetheless roots that change of tone firmly in a recognition of something that they all share in Christ: grace and peace. In fact, Galatians has an *inclusio* (that is, a shared feature at the beginning and the end) that builds on the word "grace," with the letter closing with the words, "the grace of our Lord Jesus Christ be with your spirit" (6:18). This closing benediction, "with your spirit," couples a plural possessive adjective ("your") and a singular noun ("spirit"). It is not too much to think that Paul sees his letter as being addressed to the "spirit" of the Galatian Christ-groups – almost a corporate personality or their collective identity. For Paul, the outpouring of divine grace is always intensely personal but never intensely individualistic; it envelops the whole of one's life in every regard and therefore is always relational in its impact. This is what Paul's benediction seems to signal: The letter is ultimately intended to reconfigure the relational interactions among the Galatian Christ-followers, in conformity to the character of the one who gave himself.

If the first paragraph of Paul's opening (1:1–5) captures the essentials of Paul's gospel as it pertains to the Galatian situation, the second paragraph (1:6–9) explores the flip side: the need for Paul to write the letter, precisely because so much has gone wrong in Galatia. Quite simply, it is here that Paul highlights how the Galatians are "deserting the one who called you" by following the so-called gospel proclaimed by others.

1:10–24: IMPRESSIONS OF ESTEEM, THE EXALTED SON OF GOD, AND APOSTOLIC LEGITIMACY

In 1:10, Paul elaborates further on the legitimacy of his apostleship. An apostle is not to play the role of being a "pleaser of people" – telling people things they want to hear in order to conjure adulation from them. Instead of being a people-pleaser,

Paul insists that he is enslaved to his master, Christ (1:10), an emphasis that reappears at the end of the letter, where Paul draws attention to the "marks [*stigmata*] of Jesus on my body" (6:17). This must reference scars from being beaten by those who opposed his message (see 2 Cor 11:23–25) – scars that serve as signs that he is "branded" as a slave of Jesus.

Paul's self-identification as a slave of Christ may have had particular resonance in his culture. Some enslaved people in the ancient world were tasked with representing their enslavers, embodying their power and authority in particular contexts (e.g., in business transactions, household management). This theme sets the context for interpreting Paul's tenacious actions in defense of the truth (as Paul will outline in 2:1–14) and helps explain the unyielding tone of the current letter.

In 1:11–17 Paul offers a narrative of how his encounter with the risen Lord disrupted the course of his life and reshaped his identity. Prior to that encounter, Paul shows himself to have been "militant [*zēlōtēs*] about the traditions of my ancestors" (1:14, CEB). If anyone could claim to have known what it means to live according to ancestral traditions, it was Paul, who points out that he outshone his contemporaries in that regard. But it isn't only nomistic observance that Paul seems to be referencing when speaking of his life "in Judaism." Being "in Judaism" is Paul's way of speaking about a posture of doing everything to guard the ethnic people of Israel from the influx of pagan influence. Paul had involved himself "in the effort against the erosion of Jewish identity" (= *en tō Ioudaismō*, 1:13–14; see 2 Macc 2:21; 8:1; 14:38). There are some commonalities between what Paul had done prior to his christophanic experience and what the new teachers were doing in Galatia. Paul probably expected these parallels to be noted by his Galatian audience.

What interrupted Paul's life story was a "revelation of Jesus Christ" (1:12) – not least, a revelation that Jesus Christ had been resurrected (1:1) and exalted to the heavenly throne (e.g., Phil 2:9–11). Although Paul was the recipient of revelational content that God had revealed to him, the way he speaks of this event permits the possibility of understanding it along other lines too. It was a revelation "to me" and/or "in me" – the Greek of 1:16 (*en emoi*) allows either, and so perhaps both. In that case, the revelation was not solely a moment of enlightenment that changed Paul's worldview; it was also a moment of enlivenment that transformed Paul to be a bearer of Jesus Christ, as the enlivened Jesus Christ was impressed within Paul's own identity.

Intimacy with a deity was a common interest among certain forms of ancient cultic devotion (not least devotion to some mystery deities). But Paul does not depict the moment of revelational enlightenment and intimacy as the crowning capstone of his private devotional interests. Instead, the revelation of God's Son propelled Paul into service as an apostle in the public sphere. Like the prophets Isaiah and Jeremiah, Paul understood himself to have been tasked with a mission to the gentile nations (1:15–16; see Isa 49:1, 5–6; Jer 1:4–5). Paul again emphasizes that his mission had nothing to do with human initiatives. Outlining his movements in the early years after encountering his risen Lord, Paul notes that he did not immediately rush to Jerusalem in order to learn from Christ-followers, and even when he did go to Jerusalem much later, his involvements there were minimal (as evidenced in his interactions only with Peter and James). Even so, Christ-followers there gave glory to God when they heard that Paul "now proclaims the faith that he once tried to destroy" (1:23).

If Paul is the central human character in this autobiographical sketch, as of 1:18 Peter enters the narrative to become the clear "supporting" character, with the narrative increasingly focusing on him as it gets closer to its climax in 2:15-21. In the process, Peter's character is shown to be ironic. On the one hand, he is someone in a position of authority within the Christ-movement. On the other hand, despite his involvement in authoritative decisions about the identity of Christ-followers and despite being entrusted with taking the gospel to the Jews (2:1-10), Peter is depicted as falling into error due to social pressures from Christ-followers (2:1-14) who, themselves, fail to understand the depths of the significance of what God has done in Christ. Paul wants the Galatians to watch this narrative keenly, recognizing something of their own story within Peter's deteriorating storyline. In the process, Paul weaves a narrative that depicts Jewish Christ-followers trying to "compel" gentile Christ-followers into adopting Jewish practices – something that shows up twice within Peter's supporting storyline and, obviously, the Galatians' storyline as well (compare Paul's use of "compel" or "force" in 2:3, 14, and 6:12).

2:1-10: AFFIRMING "THE TRUTH OF THE GOSPEL" BY APOSTOLIC AGREEMENT

In 2:1-10, Paul recounts an episode in which he went to Jerusalem for a discussion of a matter of theological urgency.[1] He makes it clear that he went not because the Jerusalem-based apostles had called on him to attend but because he had received a directive issued by God alone: "I went there in response to a revelation" from God (2:2).

---

[1] It is not wholly clear whether the phrase "after fourteen years" (2:1) dates from Paul's encounter with the risen Lord (in 1:15-16) or the three-year period mentioned in 1:18.

In Paul's account, three different groups were present at the consultation:

1. Paul, his mission partner Barnabas, and their associate Titus;
2. The "influential leaders" of the Christ-movement, who are named toward the end of the text unit as James (the brother of Jesus), Peter (who is also referred to by his Aramaic name, "Cephas"; see John 1:42),[2] and the apostle John; and
3. A group of unnamed Christ-followers, whom Paul calls "false" believers (2:4).

Paul's account suggests that the meeting was intended to be held privately between the first two groups, "to make sure that I wouldn't be working or hadn't worked for nothing" (2:2). While Paul tips his hat to the authority of Jerusalem-based influential leaders, it is hard to believe that he would have adjusted his message if they had disapproved of it.

Even though the discussion is being held in Jerusalem, the issue at stake is precisely the one the Galatians themselves were being faced with – whether circumcision should be expected of male gentile Christ-followers. And just as in the Galatian situation, there were some Christ-followers who were advocating precisely that at the Jerusalem meeting. Paul has nothing good to say about those people. They "were brought in secretly" in order "to spy on our freedom, which we have in Christ Jesus, and to make us slaves" (2:4). Paul indicates why the incident is important to the Galatians themselves in the middle of his account: "We didn't give in and submit to them for a single moment, so that the truth of the gospel would continue to be with you" (2:5).

---

[2] Paul uses Peter's Aramaic name in Gal 1:18; 2:9, 11, 14; 1 Cor 1:12; 3:22; 9:5; 15:5.

In this way, Paul expected the Galatians to draw a line of continuity from his defense of the "truth of the gospel" in Jerusalem to their own reception of the gospel. It is Paul's consistency in defending the truth of the gospel, even in the face of concerted opposition, that the Galatians are to recognize and appreciate. And among the various people within the Jerusalem incident, the Galatian Christ-followers are expected to see themselves represented by Titus, whose identity as an uncircumcised Christ-follower was affirmed by the influential leaders of Jerusalem Christ-groups (2:3). In fact, Paul highlights that the influential leaders among Jerusalem-based Christ-groups "did not add anything to what I was already preaching" (2:6). Instead, they "recognized the grace" that God had given him – the "grace" that propelled Paul in the task of spreading the gospel to the gentiles. Paul's reconstruction of the Jerusalem incident gives the Galatians insight into how things should rightly be working among their Christ-groups. That is, Paul's gospel is to be welcomed by gentiles who should not be instructed by "false" Christ-followers and should not be led to believe that Torah observance is essential to their Christ-devotion.

What the Jerusalem incident revealed, however, is that the gospel of the early Christ-movement can be articulated in different ways for different groups – as long as the essentials are not compromised. This diversity of presentational expression seems to be part of the recognition that Peter (and others) would take the gospel "to the circumcised" and Paul (and others) would take the gospel "to the uncircumcised" (2:9). The different "target audiences" required different forms of presentation.

Although the profiles of Jesus-groups will inevitably differ in relation to the way each group is populated, there is nonetheless to be some commonality between them, and this is found in the articulated conviction that "the destitute" should be "remembered" (2:10). Wherever the gospel takes hold, this should be a characteristic of all Christ-groups.

2:11–21: AFFIRMING "THE TRUTH OF THE GOSPEL" IN THEOLOGICAL DISCOURSE

This section of Paul's text starts out fairly straightforwardly, with Paul recounting another incident in the early history of the Christ-movement. This relatively uncomplicated account of what happened (in 2:11–14) quickly becomes a deep dive into theological complexities of what God has done in Christ (in 2:15–21). Paul probably did not see these as two separate units. The one flows into the other, with Peter's actions in Antioch (2:11–14) requiring Paul to offer a response articulating theological first principles as he saw them, with that speech to Peter starting in 2:15.

The full extent of Paul's speech to Peter is not clearly delineated. It is understandable to think that Paul loses sight of Peter along the way, with his initial response becoming increasingly detached from the Antioch situation and tilted toward the Galatian situation. Nonetheless, this does not mean that Paul's discourse is only directed to Peter in 2:14 and perhaps one or two verses beyond that. The Galatians are probably to see the whole of 2:15–21 as Paul's speech to Peter. Before Paul directly addresses the Galatians about their situation in 3:1–5, he offers an overview of a speech of rebuke that he directed to Peter in Antioch, with Paul's discourse in Galatians 3–4 (and beyond) seen as an expansion of the theological first principles that Paul and Peter held in common, as articulated in 2:15–16. If the new teachers in Galatia are appealing to Jerusalem and its leadership for the authentication of their gospel, the irony is that Paul has already chastised Peter for adopting a view that can be seen as analogous to the view of the new teachers who have arrived in Galatia.

Paul lays out the background of the incident in 2:11–14. In earlier days at Antioch, Peter had interacted with gentile Christ-followers freely, even to the extent of "eating with gentiles" (2:12).[3] In Paul's recounting of the episode, Peter's early behavior in Antioch was in complete accord with how Paul understood the "theological first principles" agreed upon by the Jerusalem apostles and Paul (2:1–10). In light of that agreement, Paul thought that the sharing of meals between Jews and gentiles made perfect sense. But Peter changed his behavior when "certain people came from James" (2:12). He "drew back" from eating with gentiles at the common meal, keeping himself "separate" (i.e., separated from gentile Christ-followers) because "he was afraid of those who promoted circumcision" as necessary for gentile Christ-followers (2:12).

Paul pivots from the "presenting situation" of 2:11–14 into one of the most powerful theological paragraphs of his surviving letters, 2:15–21. He begins by noting the identity he and Peter share: "We, Jews from birth, are not 'gentile sinners'" (2:15). But even as Jews by birth, Paul and Peter nonetheless agree on a point that is critical to the identity of Jewish Christ-followers: "A person

---

[3] When Paul says that Peter was living "like a gentile and not like a Jew," he probably does not mean that Peter, the apostle to the Jews, was eating pork and shellfish and the like. (Presumably Peter ate kosher food in the company of gentile Christ-followers, who ate nonkosher food.) Paul may be repeating the criticism articulated by those who came from James (who saw his relaxed attitude to interaction as an abandonment of Jewish identity); Paul now recasts the charge in order to work it along different lines in 2:14. Other options are also possible.

is not seen to be righteous [i.e., by God] by means of works of the Torah, but through the trust that pertains to Jesus Christ" (2:16).[4] For emphasis, Paul repeats the point a second time in order to expand the point: "By the works of the Torah no one will be seen as righteous." Here Paul seems to echo the words of Ps 143:2 (142:2 in the LXX), adding the words "the works of the Torah" into the claim of the Psalm. Paul and Peter agree that "the hope of righteousness" (5:5) is not in the works of the Torah, and for that reason "we have placed our trust in Christ Jesus."

This introduces a question that may already have arisen in Paul's ministry and one that he felt the need to address in subsequent letters as well.[5] Paul phrases the question this way in 2:17: "If we [Jews] are ourselves found to be sinners as we seek to be seen as righteous in Christ, then is Christ a servant of [the power of] Sin?" The question has some force, especially when "Sin" is understood as a power that has influence over people within "the present evil age." That is, Paul is not really thinking specifically of the sins of people at this point; instead, those sins (as in 1:4) testify to the presence of a power of Sin that stands hawkishly over people, ensuring that their lives are characterized by sinfulness. This seems to be what Paul means later in the letter when he speaks of people being "under the power of Sin" (3:22). So the question of 2:17 is ultimately about whether Paul's "good news" is really good news at all, since it could be argued that Paul's gospel simply makes Christ subordinate to ("a slave of") the power of Sin. Isn't it in the interests of the power of Sin to break down the distinction between the idolatrous "gentile sinners" and the nonidolatrous "Jews by

---

[4] For an explanation of the phrase "the trust that pertains to Jesus Christ," see Chapter 6. On the phrase "seen to be righteous," see Chapter 9.
[5] See, for instance, 1 Cor 6:12; 10:23; Rom 3:7–8; 6:1, 15.

birth" so that the number of sinners actually increases? If the "good news" means that the term "sinners" applies across the board in a fashion that problematizes the very distinction between the people of Israel and the pagan nations, isn't this good news only for the power of Sin? Doesn't Paul's gospel show God to have been thwarted by the power of Sin?

"Absolutely not!" replies Paul in the final two words of 2:17 (*mē genoito*). The question misunderstands the fundamental point on which Paul and Peter seem to have agreed – that is, that the grip of the power of Sin on all people undermines the expectation that the distinction between Jews and gentiles holds a position of primary importance in the adjudication of righteousness for those in Christ. Paul explains further in the four verses that follow (2:18–21), where the reasoning is both complex and terse. But in many ways the chapters that follow develop his negation in 2:17.

The conclusion of Paul's response to Peter is found in the short statement of 2:21: "If righteousness could come through the Torah, then Christ died needlessly." When read in relation to the question of 2:17, this means that the power of Sin is not dethroned by the Torah; it is only through the crucifixion of Jesus Christ that the power of Sin is defused of its explosively catastrophic control over all people. Again, there is more of this to follow.

Already in 2:18–20 Paul has set up the theological context for understanding the claim of 2:21. In 2:18–19a, Paul suggests that the Torah itself is onboard with this eradication of the distinction between "Jews" and "gentile sinners." This seems to be the force of his all-too-succinct claim in 2:19: "Through the Torah I died to the Torah," and the purpose of this was "so that I can live for God" in Christ. To erect the distinction between "gentile sinners" and "Jews by birth" is, then, to be a transgressor – a transgressor before God, certainly, but perhaps even a transgressor of the Torah itself. If the latter connotations are in play, Paul is highlighting an irony in the position of the new teachers, since any gentiles who adopt Torah observance in Christ would actually become Torah offenders. Either way, Paul's goal is to demonstrate that any attempt to restrict the label "sinners" to the gentile nations alone creates transgressions – and ironically this plays right into the hands of the power of Sin itself. This is because, in effect, it prioritizes Jewish identity. When Paul says he has "died to the Torah," he means that he no longer allows the power of Sin to prioritize that part of his identity over the identity of others.

In 2:19b–20, Paul pivots around the image of death – an image first used in the phrase "I died to the Torah" in 2:19a.[6] Paul makes what is perhaps his most programmatic statement in Galatians, where talk of death shifts to talk of life: "I have been crucified with Christ. I no longer live; instead, Christ lives in me." Paul amplifies this in the second half of 2:20, but notice already the significance of this claim. This is not "Christ died so that I don't have to die"; instead, it is "Christ died in order that I too can die with him." Paul insists that this is good news, gospel. In fact, the whole of the gospel is dependent on this claim. It is important to keep in mind that Paul's discourse in 2:20 is framed by the issue of the power of Sin that engulfs all people-groups (2:17–18). In this context, what has died, what has been crucified with Christ, is the person in the clutches of the power of Sin – that is, the "sinner-under-Sin." Christ-followers become incorporated into the death of Jesus

---

[6] Note that in some translations 2:19a is simply 2:19, and 2:19b is treated as part of 2:20. The point is not important except to clarify any confusion in the enumeration of verses between the standard versification of the Greek text and the various verse enumerators in different translations.

Christ, dying with him in their all-engulfing and undifferentiated identity as sinners under the power of Sin.

Christ-followers die with Christ. Paul is also convinced, however, that Jesus Christ comes alive not only in his resurrection (1:1) but in the lives of those who die with him. Here we witness the depths of Paul's theological convictions and the heart of his theological discourse in Galatians. Christ-followers enter into aspects of Christ's identity in order for that identity to flood their lives. Christ-followers are dead people, in a very real sense; their identities prior to being in Christ are no longer operative as identity priorities.

What does it look like for Christ to live in his followers? Paul explains that in the second half of 2:20: "The life I now live in the enfleshed body I live by the trust that pertains to the Son of God, who loved me and gave himself for me." The Christ who comes alive in Paul, and in all Christ-followers, is characterized by "love," which itself is virtually explained by the final clause: "He gave himself." For Paul, "love" is not so much an emotion as an action, an action of self-giving (as he highlights already in 1:4). We will see more of this in Galatians 5–6. For now, it is enough to see that what comes alive in Christ-followers is the character of Christ himself. As sinners from all people-groups who have died with Christ, Christ-followers have their self-giving (and resurrected) Lord empowering their newly animated lives. Paul will go on to call this "new creation" (6:15).

3:1–9: THE SPIRIT, TRUST, SCRIPTURE, AND THE CROSS, #1

Paul now turns to address the situation of the Christ-followers in Galatia directly. It is one thing to reason out the good news, with an echo of Ps 143:2 thrown in, as Paul has done with stunning conciseness in 2:15–21; it is another thing to engage that discourse with the part of scripture that had caught the attention of the Galatian Christ-followers – that is, the story of Abraham in Genesis. That story is one of the most foundational stories of God's dealings with God's people, being a prime example of how an idolater abandons his deities to serve the living and true God.

In Paul's view, the new teachers' interpretation of that story is disastrous – much like Peter's actions in Antioch. Just as Peter had started out along the right path and had then been nudged into a different trajectory altogether, the same is true of the Galatians. And as Paul rebuked Peter, so too he rebukes them ("foolish," 3:1). Their instability is putting in jeopardy the thing they cherish most: the presence of the Spirit among them. "Having started with the Spirit, are you now being perfected by [or 'finishing with'] the flesh [*sarx*]?" (3:3). The Greek word *sarx* is difficult to translate and is always context-dependent in its meaning. In this context, "flesh" does not connote "the sinful body"; instead, Paul is referencing a way of life that runs contrary to the Spirit, foregrounding patterns of life that are ultimately at odds with the message of Christ crucified (3:1).[7] Paul likens the Galatians to victims of a malignant form of spiritual power: "Who has cast the evil eye upon you?" (3:1). The "evil eye" is a phenomenon in which people with malignant character (in this case, the new teachers) draw the health out of others to use for their own benefit, to the detriment of their victims (see Chapter 8).

Paul's main point in this transitional paragraph (3:1–5) is that the Galatians had already benefited from the Spirit being in their midst as a result of their acceptance of the good news; how could

---

[7] This is also the predominant use of the word in Galatians 5–6.

they jeopardize that by thinking that they should observe the Torah? This paragraph is often presented as a self-contained unit, and the same is true for 3:6–9. But, in fact, Paul seems to want to run the paragraphs together as a single text unit. So he starts 3:6 with a word that joins what he is about to say with what he has just said (*kathōs*, "just as" or "in the same way").[8] This is because 3:6–9 functions, in a sense, as a very short demonstration of how the Galatians' life of trust (already referenced in 3:1–5) aligns with Abraham's story.

In 3:6–9, Paul foregrounds two scriptural quotations. The first is Gen 15:6, cited in 3:6: Abraham "trusted God and it was credited to him as righteousness." Paul's point is simple: What was true of Abraham is true of the Galatian Christ-followers. They have trusted God by putting their trust in Jesus Christ, and so they are seen as righteous by God (3:8). In fact, their trust is a fulfillment of a second scriptural passage – Gen 12:3 (see also 18:18), cited in 3:8: "All the gentiles will be blessed in you." God made this promise to Abraham – or, as Paul phrases it, "scripture preached the gospel in advance" to him.[9] Gentile Christ-followers are brought directly within the story of Abraham in Genesis, by means of their trust (3:7, 9).

The kind of trust Paul has in mind is not just blind faith in obscure things; it is trust that God is faithful to God's word of promise. This trust in God's own trustworthiness, God's faithfulness, is ultimately what links Abraham and Christ-followers. Abraham had the promise pre-preached to him ("all the gentiles

---

[8] For this reason, some translations divide the paragraphs as 3:1–6 and 3:7–9.
[9] There seems to be no dispute that ethnic Jews themselves would enjoy "the promised Spirit" (3:14) in Christ. Paul's discourse in 3:8 focuses on how gentiles enjoy the same blessings.

will be blessed in you"), and he trusted God to be faithful to carry out that promise; the Galatians had the proclamation of God's trustworthiness vividly preached to them (see 3:1), and, hearing that proclamation, their own trust in a trustworthy God was elicited (3:2, 5).[10] Here human trust itself seems to have its origins in divine initiative, being sparked in the Galatians in relation to the message that Paul vividly narrated in his graphic portrayal of Christ's crucifixion (3:1). The same is then implied with reference to the trust of Abraham, who was receptive to God working through him. With the blessing announced, God inspired trust within Abraham, who trusted that God would be faithful to God's promised blessing.

3:10–14: THE SPIRIT, TRUST, SCRIPTURE, AND THE CROSS, #2

Concentrated within this section of Galatians are four scriptural passages that Paul interacts with. The key to understanding those critical passages lies precisely in Paul's editorial comments, as he strings these passages together in a way that sheds new light on them so that they speak in accord with the gospel he has articulated in 2:15–21.

The first scriptural passage is Deut 27:26, which he cites in this way: "Everyone is cursed who does not continually practice [*emmenei*] all the things written in the book of the Torah." Cited baldly in this way, the passage looks to support precisely the view of the new teachers. For this reason, the passage from Deuteronomy was probably used by the new teachers to support

---

[10] I take the difficult Greek phrase *akoē pisteōs* in 3:2 and 3:5 to be "the report [*akoē*] that elicits [our] trust [*pisteōs*]." On this phrase, see Brewer 2025.

their position about the need for circumcision (and, beyond that, full observance of the Torah). They might well have said something like, "Isn't the God who raised Jesus Christ from the dead the same God who gave the Torah to the people of Israel? To dislodge christocentric trust from Torah observance is to leave yourselves exposed to the curse mentioned in Deut 27:26."[11] Paul isn't about to concede the passage to the new teachers, however. Instead, he adds a sentence that illustrates how he wants the scriptural passage to be understood: "Those whose identity is defined by the works of the Torah are under a curse" (3:10). With that lens for interpreting Deut 27:26, Paul is implicitly building on what he and Peter had agreed upon in 2:16: "a person is not seen as righteous by the works of the Torah" and "by the works of the Torah no one will be seen to be righteous." With Peter's agreement in Paul's back pocket, Deut 27:26 no longer looks like an obvious support for the view of the new teachers.

In fact, that is even more the case when Paul does in this paragraph what he has already done in 2:16, driving a wedge between trust and "the works of the Torah" so that the two contrast with rather than complement each other. He does this by citing two other passages. In 3:12, he cites Lev 18:5: "The one who does these things [i.e., the works of the Torah] will live by them." Paul's lens for interpreting this verse appears prior to its citation, when he writes, "The Torah is not based on trust" but, instead, is based on doing. Accordingly, the force of Lev 18:5 is shown to run contrary to what Paul and Peter have already agreed regarding the gospel in 2:16. If no one is righteous before God by

---

[11] They might also have referenced other passages in this regard, such as Deut 29:20–21.

the works of the Torah (as in 2:16), then no one lives by doing them (in contrast to Lev 18:5). The force of 2:16 is repeated with emphasis in 3:11: "No one is seen as righteous before God by means of the Torah." Paul enriches his point with a citation from Hab 2:4: "The righteous will live on the basis of trust" – trust in Christ Jesus, as in 2:16 once again.

But Paul also knows that the citation of Deut 27:26 still hangs over the discussion. He has to explain what happens to the curse pronounced by the Torah. Another passage from Deuteronomy offers an answer: "Everyone who is hung on a tree is cursed" (Deut 21:23, cited in 3:13). Paul reads this christologically, and exclusively christologically, as he says just prior to the citation: "Christ redeemed us from the curse of the Torah by becoming a curse for us." For those in Christ, the crucifixion of Christ deflects the Torah's curse. Paul does not say that the curse no longer exists; it simply does not apply to those in Christ. It still applies to any outside of Christ who see themselves as "those whose identity is defined by the works of the Torah," as Paul describes them in 3:10.

Deuteronomy makes clear that the opposite of being cursed is being blessed, and Paul has already spoken of those who trust in Christ as being "blessed" with Abraham who trusted. In 3:14 Paul picks up on "the blessing of Abraham," saying that this blessing has come in Christ Jesus. What is the blessing that was promised? The blessing flows as Christ-followers, through trust, receive "the promise of the Spirit" – which is to say, "the promised Spirit." Once again, Paul has aligned gentile Christ-followers with the story of Abraham and placed the giving of the Spirit within that storyline. This is a more elaborate form of discourse than the one we saw in 3:6–9, but it arrives at much the same place. Gentile Christ-followers in Galatia can see their trust as aligning them with the promise made to Abraham. Their reception of the Spirit (which Paul had highlighted in 3:1–5) is their blessing, exclusively through trust in Christ.

3:15–29: ABRAHAM'S PROGENY, THE TORAH, THE POWER OF SIN, AND CHRIST

This section of Galatians continues to do what previous sections have done – embed Christ-devotion in the story of Abraham. Two verses carry the most weight in this regard: 3:16 and 3:29. In 3:16, Paul picks up on a phrase that occurs in the Abraham story of Genesis and reads it (in the first instance) wholly in relation to Jesus Christ: "The promises were made to Abraham and to his progeny." Paul notes that the referent is singular, not plural (i.e., "progenies"), so the single progeny is Christ. This stunning claim arcs to the final verse of the chapter (3:29). Because Paul believes that Christ-followers are immersed in Christ (as in 2:19b), he believes them also to be "Abraham's progeny, heirs according to the promise" (3:29). This is the third time in the course of Galatians 3 that the story of Abraham has been shown to encompass Christ-followers. Each time, Paul has engaged with scripture, reading it in light of Christ to demonstrate that the gospel about Jesus Christ has nothing to do with requiring Torah observance of gentile Christ-followers.

Paul knows, however, that his reading of the Abraham story leaves questions in the air. Why was the Torah given in the first place? Paul first clarifies that the Torah and the Abrahamic promise function in different ways in the purposes of God. In 3:15, Paul offers "an example from everyday life" to make his point: After a covenant (*diathēkē*) has been made between two parties, a single party can't just cancel it or make additions to it.

Paul elaborates further, noting that the Torah was introduced 430 years after God's "covenant" with Abraham (3:17); as such, the Torah is neither a cancellation of the Abrahamic covenant nor its supplement.

The "either-or" perspective involving Christ and the Torah that Paul established so clearly in 2:21 is restated in 3:18: The inheritance (that is, the presence of the Spirit among the Abrahamic progeny in Christ) cannot come through the Torah; it is linked exclusively to the Abrahamic promise, where God's personal word of grace is operative (3:18; compare 2:21). There is no direct link from the Torah to (eschatological) life: "If a collection of instructions [*nomos*] had been given that was able to generate life [i.e., eschatological life], then righteousness would indeed have come by the Torah [*nomos*]" (3:21).[12] But since the first is negated, so too is the second.

Paul presents the giving of Torah in a way that implies distance and separation between God and the recipients of the Torah. In between the divine source and the ethnic people of Israel are "angels" and "a mediator" (i.e., Moses; 3:19). Paul is laying the groundwork for his depiction of the intimate relationship Christ-followers have with God, as expressed in 4:6. That intimate relationship (represented in the cry "Abba, Father") is much different from the mediated relationality between God and the people of Israel.

The mediator, says Paul, is "not of one" (3:20). By this cryptic phrase, Paul seems to be saying something like, "A mediator

---

[12] Unlike the initial occurrence of the Greek word *nomos* in 3:21, these two occurrences of the word do not have a definite article. The second occurrence seems to reference the Torah; the first, however, is slightly playful, almost speaking about a general situation.

stands between two parties." Paul is setting up a claim that builds on the notion of "one." Instead of a mediator between two parties, "God is one" (3:20) – an affirmation that lies at the heart of Jewish monotheism. If the Galatians are seeking to ensure that they have abandoned pagan polytheism for monotheism, Paul's gospel is aligned with that intention. Proper relationship with the only true God involves a relational intimacy that the Torah is not configured to offer.

So what purposes did this Torah of mediated relationality (through angelic and human mediators) serve? In 3:19–25, Paul suggests two ways (at least) of understanding the purposes for giving the Torah. First, he says it was added (430 years after the promise) "because of violations" (3:19). By this curious phrase, Paul seems to suggest that the Torah offers a checklist of violations where previously there was simply a morass of intertwined sinfulness. This coheres well with Paul's claim in 3:22 that scripture (understood as the concentrated divine voice within the Torah and beyond) "locked up all things under the power of Sin." The Torah offered a taxonomy of violations, and in doing so, revealed the extent to which the power of Sin reigns in this world. The effects of the power of Sin are now recognizable within people's lives through the Torah's taxonomy of identifiable violations. The concentrated divine voice within the given Torah "locked up" the sinfulness of all things in the "power of Sin" column, lest there be any mistake about the identity of the overlord of sinfulness.

Notice the breadth of Paul's vision about "the problem." "Violations" that reveal the sinfulness of humanity are certainly in play, but so too is something bigger than human sins. Those sins themselves testify to the influence of "the power of Sin" in the present evil age. And what that overarching power has in its control is not simply "all people" (*pasa sarx* in 2:16) but "all things" (*ta panta* in 3:22). Here, Paul seems to be thinking about overarching systems, with people being enmeshed within enveloping entities, all of which are engulfed by the power of Sin. When he assured the Galatians at the outset of the letter that Jesus Christ "gave himself for our sins in order to redeem us from the present age of evil," Paul knew that he would foreground not only the sins of people ("all flesh," Jews and gentiles alike) but also the systems that contribute to the shaping of people's identities within this world – placing all of this under the overlordship of the power of Sin.

It is against this backdrop that Paul introduces another purpose for the giving of the Torah. That is, the Torah served as a custodial "pedagogue" (3:24–25). In the ancient world, pedagogues (almost always household slaves) were tasked by householders with the responsibility of overseeing children during their years as minors. While various tasks could be included in this role, the pedagogue's overarching responsibility was the protection of the minor in an otherwise injurious world. Whatever else a pedagogue did, the children under a pedagogue's care were to be protected from trouble that would otherwise endanger them. Paul uses this metaphor to describe the Torah, given not to all people but to the Jewish people in particular ("by the hand of a mediator," Moses). The pedagogical Torah was a form of protection from the dangerous ravages of maliciously intentioned phenomena – which, when pegged to Paul's discourse in Galatians, would correspond to the singular power of Sin.

In what way could this be? What made the ethnic people of Israel different from the other nations? Probably any Jew of Paul's day would answer this with the response, "Unlike the gentile nations, we Jews are meant not to be idolators, because idolatry is prohibited in the Torah."[13] This is how non-Jews seem to have thought of Jews – as offering exclusive worship to their sole deity (see Tacitus, *Hist.* 5.5.4; Juvenal, *Sat.* 14.97). Whether or not Paul had anything else in mind, this single characteristic of Jewish identity must have been at the forefront of his thinking when likening the Torah to the pedagogue of the ethnic people of Israel.

Because the Torah was a system of social order that was not "unto life," Paul thought it to have had a negative aspect, as in his characterization of the Jewish people as "locked up" under the Torah (3:23). The Torah might have prevented them from the worst ravages of idolatry, but at the same time it systematized a way of life that was not "unto [eschatological] life." What Paul calls being "locked up," or being "under the Torah," or being "under a pedagogue" in 3:23–24 he will later call "being enslaved" in Galatians 4. This is because the situation has changed with the coming of Christ. Like the pedagogues of Paul's day, the Torah was not intended to serve its custodial purpose endlessly. It would be a social atrocity for pedagogues to be tending to adults; those adults would be the laughingstock of all the local residents. So too the Torah was to perform a custodial purpose only "until Christ" (*eis Christon*, 3:24), with the people of Israel "guarded ... until the trust that was coming would be revealed" (3:23). "Now that Christ has come," Jews in Christ "are no longer under a pedagogue"; with the coming of Christ there is now a more effective way to avoid idolatry, which Paul explains in Galatians 4.

Of course, Jews in Christ can still observe the Torah, but in Christ they are not "under" it – which is to say that they do not put any salvific hope in it, nor do they prioritize their Jewish

---

[13] See, for instance, Philo, *Spec.* 2.166.

identity before God and others.[14] But Paul is uncompromising in his vision of Christ-groups as comprised of people with necessarily different identities except that they belong to Christ. Differences in identities still exist in Christ, but in Christ they are no longer aligned unproductively (and often confrontationally). Paul makes this point in 3:28: "There is neither Jew nor Greek; there is neither enslaved nor free; nor is there male and female, for you are all one in Christ Jesus" (CEB). In Christ Jesus, diverse identities are united rather than weaponized. This is because, in their baptism into Christ, Christ-followers are clothed with Christ, whose identity is shared among them as their common macro-identity, despite the differences of their micro-identities. Just as "God is one" (3:20), so too God's people are one in Christ Jesus. For Paul, this is what it means to be "children of God through trust in Christ Jesus" (3:26); this is what it means to be "Abraham's progeny" (3:29).

4:1–11: DIVINE SENDING AND REDEMPTION FROM THE SLAVERY OF THE *STOICHEIA*

If this is a new text unit, it nonetheless draws heavily on the preceding section, expanding on Paul's notion that the Torah's custodial function was limited to a period of time. In 4:1–2 Paul notes that children are under custodial care but that (unless disaster strikes their young lives) they eventually leave that situation behind. Paul wants to move that analogy to a different level, however. Because children are under the control of others

---

[14] They may even find that some aspects of Torah observance get reinterpreted, revalued, or relinquished in the process – not least aspects of the sacrificial system in the Jerusalem temple.

(i.e., trustees and guardians, at least for children in economically "secure" households of Paul's world), in that way they are no different from enslaved people (who were also under the control of others). Paul identifies the enslavers as "the *stoicheia* of the world" (4:3, or simply *stoicheia* in 4:9).

It is hard to know precisely what Paul means by this term. In Chapter 4, it will be suggested that the *stoicheia* that exist in this world are something like "the formative influences of all kinds that collectively shape the world's systems and all social identities within them, under the power of Sin." In short, the *stoicheia* are "identity influencers conscripted by the power of Sin." Paul understood, for instance, that cultural mechanisms were deeply in place; that whole systems of life were whirring away; that structures processing opportunities, options, and hindrances had long been established; and that a myriad of forces shaped the contexts of life. All of those phenomena are, according to 3:22, vulnerable to becoming pawns of the power of Sin and so are "under" its control, at its beck and call.

When Paul speaks of "we" in this context ("we were enslaved to the *stoicheia* of this world"), he is probably referring to all people. The Jewish people may have been safeguarded from the worst forms of idolatry, but even Jews were firmly embedded in the web of interlocking systems, none of which were unto life, all of which were enslaving. Jew and Greek, enslaved and free, male and female – people of all identities were alike "under the *stoicheia* of the world."

But then God's organization of time came to the point of perfect culmination – "the fulfillment of time" (4:4, recalling the time "appointed by the father" in Paul's analogy at 4:2). Time's fulfillment, the moment that all of time is oriented around, came when God the Father sent the Son into this quagmire of enslavement that the power of Sin had orchestrated. Paul outlines the consequences of that divine sending in 4:4–7, a passage characterized by lucid brevity. But even here we find the same sort of thing we have already seen in 2:19–20 and in 3:26–29 – that is, the incorporative, participatory aspect of Paul's theological worldview, where the Christ-follower is in Christ and (or "so that") Christ is in the Christ-follower (i.e., the Spirit of God's Son takes up residence there). Christ-followers are no longer "under" anything; they are no longer, then, enslaved. Instead, being set free from enslavement (being "redeemed"), they are "adopted as sons" (4:5, which we might translate as "as sons and daughters").

Paul wants Galatian Christ-followers to see themselves as former slaves who have been brought into the most magnificent of family households – what Paul will call "the family of trust (in Christ)" in 6:10. As adopted members of that household, they are also inheritors of the household's blessing (4:7). Paul first mentioned "inheritance" in 3:18, linking it to Abraham "through the promise." What is it that members of this family inherit? The Spirit, the abundant blessing that (as explained in 3:6–14) comes to Abraham's progeny as a result of God's commitment to bless the nations who are seen to be righteous in Christ.

If the Spirit had already manifested powerful works among the Galatian Christ-groups (3:5), more importantly (at least in Paul's Galatian discourse) the Spirit brings intimacy with God, so that the Spirit cries out within the hearts of Christ-followers, on behalf of Christ-followers, "Abba, Father" (with the Aramaic "Abba" being reminiscent of Jesus's own address to God; see Mark 14:36). These words are not simply uttered vocally; they are uttered within the hearts of Christ-followers, where the Spirit accesses their inner identities (4:6). The words of obedience, uttered by the self-giving Jesus Christ, can come alive in the hearts of Christ-followers because Christ himself, by the Spirit, comes alive in the inner recesses and fundamental core of their diverse, individual identities. This might be why Paul surprisingly but importantly shifts from plural referents ("we," "our," "you [plural]") to singular referents: "You" in the singular seems to suggest "each one of you personally" (4:7).

Here the intimate relationship with God is to be understood in such profound and overwhelming terms that, consequently, interest in any other forms of identity before God is completely undermined. So Paul takes the opportunity to put the Galatians' current interest in Torah observance into perspective. Running throughout 4:8–11 is a contrast between the "then" and the "now" of the Galatians' life narrative. Back "then," the Galatian gentiles were enslaved in a world of idolatry – "enslaved to things [i.e., the *stoicheia*] that by nature aren't deities at all" (4:8).[15] With irony and exasperation, Paul regards the Galatians as abandoning their current enjoyment of sonship in Christ and "turning back" to a pre-Christ situation of enslavement. In Paul's view, if the Galatian gentiles were to prioritize Torah observance as a new form of identity, they would in fact be returning to an old form of identity – one of enslavement. So Paul asks, "How can you want to be enslaved to them again?" (4:9). Intending to avoid idolatry by observing the Torah, the Galatians would end up observing (and perhaps were already beginning to observe) certain "days, and months, and seasons, and years" prescribed by the Torah (4:10). Those temporally determined practices resemble the

---

[15] The Greek *tois* could have a masculine referent, "beings" (i.e., "beings that by nature aren't deities"). Alternatively, it could have a neuter referent, "things," referring specifically to the *stoicheia* that are soon to be referenced (4:9).

ordinary forms of Greco-Roman idolatrous rituals that were also regulated by calendrical measurements. In this way, Paul correlates gentiles adopting Jewish practices on the one hand with pagan observance of idolatrous practices on the other. He sees things in stark either-or terms (see 2:21; 5:2). So Paul says bluntly at this point, "I am afraid for you, that my efforts on your behalf may have been in vain" (4:11).

4:12–20: A THEOLOGICAL INVENTORY OF A RELATIONSHIP

Paul's comments in 4:11 about his efforts on behalf of the Galatians serve as the pivot into the next section of his letter, where Paul takes stock of his relationship with the Galatians. Paul explores that relationship in light of the theological vision he has been articulating. For Paul, a relationship inevitably testifies to the theological commitments of the people within that relationship. Paul was an expert in the theological interpretation of relationships, and that's what he puts his mind to here.

Up to this point, Paul has tried to dissuade the Galatians from taking a particular course of action. From this point on, Paul will regularly articulate what he wants them to do. The first occurrence of that is the first verse of this section: "Become as I am." Here the autobiographical presentation of Galatians 1–2 is probably in view, with Paul saying, in effect, "Stand fast in the truth of the gospel, as I have done over the course of the years, despite pressure to do otherwise."

In 4:12b–15 Paul has some very positive things to say about his early days with the Galatians, which we will look at more closely in Chapter 8. But he notes that things have changed since then. Under the influence of the new teachers, Paul has come to be seen as the Galatians' "enemy" (4:16). The new teachers want to "exclude" the Galatians from the very "blessedness" that the Galatians had already enjoyed. Paul takes the occasion to question the moral character of the new teachers. They are "courting" the Galatians but for no good purpose; they are motivated by their own selfish interests, in the hope that the Galatians will attach themselves like groupies to the new teachers (4:17).

It has all been utterly devastating to the well-being of the Galatians. Paul is at a loss regarding their current calamitous situation (4:20). He wishes them to be restored to health, even restored to life: "My children, I am again experiencing labor pains, until Christ is formed among you" (4:19). The maternal imagery is profound. Christ lives in Paul (1:16; 2:20), whose service to the Galatians is to bring Christ alive in Galatian Christ-groups. It was all going so well, until the new teachers put Christ's presence among them in jeopardy. With this, Paul is ready to return to the Abraham story one final time in the letter, in 4:21–31.

4:21–31: ABRAHAM'S PROGENY AND THE DIRECT SPEECH OF SCRIPTURE

The main features of Paul's case to the Galatians are largely in place. And so now he pulls the trigger in this text unit, drawing from the story of Abraham an instruction as to what the Galatians need to do now. He does this in light of what he has already shown: (1) the Galatian Christ-followers are linked to the story of Abraham in no other way than by their trust in Christ; (2) for that reason they have the promised Spirit in their hearts and in their midst; (3) all this has been jeopardized by the influence of the new teachers, in contrast to Paul's own divinely legitimated apostolic ministry. With those elements in place, Paul will now show the

Galatians that the same story of Abraham snaps back at the new teachers to delegitimize their influence among the Galatians.

Picking up the details of the Abraham story, Paul reminds the Galatians that Abraham had two sons: "One was born by an enslaved woman [i.e., Ishmael, born through Hagar] and one born by a free woman [i.e., Isaac, born through Sarah]" (4:22). Paul has already used the simple contrast of slavery and freedom to depict Christ-followers as having moved from enslavement to freedom through their trust in Christ; consequently, already in 4:22 we can see where he is leading – trust in Christ places Christ-followers in line with Abrahamic descent through Isaac and the free woman, whereas following the bad news of the new teachers places Christ-followers in line with Abrahamic descent through Ishmael and the enslaved woman. But there is more: "The son born by the enslaved woman was conceived biologically [*kata sarka*], but the son born by the free woman was conceived through a promise" (4:23). This recalls the very promise that Paul references in 3:6: Abraham "trusted in God" that the nations would be blessed in him.

Central to this scriptural "allegory" (as Paul calls it in 4:24) is Isa 54:1 (cited in 4:27). That passage initially likens Jerusalem to a barren woman, whose barrenness will be offset by God's enlivening power, blessing her with numerous descendants, in contrast to the woman who conceives through natural means. In the interplay between the Genesis account (largely Gen 16–22) and this Isaianic passage, the present-day Jerusalem is said to be in enslavement together with her children, like Hagar, represented in the covenant from Mount Sinai (4:24–25). This is in contrast to the Jerusalem that is above, which is free and which is the mother of those who are free in Christ (4:26).

The "punch" of all this comes in 4:29–30, where Paul cites a passage from scripture (4:30) after explaining the context for interpreting that passage (4:29). The two verses on either side (4:28 and 4:31) frame how the Galatians' identity in Christ impacts the reading: The Galatians are "children of the promise, like Isaac" (4:28; see also 3:29); they "aren't the children of the enslaved woman but children of the free woman" (4:31). The narrative context fits into this: "the one who was conceived biologically [*kata sarka*] persecuted the one who was conceived by the Spirit [*kata pneuma*]" and "the same thing is happening now" (4:29) – as the new teachers are effectively "persecuting" the Galatians (by diminishing the importance of gentile identities).[16]

So, if the Galatians are so interested in the Abraham story, what does "scripture" tell them to do in this instance? "Throw out the enslaved woman and her son" – that is, throw out the new teachers who peddle the bad enslaving news. These are the words of Gen 21:10. Paul wants Christ-followers informed by the gospel of freedom to "listen to the Torah" (4:21). What happened in the Genesis account should inform what happens in Galatian Christ-groups. The new teachers have tried to separate Paul from the Galatians (4:17); now Paul shows how scripture informs the Galatians to separate themselves from the new teachers. This is, after all, the same God who had set Paul apart for his apostolic ministry, the same God who revealed his Son to and in Paul in order for Paul to preach to the gentiles (1:15–16; see also 1:1). This is the same Paul who has never been a people-pleaser, the Paul who is a slave of Christ, whose gospel came through "a

---

[16] This aspect of the story is hard to find in the Genesis account itself but was elaborated in later developments of the story, to explain Sarah's rather callous treatment of Hagar and Ishmael (Gen 21:9–10; contrast 21:14–21, where God is shown to preserve Ishmael). Reading between the lines of the story, interpreters came to think that Hagar and Ishmael had been sent away because Ishmael had severely mistreated Isaac.

revelation from Jesus Christ" (1:14). The scriptural narrative that the new teachers presented in support of their teaching has now been turned around, with Paul showing it to indict the new teachers, forming a basis for their removal from the Galatian Christ-groups.

5:1–12: CIRCUMCISION AND THE WORK OF TRUST

Much of the text unit that follows restates points Paul has made earlier. He reasserts the either-or that we saw most clearly in 2:21 and have seen throughout: Trust in Christ is the only form of identity that prompts God's declaration of righteousness. In 5:2 this is presented as a "Christ or circumcision" decision. In 5:4 the same either-or is reframed as a "Christ or the Torah" decision. This is because in 5:3 Paul expands the Galatians' primary focus from circumcision to complete observance of the Torah. This most likely was no great surprise to anyone; full observance of the Torah was probably the ultimate goal of the new teachers, and the Galatians probably understood that. But Paul has a way of taking the spin off a serve and returning the ball with a different spin altogether, and that might be what's going on here. "Don't forget, once you gentiles start circumcising yourselves, there's a lot more that you'll be expected to do." In fact, the Torah requires sacrifices to be made; are the Galatians "wanting to be made righteous" in that way, in a temple embedded in a city that is "in slavery with her children" rather than free (4:25)?[17] "Christ will be of no benefit to you at

---

[17] There were various kinds of sacrifices, including sacrifices of thanksgiving. Not all sacrifices were for purposes of atonement. Luke depicts Paul offering a votive sacrifice at the Jerusalem temple in Acts 21:23–26.

all" if you "cut yourselves off from Christ" and fall "away from grace" that is in Christ (5:2, 4).[18]

In 5:5–6 Paul gives a glimpse of where he will be going in the second half of Galatians 5 and the first half of Galatians 6. In 5:6 he highlights what really matters: "trust that continues to work in practical ways [*energoumenē*] through love." Trust works. Trust in Christ is inherently outward-looking, toward the needs of others, precisely because Christ comes alive in his followers (4:19). That's what matters for those in Christ Jesus. What doesn't matter is Jewish or non-Jewish identity, neither of which can serve as a primary feature of one's standing before God. Paul's discourse throughout the letter indicates why this is so.[19] Paul frames this in 5:5 with important qualifiers that do not surprise us: "through the Spirit" and "by trust." But one aspect of that verse is new and relatively unique in Galatians: "as we eagerly anticipate the hope of righteousness" (5:5). Christ-followers are already seen to be righteous by God because of their trust in Christ, but that situation is itself an advance on the eschatological divine pronouncement in the throne room of justice. We will look more closely at this in Chapter 9.

With that end in sight, Paul turns again to focus on the new teachers in 5:7–12. They are impeding the Galatians' way. They have introduced forms of persuasion that do not originate with God. They will pay the penalty (presumably, in the throne room of justice). In the meantime, Paul articulates his own exasperated annoyance. If the new teachers are so interested in cutting penises,

---

[18] It is critically important that Paul is talking here to gentile Christ-followers considering circumcision; he is not condemning Jews circumcised on the eighth day (a legitimate micro-identity in Christ).
[19] There is another sense, of course, in which these identities do, in fact, matter significantly in Christ. See Chapter 7.

"I wish they would castrate themselves!" (5:12). And with that, he turns in the next text unit to elaborate what it means for trust to work in practical ways through love.

5:13–6:10: MORAL CHARACTER, THE SPIRIT, AND THE PROPENSITY TOWARD SELF-CENTERED LIVING

Paul now offers guidance on what it means for trust in Christ to work in practical ways through love (5:6) – that is, for Christ to be born "among you" (4:19). Repeatedly he will contrast it to *sarx*, a Greek word commonly translated simply as "flesh." Elsewhere in Galatians the word has referred to a number of different things: the physical body (2:20; 3:3; 4:13–14; see also 6:13), the body's biological functions (4:23, 29), or the human constitution (1:16, "flesh and blood"; 2:16, "no flesh" = "all humanity"). In this section, however, as Paul crafts a moral vision for the community, the word "flesh" takes on connotations of corporate destructiveness – in particular, the propensity for living to benefit one's own self at the expense of others. Paul does not connect this attitude with the body per se; it is not "bodiliness" that Paul wants to uproot. It is the "fleshly" attitude, an inner world of willful self-determinacy without regard for (or even at the expense of) others. This, then, is the opposite of trust that works through love. This is the deeply engrained human "propensity for self-centered living."

Paul begins this section (in 5:13) much like he did in the last section (in 5:1) – emphasizing freedom. But this time, he adds two qualifications. First, "do not allow your freedom to become an opportunity for self-centered living"; second, "be enslaved to each other through love." Paul has been emphasizing how Christ-followers are free rather than enslaved; in the course of one verse, he moves remarkably from highlighting the freedom of Christ-followers to exhorting them to become mutually enslaved. The key is the potent phrase "through love." A life of enslavement to each other through love is, in fact, how a community of Christ-followers can see the "whole of the Torah" being fulfilled in their midst (5:14, citing Lev 19:18). As trust works through love, as the Galatians enslave themselves to each other through love, their corporate lifestyle together will be a fulfillment of the whole Torah, without living "under the Torah." The alternative is to live in the realm characterized by the propensity for self-centered living, which is portrayed proverbially in "dog-eat-dog" terms in 5:15: "If you continually bite and devour each other, watch out or you'll be entirely obliterated by each other." Once you get started down that road, there will be no end to it. The same concern to avoid hostility within Christ-groups is highlighted eleven verses later: "Let's not become arrogant people; let's not become people who shout each other down; let's not become people who envy each other" (5:26).

Paul exhorts the Galatians to "be guided by the Spirit" (5:16) and to be "led by the Spirit" (5:18). Paul sees the Spirit and the propensity for self-centered living as fundamentally "at war" with each other (5:17). So he offers two lists: one filling out what it looks like to be guided by the Spirit, the other filling out what self-centered living looks like. The list of "practices that characterize the propensity for self-centered living" (or the "works of *sarx*," 5:19–21) begins and ends with entries that might be considered standard Jewish reflections on things to avoid. Heading the list are "sexual immorality, corruption, doing whatever you want, idolatry, sorcery," while "drunkenness, orgies, and things like that" conclude the list. In the middle we find entries that pertain to Paul's concern about the rise of hostility (potential or actual) within Galatian Christ-groups:

- acts motivated by hostility toward other people (*echthrai*),
- fighting between people (*eris*),
- envious jealousy between people (*zēlos*),
- acts motivated by anger toward other people (*thymoi*),
- acts motivated by competitive rivalry toward other people (*eritheiai*),
- acts motivated by group rivalry (*dichostasiai*),
- acts of tribalistic loyalties (*haireseis*),
- acts motivated by selfish envy of other people (*phthonoi*).

The entries that begin with the translation "acts" appear in the plural in the Greek text, suggesting that Paul is thinking here not simply of attitudes (for example, the feeling of anger) but of actions undergirded by those attitudes (that is, acts of anger). As Paul says in 5:24, "Those who belong to Christ Jesus have crucified the propensity for self-centered living, with its passions and its desires." Consequently, "those who do these kinds of things won't inherit the kingdom of God" (5:21) – in contrast to those who "anticipate the hope of righteousness through the Spirit" (5:5).

Paul's list of "the fruit of the Spirit" (5:22–23) is relatively simple (with all entries being in the singular): "love, joy, peace, patience, kindness, goodness, faithfulness, gentleness, and self-control." As Paul shrewdly says in 5:23, "the Torah is not against things like this," complementing his point in 5:14 about the Torah being summed up in love.[20] These particular entries are

---

[20] The Greek is often translated so that the word *nomos* is not a direct reference to the Torah: "There is no law [*nomos*] against things like this." It is also possible that the Greek plural *tōn toioutōn* is not to be understood as neuter ("such things") but as masculine ("such people"). In this case, Paul's case would be playing off the curse of the Torah in 3:13. That is, whereas all those who try to observe the Torah inevitably come up against its curse, the Torah is not at all opposed to Christ-followers who live by the Spirit.

descriptive of a moral orientation, out of which actions will emerge in refreshing ways within the corporate life of Christ-followers. In this context, Paul expects everyone to agree to his call to arms: "If we have the power of life by means of the Spirit, let us also keep in step with the Spirit's guidance" (5:25).

Knowing that "trust works" and that the fruit of the Spirit is manifest in relationality, Paul moves in 6:1–10 to offer examples of the kinds of things he does and does not imagine transpiring within Christ-groups. These are, then, concrete illustrations that amplify what the "fruit of the Spirit" looks like with a bit more specificity. In particular, Paul urges the Galatians to "carry the burdens of one another; in this way you will be fulfilling the *nomos* of Christ" (6:2). The gist of this is quite straightforward: Christ-followers are to be involved in offsetting the needs of one another – with the metaphor of carrying burdens overlapping considerably with the metaphor of being enslaved to each other in 5:13. If this is straightforward, it is also completely unsurprising in a text where the identity of the self-giving Lord comes alive within the lives and communities of his followers. What is surprising is the term "*nomos* of Christ." As Christ-followers live into their corporate identity as those who carry the burdens of one another, the axiomatic character of Christ (or the pattern of his life) is "filled full" within their communities.

Paul's exhortations in 6:1–10 are notably concise. Have a realistic evaluation of yourself (before God), not imagining that you are all-important within the group (6:3, in line with Paul's exhortation not to be arrogant in 5:26). Don't compare yourselves with others in a competitive spirit (in line with Paul's exhortations against jealousy and envy in 5:20–21 and 5:26). Instead, turn the evaluative scales on yourself (6:4–5), considering your life in relation to the self-giving that comes from trust in Christ, in light of the future eschatological judgment (6:7). In that judgment, eternal life will be the reward for those who live "for purposes of the Spirit by means of the Spirit" (6:8). This includes financial generosity – an extension of the "goodness" in the list of the fruit of the Spirit (5:22). So, support those who teach the word properly (6:6, perhaps preventing charlatans like the new teachers from getting a foothold in a community that has not supported legitimate teachers). But that same generosity of spirit should be a permanent characteristic of Christ-groups, always working good things in the lives of others, not least those within the family (or household) of trust in Christ (6:9–10).

6:11–18: SOCIAL REPUTATION, THE CROSS, AND NEW CREATION

The closing section of Galatians focuses on the cross of Jesus Christ and, in light of the cross, the failings of the new teachers who have caused so much trouble in the Galatian communities. In 6:12–14, Paul depicts himself and the new teachers as boasters, but each party boasts in different things. Paul boasts in "the cross of our Lord Jesus Christ," and because Paul has been crucified with Christ, "the world," he says, "has been crucified to me and I have been crucified to the world" (6:14). Paul does not live by the world's systems of honor-based, status-based competition. And he can prove it by showing "the marks [*stigmata*] of Jesus on my body" (6:17). Paul's body displayed physical scars as a consequence of people persecuting him for his proclamation.[21] Did some think Paul to be a people-pleaser? His own body testifies against the charge.

---

[21] Compare 2 Cor 11:23–27 (with 2 Cor 1:8–9 and 6:3); also Acts 14:19–20.

The new teachers also boast but not in the cross of Christ, says Paul. The new teachers are immersed in "the propensity for self-centered living" (*sarx*), hoping to use the circumcised body (*sarx*) of the Galatians to enhance their own social prestige (6:12–13). Paul's exploration of moral character in 5:13–6:10 now provides him with a further lens with which to see the new teachers – in this case, they are living in that disposition of self-centeredness, thereby betraying the self-giving Lord and his cross, through which and through whom that world no longer exists for those who truly belong to Christ. They are motivated only to look good, to "gain face" (*euprosōpēsai*) in the eyes of others, and "to avoid being persecuted for the cross of Christ" (6:12). Who, in Paul's view, are the new teachers trying to impress? Probably believing and nonbelieving Jews in Jerusalem – the "present-day Jerusalem" that is "in slavery with her children" (4:25). The irony, according to Paul, is that the new teachers "do not themselves obey the Torah," a charge that is hard to parse out, but perhaps Paul is implying that the very people whom the new teachers are trying to impress would find the new teachers themselves to be deficient in some matters of Torah observance.

In contrast to the curse that should fall upon the new teachers (as articulated in 1:8–9), in 6:16 Paul pronounces a blessing of peace upon those who live in accordance with "this standard," as articulated in 6:15: "Being circumcised doesn't count for anything, just as not being circumcised doesn't count for anything; the only thing that matters is new creation." This slightly expansive translation fills in a gap that Paul probably leaves intentionally empty for the purpose of rhetorical force: in Greek, his final three words are simply and starkly "but new creation." Notice the parallel between this verse and 5:6: "In Christ Jesus, being circumcised doesn't matter, just as not being circumcised doesn't matter, but trust that continues to work in practical ways through love." Circumcision, together with its opposite, carries no significance in one's standing before God. In that context, what matters is one thing: new creation.

Paul also includes in 6:16 a reference to "the Israel of God." Precisely what he means by this is contested. We will discuss this further in Chapter 9.

In a final sentence (6:18), Paul relates to the Galatians in familial terms; they are, after all, "brothers and sisters" (*adelphoi*) in Christ. In the course of the letter, Paul has said harsh things to them. Here he wants them to know that he has done so as a brother in Christ, with his reference to "brothers and sisters" reinforcing the eight previous occurrences when he refers to them as fellow siblings in Christ (1:11; 3:15; 4:12, 28, 31; 5:11, 13; 6:1). His blessing is simple: "May the grace of our Lord Jesus Christ be with your spirit [*pneuma*]." It is the same blessing that Paul will later use to conclude other letters as well, such as Philippians (Phil 4:23) and Philemon (Phlm 25). It is important to note that in Philippians Paul instructs the Philippians to "stand firm in one spirit [*pneuma*]" (1:27), so that they can live together "in a manner worthy of the gospel of Christ." Paul wants the Philippians to share a corporate "spirit" that informs their corporate relationships among them. In Galatians, this corporate focus is expressed in terms like "Christ is formed among you" (4:19). The same may also be true in the final verse of the letter, when Paul pronounces a blessing on their "spirit" – perhaps not only their individual "spirits" but, in fact, the corporate spirit that they share and that nurtures their individual lives in Christ. Grace be with your corporate spirit. Let it be (*amēn*).

PART II

Probing the Theology of Galatians

The chapters that follow will probe selected parts of Paul's discourse thematically. Chapter 4 discerns Paul's presentation of the "problem" in its layered aspect – that is, its multifaceted character, with different aspects of the problem stratified in terms of their agencies and effects. Chapter 5 places Paul's discourse about the Torah in relation to the corresponding layers of the stratified problem. Subsequent chapters explore Paul's participatory theology of Christ-followers dying with Christ (Chapter 6) and discern Paul's decentering of micro-identities in Christ-groups (Chapter 7) and his centering of "Christ-full-ness" in the corporate life of those assemblies (Chapter 8). Chapter 9 interprets the meaning of "righteousness" in Galatians, highlights the faithfulness of God as essential to the coherence of Paul's discourse, and considers the ethnic people of Israel in relation to both "the hope of righteousness" and the faithfulness of God.

CHAPTER 4

The Problem in Layered Perspective

It is worth spending time considering the problem that Paul's theological discourse reveals. To understand the significance and richness of the "solution" Paul presents in Galatians, it is helpful to appreciate the complexity of the "problem" presented in that text. This involves (1) recognizing the "transgressive" nature of Paul's analysis of the "social Darwinism" of his day, and (2) articulating the way in which the problem itself features stratified layers of interlocking phenomena.

THE TRANSGRESSIVE CHARACTER OF PAUL'S DESCRIPTION OF THE PROBLEM

In the Roman world, people formed groups quite frequently – "associations" that met about once a month to dine in celebration of some shared form of identity. The members may have belonged to a common occupation, or come from the same ethnic group, or resided in the same neighborhood, or gathered under the auspices of a particular deity. Groups of this kind frequently went out of their way to demonstrate their beneficial place within society. The civic elite were often suspicious of people gathering in groups, however, since groups had the potential to exert power over their adherents in ways that might transgress societal norms. This was especially true of groups devoted to deities that were not part of the cohort of traditional Greco-Roman deities, and/or deities who in one way or another were thought to threaten the stability of society.[1] For instance, groups devoted to Dionysos (or Bacchus, as he was known to the Romans) were highly suspect at various times in the Greco-Roman world, not least because the wild madness induced by Dionysos was thought to have the potential to cause social havoc.

In a first-century context, Paul's letter to the Galatians can easily be read as if it were planting Christ-groups on the wrong side of this divide of social repute and disrepute. Even prior to writing Galatians, Paul already had a reputation for establishing Christ-groups that were socially transgressive. Writing to the Thessalonians in the spring of 50, Paul reveals the extent to which Christ-followers in that city had experienced persecution (1 Thess 1:6; 2:2–4; 3:7) – a persecution arising from the suspicion that Christ-followers were transgressors of the established social order. In that context, Paul denounces those who are immersed in the gospel of Roman control (i.e., "peace and security"; 1 Thess 5:3). Moreover, he reconfigures the worldview of the Thessalonian Christ-followers so that they see their world not as the space-time continuum of Rome and its deities but as the space-time continuum of the deity Paul proclaimed as Lord.[2]

With the presenting situation in Galatia being quite different, Galatians is not as explicit in targeting a particular religiopolitical order. Nonetheless, Galatians is relentless in constructing a worldview in which the space-time continuum is in the control of Paul's deity rather than the deities that propped up Rome's purportedly eternal reign. Even in Galatians Paul's deity is shown to control

---

[1] On this, see Brewer 2022.   [2] See B. Longenecker 2022; 2024a.

time: "When the fulfillment of time came, God sent his Son" (4:4). Rooting out the ultimate cancer in "this present age of evil" (1:4), Paul's deity does not share sovereignty with the deities of Rome. Paul's discourse implies, without it needing to be said, that the purported sovereignty of those deities left the power of Sin free to roam rampantly throughout the world. Paul's deity, on the other hand, transcends the deities that populated the ancient mind – all belonging to the realm of things that "by nature are not deities." In this regard, although Paul's discourse in Galatians does not directly denounce the ideology of the Roman imperial order, Galatians nonetheless is just as strident as 1 Thessalonians in constructing a worldview in which the deities of the Roman world were implicitly stripped of their authority, their effectiveness, and even their ultimate existence.[3]

For people of Paul's day, Christ-followers might have appeared to be devotees of a new deity, Jesus Christ. The birth of Jesus Christ ("born of a woman") predated the writing of Galatians by only fifty years or so and the death of Jesus Christ by twenty years or so. Paul's deity might well have looked like a newcomer, a fledgling foreigner to the panoply of deities. Christ-groups were, in one important sense, "the new kid on the block" of devotional groups, worshipping a "Lord Jesus Christ" who, named as such, had never been the object of devotion previously.

This would have been of some concern to those who oversaw social stability in Paul's world (see Acts 16:20–21; 17:6–8). In Paul's day, novelty was often seen as dangerous. Devotional novelty could introduce powerful forms of social instability, and social instability could be the thin edge of the wedge for societal rupture, with troublemakers of this kind attracting the wrath of

---

[3] Along somewhat similar lines, see Barclay 2011:363–87.

the Greco-Roman deities upon themselves and, perhaps, upon society itself.[4] Groups with long-standing credentials or groups devoted to the traditional deities were thought to have played their part in propping up the long-established structures of society and ensuring the continuance of divine blessings upon society. Christ-groups were, in one sense, novelties in the neighborhoods of Greco-Roman cities, worshipping a deity who had not been tried and tested and who had not yet proven his merit to society. Novel patterns of life might spring up among such groups that could intimidate, compromise, and ultimately imperil patterns of civic life from which the purported benefits of society flowed. No matter how small their size or how socially insignificant they might have seemed, groups devoted to newly discovered deities or to deities that subverted the order of things were prime candidates for cultural suspicion.

If Paul's deity looked dangerously new and newly dangerous, Paul would have said that the deity proclaimed in his gospel is not, in fact, a new deity. The exclusively sovereign deity cannot be a new deity. Paul's deity was not only the sole primordial deity (and, in that sense, the only true deity) but his deity had also been involved in significant historical initiatives even prior to the birth of Jesus Christ. Paul depicted his deity in terms that differed from the way some Epicurean philosophers thought of the deities in general – that is, simply residing in the heavenly realm of the divine, separate from human affairs, having nothing to do with people, people-groups, nations, the world, and the histories that intertwine these things. The deity Paul proclaimed had been active in history. As Paul articulates things in Galatians, God had long ago overseen the articulation of a "pedagogical" guide

---

[4] See case studies in Barclay 1993; B. Longenecker 2024b.

to benefit the ethnic people of Israel (albeit through a series of mediators and in a fashion that retrospectively is seen to be constraining rather than freeing). Hundreds of years before that, the same deity had selected Abraham to be a conduit of blessing within the world (through his single progeny). First-century readers would have taken note of the ancient credentials of Paul's sovereign deity.

But in Galatians Paul combines those reassuring credentials with other features that could easily have been seen as troubling. In Paul's discourse, the exclusively sovereign deity who has acted beneficially in history is also one who rescues people from the formative influence of the *stoicheia* of this world. This could be good news for some, but for those entrusted with keeping those structures robust and for the many who sought to work within them for their own advancement, a message of this kind might have raised eyebrows. In fact, Paul characterizes the structures that produce the multitude of identities in "the present evil age" as themselves being the enslaved victims of an overarching detrimental force: the power of Sin. Christ-followers do not take their marching orders from those societal structures; instead, their identities are open to redefinition in Christ. It would not be surprising if such claims were interpreted as having the potential to be socially transgressive.[5]

If others saw the structures of their world as empowering all that is good, Paul saw things in other terms altogether. In the second half of Galatians 5, for instance, Paul offers a rough sketch of what life looks like beyond properly functioning Christ-groups. His description largely corresponds with what has been called

---

[5] On the transgressive nature of Gal 3:28 in relation to the contrast of enslaved and free in the first century, see B. Longenecker 2018b.

"social Darwinism" – essentially, the "survival of the fittest" played out by people in dog-eat-dog relationships. That is, Paul unmasks the world outside Christ-groups by revealing its moral character within social relationships. Getting behind the hype, going beyond the propaganda, looking past the facade of public opinion, Paul focuses the Galatians' attention on the moral configuration of that world. If Christ-followers fall out of step with the Spirit, they will begin to adopt the moral characteristics of those immersed in "the present evil age," with relationships between people of different identities marked out by "biting and devouring each other," as people become "entirely obliterated by each other" in the process (5:15). In his list of practices that characterize "the propensity for self-centered living" (5:19–21), Paul seems especially interested in registering entries that focus particular attention on aggressively antagonistic actions driven by polarizing animosity: acts of hostility, fighting, jealousy, anger, competition, rivalry, tribalistic loyalty, and envy. Paul captures the moral character of the world beyond the Spirit in the word "arrogance" or "conceit," together with downgrading the identity of others (i.e., shouting each other down, *allēlous prokaloumenoi*) and envying them (5:26). When Paul looks to the world apart from Christ, he sees nothing but people's numerous partialities for themselves, their unbounded forms of self-preferentiality, at the expense of any whom they might be able to take advantage of.

Paul is not alone in this kind of assessment of the moral character of the ancient world. The philosopher Lucretius (first century BCE) would have largely agreed with Paul's diagnosis of the symptoms of social dysfunction. Foregrounding politicians as the best representatives of how the world actually works, Lucretius encouraged his audience to see them for what they really are: "contending with their wits, fighting for precedence, struggling night and day with unending effort, climbing, clawing their way up the pinnacles of wealth and power" (*On the Nature of Things* 2.11–13). To this, Lucretius added the following comment: "O miserable minds of men! O blind hearts! In what darkness, among how many perils, you pass your short lives!" (2.14–16). Caught up in this world of agonistic survival, Lucretius estimated that "deep in every home were aching hearts and torments of the mind, all hapless, self-inflicted without pause, and sorrows breeding furious laments" (6.14–16).

Similar is the *Hymn to Zeus*, a popular piece of poetry by Cleanthes, a Stoic philosopher who lived around 320–230 BCE. Cleanthes depicted the "orderless" living of "the wicked ... in their strange madness" in these terms: "They rush unthinking after ill – some with a shameless zeal for fame; others pursuing gain, disorderly; still others folly, or pleasures of the flesh." And in his satirical novel *The Satyricon*, the Roman novelist Petronius (c. 27–66 CE) has one of his characters curse civic magistrates for rigging the system in favor of themselves, at the expense of the people: "You scratch my back and I'll scratch yours," they say to each other, resulting in situations where "the little people come off badly" since "the jaws of the powerful are always keeping carnival" (*Satyricon* 44). Examples of the inevitable abuse of power in Paul's world could easily be multiplied by other ancient observers. As one scholar has characterized things, this was a "system that encouraged a gnawing hunger for prestige in its citizens, that seethed with their vaunting rivalries, that generated a dynamism so aggressive that it ... overwhelmed all who came against it."[6] (We will see something along similar lines in Chapter 7 in terms

---

[6] Holland 2003:29. (This is as true of the Roman imperial age as it was of the republican age, which Holland's quotation describes.)

of destructive "ethnic hierarchies" that were rampant in the ancient world.)

Paul's analysis of the moral ethos of the world has parallels among some who chose to comment on the configurations of social power in the ancient world. Apart from what God has done in Christ, Paul saw the world as a place of cutthroat competitiveness and aggressive hostility. In Paul's assessment, a cancer of unbridled self-interest had spread into every sector of human life – whether individual, corporate, cultural, societal, national, or international. Self-interest at the expense of others is the fundamental modus operandi characterizing "the present evil age." Paul exposed the essence of the domination system, with a relational cancer infesting all arenas of life.

As noted in Chapter 3, there are "layers" to Paul's understanding of the problem. Beyond the propensity for self-centered living (or *sarx*) lie the *stoicheia* of the world (4:3, 9) and the cosmic power of Sin (2:17, 3:22). This multifaceted way of looking at the problem requires some clarification, not least because we are generally not accustomed to think in terms of *stoichei-ic* influences and cosmic powers. Although these two phenomena are intricately intertwined in Paul's thinking, they are also distinct from each other and will be considered separately here.

CONCEPTUALIZING THE POWER OF SIN

On two occasions Paul's theological discourse foregrounds the "power of Sin" (2:17; 3:22) – a power that has all things within its grip, apart from what God has done in Christ. Paul's sense that a power of Sin exists within "the present evil age" may not come naturally to many people today. In modern Western cultures, it is common to think that existence is primarily lived out within the

The Problem in Layered Perspective 75

material world. For some people, there might be a spiritual add-on (in a sense), and for those who are religious, the human spirit might be in touch with a divine realm beyond the material realm. But the world we live in is predominantly thought to be a material world where what meets the eye is (pretty much) all that is real. In Paul's world, people usually thought much differently. What meets the eye was thought to be animated by spiritual forces of one kind or another, with the material world being the playing board for a competition of spiritual forces.

A quick sideways glance into another Pauline letter allows us to see this perception of the world and how a discourse about cosmic powers plays into Pauline theological discourse about what God has done in Christ. According to Eph 6:12, the struggle of the Christ-follower is not against things or people of the material world but is directed "against the rulers, against the authorities, against 'the cosmos grabbers' [*kosmokratores*] of this dark world, against the spiritual powers of evil in the heavens." This verse articulates the Pauline view that suprahuman forces impact the material world, clutching to get their "hands" on God's cosmos. Whatever God is doing in Christ must pertain to those "spiritual" realities. Ephesians speaks of those realities inducing hostility between people ("the wall of hostility that divided us," 2:14–16). The biggest trick of those suprahuman powers is ensuring that people engage in demonizing each other. Unmasked, the social chaos that results is itself a testimony to the overlordship of the powers in this world. But the letter to the Ephesians also highlights the various assemblies of Christ-followers as the places where relational realignment takes place, with a different spiritual force permeating their gatherings. Precisely in that ethos, Christ-groups are where "the wisdom of God in its rich variety" is being made known "to the rulers and authorities [i.e., the spiritual forces] in the heavenly places" (Eph 3:10). In embodying a different ethos of relationships (a different "spirit-uality"), Christ-groups embody proclamations to spiritual forces that they (those forces) are not sovereign. Christ-groups are to be extracted from the antagonism induced by those spiritual forces, with Christ-followers joining together in harmonious and fruitful unity in Christ and worship of God as a testimony against those spiritual forces.

In Galatians Paul covers similar theological terrain when speaking in 3:22 about the power of Sin that engulfs "all things."[7] Paul's discourse about the problem works well when the power of Sin is understood to inflame the differences in people's identities. The power of Sin is not simply an amalgamation of all of our single sins, our transgressions grouped together that weigh us down under their accumulated density. Paul has space in his discourse for highlighting human sinfulness, of course (1:4; 2:17–18; 3:19), and the propensity for self-centered living (*sarx*) is firmly of central concern to him.[8] But human sinfulness is not in his sights when he speaks of Sin. That power is beyond human agency, is more than human sinfulness in the sum of its parts. The power of Sin seems almost to have its own intentionality, agency, and program, resulting in a situation in which sinfulness permeates all realms of life. Of course, we might want to imagine the power of Sin as a projection or personification of personal sinfulness – an abstraction of collective human sins. But that is not how Paul presents things in Galatians (and elsewhere). Paul externalizes Sin

---

[7] This view of Sin as an overlord of creation reappears in Rom 5:21 and permeates Paul's discourse in Romans 6–7. See also his claim that all people are "under the power of Sin" in Rom 3:9. See B. Longenecker 2020c.

[8] On sins in Paul's letters, see Gathercole 2018. On the relation of sins and the power of Sin, see Dunn 1998:102–27; Carter 2005; B. Longenecker 2020d.

as a power roaming around in "this present age of evil," and this externalization gives him more space to conceptualize things in vivid fashion. We need to honor that way of looking at things if we hope to capture the full force of Paul's theological discourse. To move the power of Sin simply into the human heart would constrain Paul's discourse in a fashion that mutes its dramatic potential – as when a full orchestral score is transcribed for a string quartet. We need to sit patiently with Paul's conceptualization of Sin as a cosmic power in order to open up the full potential of his presentation.[9]

CONCEPTUALIZING THE *STOICHEIA* OF THE WORLD

What, then, are the *stoicheia* that Paul introduces in Gal 4:3 and again in 4:9, and how are they interfaced with the power of Sin? As we will see, the *stoicheia* are (1) identity influencers and (2) conscripted by the power of Sin. Both of these aspects require some explanation, but it is important to note at the outset that for something to be *stoichei-ic*, both of these aspects must be in play. This is why I prefer to translate *stoicheia* with the expansive paraphrase, "the formative influences of all kinds that collectively shape the world's systems and all social identities within them, under the power of Sin" – or, in abbreviated form, "identity

[9] Nor should the power of Sin be confused with Satan. Paul does not reference Satan in this letter. In other letters where Satan is mentioned, Paul speaks of cosmic powers in a way that differentiates them from the Satan figure. We inevitably want to know more – about the differentiation of and relationship between powers and Satan, about the cosmological origins of these things, etc. Paul might give clues here and there, but in general he does not give us much to work with, and in Galatians he gives us nothing at all along these lines. That silence is something we simply need to accommodate, despite our desire to know more about what Paul might have thought.

influencers conscripted by the power of Sin." In each case, both aspects need to be kept in view.

Note, however, that some identity influencers can be freed from servitude to the power of Sin, in which case they are no longer *stoichei-ic*. For Paul, certain phenomena take on characteristics when immersed in one overarching power domain (i.e., under the power of Sin) and other characteristics in another power domain (i.e., the power of the Spirit).[10] Identity influencers conscripted by the power of Sin fall under the label *stoicheia*; but some of those same identity influencers can be empowered by the Spirit in alignment with the purposes of God in Christ, in which case they are no longer among the *stoicheia* (see especially the discussion in Chapter 7).

THE *STOICHEIA* AS IDENTITY INFLUENCERS

People in the ancient world identified different things as *stoicheia*. Consequently, scholars have tried different interpretations in relation to those various *stoicheia*, sometimes shoehorning specific kinds of *stoicheia* into Paul's argument in the hope that one context will explain the flow of Paul's discourse in Galatians more suitably than any other.

It seems, however, that the very variety of *stoicheia* recognized by the ancients is itself more important to Paul's argument than a particular set of *stoicheia*. For instance, earth, wind, fire, and water were commonly thought of as *stoicheia* (Philo, *Opif.* 131; *Her.* 197; 209; 226; *Contempl.* 3–5; *Mos.* 1.96), but so too were the letters of the alphabet (Plato, *Crat.* 422A; Aristotle, *Metaph.* 998.A26); so too were the rudimentary assumptions that inform a person's

---

[10] On this, see Snodgrass 1988.

worldview (Plato, *Laws* 7.790C); so too were numbers (Philo, *Her.* 190); so too were individual musical notes (Plutarch, *Prim. frig.* 7); and so too (at least by the second century but perhaps earlier) were the astral bodies (i.e., the sun, the moon, the stars; Justin, *2 Apol.* 5:2; Theophilus, *Autol.* 2:35; see Wis 13:1-9).[11] Paul did not intend his audience to debate which one of these best fits his argument. His use of the term does not reference any of these phenomena in particular but instead looks more expansively at all the various subparts within the world's network of interlocking systems – systems that influence people's identities in one way or another.

In fact, Paul seems to have conceived of the *stoicheia* (as was commonly done) as the basic components of larger systems in which they were embedded, with those systems giving shape to phenomena that they influence.[12] The *stoicheia* were things that could not be broken down into smaller parts – the primary, indivisible constituents of larger phenomena. In his *Metaphysics* (5.1014a-1014b), Aristotle noted that the term was understood differently by different people, but what the *stoicheia* have in common is that "each of them, being a simple unity, is present in many [further] things" (5.1014b). For instance, as *stoicheia*, the letters of the alphabet are basic to systems of language, thought, and expression; as *stoicheia*, numbers are basic to systems of

---

[11] For overviews of the *stoicheia*, see Wink 1984:67-77; de Boer 2007; Moses 2014:134-47; deSilva 2018:348-53; Wasserman 2018:151-55.

[12] A different way of envisaging them makes them the very basic aspects of something that more developed phenomena leave behind. This is how the author of Hebrews presents things in Heb 5:12. The author wishes that his audience could leave behind the *stoicheia* of diet (i.e., milk) in order to move on to solid foods. Here, the basic *stoicheia* are not basic components of more developed forms.

mathematics, physics, and astronomy; as *stoicheia*, musical notes are basic components of musical compositions; as *stoicheia*, assumptions are basic starting points from which further conceptual constructs develop; as *stoicheia*, earth, wind, fire, and water are basic to physical systems of all kinds; as *stoicheia*, astral bodies are determinative of realities beyond themselves; and so on. It is true that the four physical elements were commonly identified as *stoicheia* in Paul's day, precisely because the ancient people held such fascination about the constructions that undergirded physical reality. But the four physical elements are only one subcategory of a much larger category of things that were recognized to be *stoicheia*. It is not the four physical elements nor the astral bodies that Paul is referencing in particular.[13] Instead, he has in mind a broad conception of the *stoicheia*, seen collectively as the plurality of elemental things that give structure to complexities of life in one way or another, in all of life's varieties.

It is important to emphasize, once again, that even things we conceptualize as immaterial and passive were recognized in the ancient world to have an active influence on the shaping of people's lives. People in Paul's world thought there were spiritual aspects to physical phenomena, each having a formative force. There is a spiritual identity to any number of material phenomena (e.g., residences, workshops, neighborhoods, towns, cities, colonies, territories, empires). We might scratch our head at the thought that things of this kind exert influence over the lives of those within their localities, but that is precisely how most people

---

[13] The fact that he can use the word *stoicheia* in 4:9 without embedding it in a larger phrase "of the world" suggests that Paul is not thinking here of a "technical term" – that is, "the *stoicheia* of the world." He is thinking of *stoicheia* that exist within the world.

of Paul's day imagined the architecture of reality.[14] They were cognizant that there were suprahuman forces shaping their identities, and they attributed those forces to a variety of phenomena, including phenomena that we would consider merely physical, solely inert, exclusively material. People of Paul's day thought it crucial to tend to these suprahuman forces of material realities, thinking the influence of those forces could be beneficial when properly honored, just as they could be malignant when neglected.

THE *STOICHEIA* UNDER THE POWER OF SIN

Paul had a breadth of nonspecified influences in mind when referring to the *stoicheia*. The term *stoicheia* refers to a variety of phenomena that shape the identities of people and are used by the power of Sin to enhance Sin's overlordship.

In Paul's view, people's identity is always formed in relation to external influences. People are not masters of their own identities; they are molded by forces that transcend them. No one is "free" in an individualistic sense, despite whatever pretenses they might otherwise have. There are always factors that shape their identities, with identities growing within a variety of cultural environments. Paul presents a scenario in which Sin had taken hold of those cultural environments, in their virtually endless combinations. These environments mold identities that, under Sin's influence, become occasions for provoking social chaos. These are the *stoicheia* that both promote differences of identity and are exploited by the cosmic power of Sin in relation to those differences. The *stoicheia* are not necessarily bad influences in themselves; they might be neutral or even good influences in

---

[14] See B. Longenecker 2020a:79–87, 212–18, 227–32.

themselves. *Stoicheia* is an overarching term that does not differentiate between phenomena based on a moral taxonomy of some sort. What all the *stoicheia* have in common is simply their influence in shaping identities and their exploitation by the cosmic power of Sin. To the extent that those things (are used to) hinder the fruitful flourishing of relational life, to the extent that they (are used to) foster hostility between people of different identities or promote injustice, those influences have (in Paul's view) come under the control of the power of Sin. Political systems, economic structures, educational institutions, social cultures and subcultures, social and religious norms, and on and on – these may be necessary and good in themselves, but embedded with influential power, they are also vulnerable to obstructing the fostering of beneficial relationships among all people. That is a *stoichei-ic* situation, with identity influencers being repurposed by the power of Sin to promote ways of life that run contrary to God's will.[15] Since all people are enmeshed within this multi-layered problem, they can never claim that a particular aspect of their identity renders them bulletproof against the machinations of Sin.

Paul gives a case study of this in Romans 7. There, the God-given Torah, which itself is "holy" and "good" (7:12, 14), is nonetheless shown to be conscripted by the power of Sin, producing "all kinds of covetousness" (7:8) that destroys healthy relationality. This is the result of enslavement "to the Torah in its connection with Sin" (paraphrasing 7:23, *en tō nomō tēs hamartias*). Here, even the Torah, a God-given identity influencer, is shown to be conscripted by the power of Sin – a situation

---

[15] See, for instance, a more general discussion along similar lines in Wink 1992:73–85.

that the word *stoicheia* seems to reference when Paul uses it in Galatians.

Paul's theology of the *stoicheia* is notably underdeveloped. He does not use a theology of the *stoicheia* to create an inventory of various identities and discuss whether or not they are sinful. The closest he comes to that sort of thing in Galatians is his list of works of self-interestedness (5:19–21). His embryonic comments about the *stoicheia* simply amount to the view that every person's identity has been formed in a matrix of some kind and, moreover, none of those matrixes provide ways out of the overlordship of the power of Sin.

IN SUM

Paul's view of the problems of his world was fundamentally transgressive. It implied that the alleged benefits brought by the Roman deities, structures, and authorities were in fact in the grip of a power propelling the world in never-ending cycles of socially destructive chaos.[16] In articulating his view, Paul differentiated two layers of the forces that regulate people's lives. Although the two are different, both the power of Sin and the *stoicheia* used by Sin are enslaving forces. People are "locked up" or "imprisoned" under them both, apart from Christ. According to Gal 3:22, all things are locked up under the power of Sin; and according to Gal 3:23 and 4:3, people were locked into the structures that influenced their identities and social relationships (as evidenced by the fact that even the Jews were locked up under Torah in a world under Sin). Apart from Christ, the forces that condition identities

[16] Here, Paul's discourse in Galatians links well to the discourse of the Johannine apocalypse.

are trapped under the power of Sin; in that context, identity influencers become *stoichei-ic* traps themselves (which Paul elaborates in 4:21–31).[17] To Sin's delight, the trapped *stoicheia* become entrapments.

Paul thought precisely that situation was taking root even within Galatian Christ-groups as one form of identity was being raised to the level of a macro-identity. This looked to Paul too much like what happens in the realm overseen by the power of Sin, where identities are made to jostle for supremacy over other identities, in never-ending cycles of social Darwinism, to the delight (we might say) of the power of Sin.

If Paul has a layered view of the problem that God solves in Christ, he also has a layered view of the Torah, as will be considered in the next chapter.

---

[17] On 4:21–31 (or 4:21–5:1), see Harmon 2010; Greene-McCreight 2020; and especially Tedder 2020.

CHAPTER 5

The Torah in Layered Perspective

In the previous chapter, we saw how Paul perceives the age before the sending of the Son to be engulfed in a layered problem, involving the power of Sin and the identity influencers that Sin conscripts for its purposes (i.e., the *stoicheia*). We now need to press into the question of how Paul perceived the Torah to function in relation to both of these layers of the problem. In Galatians, Paul depicts the Torah as functioning in relation to at least two purposes: (1) a purpose pertaining to the ethnic people of Israel and (2) what might be called a "cosmic" purpose. It is important to disentangle these two functions. But disentangling them also reveals the significant extent to which they are also intertwined.[1]

THE MEDIATED TORAH

After discussing the promise given to Abraham and his progeny (3:16), Paul declares that the Torah was introduced 430 years after that (3:17). Two verses later, Paul speaks of the Torah having been added *di' aggelōn* (3:19) – a Greek phrase that is open to

---

[1] On the multifaceted character of Paul's discourse on the Torah, see Dunn 1998:128–61.

interpretation regarding the role of angels. Does the phrase denote angels as the primary agents (as its source or origin), in which case the Torah was given *by* angels? Or does it denote angels as the secondary agents (as intermediaries or go-betweens), in which case the Torah was given *by means of* (or *through*) angels?

For some interpreters, Paul saw the situation in Galatia to be so dire that he was forced to portray the Torah in quite a negative light. In this frame of reference, angels easily slip into the role of being the originators of the Torah. Perhaps the angels were even working against God's purposes, either intentionally (if they were evil) or incidentally (if they were somewhat inept at expressing God's will correctly). In interpretations of this kind, when Paul talks about Christ having died "to set us free from the present evil age" (1:4), one of the things he has in mind is redemption from the Torah, given by angels who messed things up (willingly or otherwise) until God intervenes in Christ. For some interpreters, the Torah can even be interpreted as "an anti-God power."[2]

Unless Paul had already instructed the Galatian Christ-followers that the Torah had its origins exclusively among angels (rather than God), it is unlikely that the Galatians would have read "primary agency" out of the Greek preposition *dia*, especially in light of the long-established Jewish tradition about the angelic mediation of the Torah.[3] If Paul wanted to turn that tradition on

---

[2] Harink 2017:110. See the basis for this estimate in Martyn 1997b:153, 155, where the Torah is a tyrant against which God enters into combat. See also de Boer 2011:231, where "the plan of the angels" was "to invalidate God's promise by adding the law."

[3] The angelic mediation of the Torah is found in the Old Testament (Deut 33:2 [esp. in the LXX], Exod 3:2, and Ps 68:17) and is developed in Jewish literature of dramatically different genres and ideologies (*Jub* 1.27–29; 4Q216 5.1; Philo, *On Dreams* 1.140–44; Josephus, *Ant.* 15.136). That diversity attests to its functionality across a wide spectrum of Jewish theological

its head, he would have needed to do much more than simply write the preposition *dia* in 3:19. It would have been easy for Paul to add a phrase indicating that the Torah was not given by God, but he didn't do that either. It is too much to believe that the Galatians could have connected the dots between the simple preposition *dia* and some grander scenario involving the "malicious intent" of the angels, who acted apart from and contrary to God's will.[4]

It seems, then, that even in Galatians the ultimate origin of the Torah lies not simply in the angelic order (*dia* as "by") but in the realm of the God who acted by means of intermediary angels (*dia* as "through"). However, whereas the angelic mediation of the Torah was traditionally seen to demonstrate the glory of the Torah, Paul sees it to indicate the relational distance between God and the recipients of the Torah. It is not the case that God was not involved in the giving of the Torah; but nonetheless, for Paul, the Torah is not God's ultimate self-revealing involvement.

In this regard, it is important to note that what fascinated people in Paul's world was how to gain empowering intimacy with deities. Devotion to the mystery deities (e.g., Dionysos, Isis) was on the rise in Paul's world precisely because those deities offered forms of intimacy that were not known to be characteristic

---

reflection. (It also appears in early Christian texts: Heb 2:2; Acts 7:38, 53.) There is little reason to think that the Galatian Christ-followers did not know of this tradition before their first hearing of Galatians. They were probably conversant with it, either through synagogue attachments (as God-fearing gentiles, perhaps), Paul's teaching, or the teaching of the new teachers.

[4] Even if the Torah is conceptualized as having its origins in angelic agency, that does not necessarily set it up as oppositional to God's will. Instead, the angelic initiative should be seen as being in compliance with the will of God.

of the traditional deities. So, for instance, the Roman poet Ovid (43 BCE–17/18 CE) can say of Dionysos, "no deity is more near" (*Metamorphoses* 3.658–59), while the Roman rhetorician Apuleius (125–180 CE) has his main character speak of how devotion to Isis brought him "face-to-face with the deities below and the deities above, and in unmediated intimacy I worshipped them" (*The Golden Ass* 11.23). A second-century altar to Dionysos describes him as "the manifest deity" (SEG 20:37). The Roman historian Diodorus Siculus (writing between 60 and 30 BCE) depicted the "manifestation" (*epiphaneia*) of the mystery deities of Samothrace to their devotees, bringing "unexpected aid" to those "who call upon them in the midst of perils" (*Library of History*, Book 5, 49.5). For many in Paul's day, intimacy with the deities was an alluring prospect.[5]

In Galatians, Paul depicts properly configured Christ-devotion as opening up channels of unmediated intimacy with the sovereign deity, who alone is "one" (3:20). This monotheistic intimacy is illustrated by Paul's own personal encounter with the resurrected Son (1:15), by the Galatians' experience of the Spirit (3:1–5), and by Christ-followers in general, in whose hearts the Spirit of Christ cries out in worshipful intimacy and intimate worship, "Abba, Father" (4:6).[6] By contrast, the Torah was given for a specific people but only in mediated relationality (through angels, at the hand of a mediator), and it was to serve as their "pedagogue" for a specific period of time – "until [the coming of] Christ" (*eis Christon*, 3:24).

---

[5] This is not seen ubiquitously, however. For starters, Epicureans did not believe the deities had any involvement in the things of this world.
[6] "Abba" does not equate to "Daddy."

THE TORAH AS PEDAGOGUE

Because there is relational distance between God and the recipients of the Torah, other figures fill the space between them. This is how Paul depicts the Torah in its role as pedagogue. The term "pedagogue" requires some attention. In our world, "pedagogy" refers to the act of teaching; in Paul's world, a teacher was different from a pedagogue, since a pedagogue had no official role in teaching a syllabus in (say) rhetoric or philosophy or mathematics. Teachers were hired for those roles. A pedagogue, by contrast, served a household in the task of overseeing the everyday life of a child, or children, within the household – somewhat like a "childminder" in Western cultures today, with the obvious difference that a pedagogue was usually an enslaved person within the household.[7] Pedagogues were charged with ensuring that the householder's expectations for their children were not derailed, that the children's lives were structured to avoid chaos, and that the children would not get sidetracked or engulfed in danger (for instance, abducted for ransom or simply for other purposes of ill intent). There is evidence that some pedagogues were harsh in their handling of children, and there is evidence that some pedagogues were cherished and loved by their charges.[8] This allows interpreters of Galatians to choose which kind of scenario they think corresponds best with their understanding of Paul's

---

[7] See, for instance, Plautus, *Bacch.* 422–23; Libanius, *Or.* 58.7; Petronius, *Sat.* 94.

[8] Fondness for childhood pedagogues appears in Cicero (*Amic.* 20.74), while the harshness of the pedagogue appears in Quintilian (*Inst.* 1.3.17) and Martial (*Epigr.* 11.39). Notably, both emphases appear in Plutarch, where fondness in one passage (*Alex.* 24.6) contrasts with the emphasis on harshness (*Mor.* 37D). On the pedagogue in the ancient world and Galatians, see R. Longenecker 1982; Belleville 1986; Lull 1986; Young 1987; Sänger 2006.

discussion of the Torah. Does Paul depict the Torah as harsh and something to be despised? Or did the Torah play a role cherished by those whom it oversaw?

Paul's discourse plays on both sides of this street. On the one hand, to be "under the Torah" is to be enslaved to it. In Paul's discourse, this is an unwanted thing, with negative connotations (in the retrospective light of freedom in Christ). Resonances of this kind can easily be heard in Paul's talk of being "locked up under the Torah" in 3:23, serving as the basis for the metaphor of enslavement that Paul develops in 4:3 and elaborates in 4:21–31. On the other hand, Paul's discussion of the pedagogue moves into another analogy in 4:2, where he speaks of a time when children are under "those who have oversight" (*epitropoi*) over others and "those who manage the household affairs" (*oikonomoi*). These are not negative functions carried out by resented people; they were essential to the good ordering of households, carried out by people entrusted by the householder.

Resonances of this more positive kind can easily be heard in Paul's talk of being under a pedagogue in 3:24–25. Both sides of the street need to be visited when touring through Galatians.[9] In that regard, we need to understand what it is about the Torah that allows Paul to see it serving a positive function.

THE PROTECTIVE ROLE OF THE TORAH

The pedagogue's primary role was not to perfect children but to protect them. But who are the protected children under the pedagogue in Galatians? Some commentators propose that Paul

---

[9] On the double character of Paul's pedagogue imagery, see Moo 2013:243; Keener 2018:160.

is not thinking of the ethnic people of Israel exclusively; these interpreters see the first-person plurals of 3:24-25 ("we were guarded," "our pedagogue," "we are no longer under a pedagogue") as referring to all of humanity.[10] But this is unlikely, and all the more so when we rid ourselves of translating *nomos* as "law" (with all the theological baggage of that term) and stick with its more natural sense of "Torah" – Torah as divine instruction and guidance. For Paul, in its pedagogical role the Torah was the instruction given to the ethnic people of Israel.[11] Paul highlights this by noting Moses's role as the intermediary between God and the people of Israel: "by the hand of a mediator" (3:19). This was an ethnic mediator for an ethnic people. And the Torah was given to that particular people to act as a pedagogue prior to the incarnation of the Son. If the Torah has other functions pertaining to people other than ethnic Israel, in its pedagogical role the Torah was articulated for the specific benefit of protecting the ethnic people of Israel.

What was this protective role? That purpose must have involved, in its primary function, the distancing of ethnic Israel from the idolatry of other people-groups. Jews were sometimes accused by their gentile peers of *asebeia*, "impiety," the failure to worship the traditional Greco-Roman deities. In Galatians, this issue of idolatry is high on the agenda:

1. It is central to the story of Abraham, who was known to have abandoned idolatry to worship Yahweh.
2. It is probably included in the resonances of the phrase "gentile sinners" in 2:15.

---

[10] See Martyn 1997a:362; de Boer 2011:238. See also the claim that being "under *nomos*" is "the (universal) human predicament" (de Boer 2011:263n393).
[11] See Wright 2021:237.

3. It is the inverse of Paul's reference to the "Shema" of Deut 6:4 in Gal 3:20: "God is one" – the Shema being the affirmation of monolatrous worship prayed daily by observant Jews: "Hear, O Israel, the Lord, our God, the Lord is one" (compare Jesus's pronouncement of the Shema in Mark 12:29–30).
4. Paul foregrounds idolatry specifically in 4:8 when referencing the Galatians' former enslavement to things "that by nature aren't deities at all."
5. Idolatry is explicitly referenced as an entry in Paul's "works of *sarx*" in 5:20.

While Paul envisioned all people-groups to have been under the power of Sin, he also carves out space for imaging ethnic Israel in a somewhat different position under Sin, being differentiated from other ethnic groups by its unique protective pedagogue, which offered something of a shelter against the worst idolatrous violations evidenced in the worship practices of the pagan nations. Of course, even the people of ethnic Israel were not free from flirting with idolatry (as Paul recounts, for instance, in 1 Cor 10:1–7), but idolatry was specifically what observance of the Torah was to curtail, minimizing its enthrallment and entanglements.[12]

This is why Galatian Christ-followers were so enamored with Torah observance; they sought to distance themselves from pagan idolatry and enhance their nonidolatrous relationship with the God of Israel. Paul saw his own gospel in precisely those terms – stripping idolatry from Christ-followers (as in 1 Thess 1:9–10). But for him, the adoption of Torah observance by gentile Christ-followers does not get them closer to that goal. The Torah had

---

[12] On Paul's reading of idolatry in scripture, see Watson 2004:363–74.

protected ethnic Israel from the ravages of idolatry that had infested the other nations prior to the coming of Christ, but that does not make the Torah the "go-to" place for Christ-followers now that "the fullness of time" has come.

There is a certain logic, of course, in the suggestion that non-idolatrous Christ-followers should observe those practices that were given as protection against idolatry. This is why Paul's image of the Torah as the pedagogue of the ethnic people of Israel makes so much sense as a way of countering what the Galatians were being taught by the new teachers. A pedagogue functions beneficially only as a protector of children; a pedagogue has no corresponding role with regard to mature adults. It would be the most outlandish thing to see a grown man attending a social meal with a pedagogue at his side, or walking through the streets with a pedagogue accompanying him as his protector, or at meals or in the public baths under the watchful eye of a pedagogue. As well as being laughable, that scenario would suggest that something has gone wrong within the man's household, as if his own upbringing had been defective.

In its pedagogical role, then, the Torah was articulated to provide some structural protection for the ethnic people of Israel in the idolatrous epoch prior to the coming of Jesus Christ. Paul is not in the least suggesting that Israel was slowly progressing by means of Torah observance, until such time as it was ready for Christ to come – or any variation on a "maturation" scenario.[13] Instead, the Torah only served to differentiate the ethnic people of Israel and the other nations with regard to idolatry.

---

[13] If anything "matured," it was time itself ("the fullness of time," 4:4). For a provocative thesis regarding Paul's view of time, see Jervis 2023.

In Chapter 7, we will see why this differentiation is important for reasons beyond the pedagogical function of the Torah. For now, notice how this pedagogical function of the Torah provides the context for Paul's claim that "God sent God's Son ... born under the Torah" (4:4). Paul does not say as much, but it is easy to see an implied connection between the protective function of the Torah and the incarnation of the Son. Could the Son of God have been sent to live his life within a polytheistic ethnic group? Evidently Paul could not imagine such a thing, and for good reason. Instead, the establishment of the pedagogue among the ethnic people of Israel differentiated them from the polytheistic pagan nations in order to provide a monotheistic context for the Son's incarnation. Although Paul does not say as much, the implication is reasonable, and Paul may well have explained this previously to the Galatians. Moreover, this implication seems to serve as the basis for Paul's claim in 4:5 that this was "to redeem those under the Torah" – as we'll see in Chapter 9.

If the Torah structured the life of the ethnic people of Israel in ways that kept idolatry in check, it nonetheless was "not able to generate [eschatological] life" (3:21) and was not able to create identities of righteousness before God (2:16, 21). It was not able to overthrow the overlordship of the power of Sin. If this inadequacy is true even for the Torah, it is certainly true for any other form of influence or status imaginable. This may be what Paul means when he calls the *stoicheia* "weak and ineffectual" (4:9).[14] Beyond the realm of those properly enlivened in Christ, these "identity influencers" inevitably are tools whereby the power of

---

[14] The term *ptōcha* in 4:9 is difficult to translate. I consider something like "ineffectual" better than most translations (NRSV: "beggarly"; CED: "worthless"; NIV: "miserable").

Sin maintains its entrenched overlordship by manipulating unending contests of identity superiority. We need to give further consideration to the Torah's function with regard to that cosmic power.

UNMASKING THE POWER OF SIN

In Gal 3:22, Paul claims that "scripture locked up all things under the power of Sin."[15] When interpreting what this clause might mean, consideration also needs to be given to a phrase just a few verses earlier, where Paul stated that the Torah was given "because of the violations" (3:19). Various interpretations have been proposed to explain this ambiguous phrase. In one interpretation, the phrase means something like "in order to atone for violations" through the sacrificial system.[16] Others think Paul means that the Torah was given to increase violations;[17] others that the Torah was meant to restrain violations;[18] and others that the Torah was given to catalog amorphous forms of sinfulness so that they can be registered as explicit forms of transgression.[19] All of these make sense, but some fit the context better than others.[20]

In the light commentary of Chapter 3, the last two options (i.e., restraining sinfulness and naming transgressions) were shown to

---

[15] Paul's use of the word "scripture" in Galatians seems centered in the notion of "the concentrated divine voice within the given Torah and beyond."
[16] Dunn 1993a:188–90.
[17] This might seem strange, but it has a foothold in one interpretation of Rom 5:20: "The Torah came *in order to* multiply the trespass." That interpretation is itself in some doubt, however, since the Greek *hina* may indicate result rather than purpose: "The Torah came *with the result* that the trespass multiplied." See Martyn 1997a:354–55; Schreiner 2010:241; de Boer 2011:230; Grindheim 2013:102–3.
[18] Lull 1986:485–86.   [19] R. Longenecker 1990:138.
[20] The "sacrificial system" interpretation is the least compelling.

be working inextricably together. In fact, probably Paul leaves the phrase "because of the violations" without immediate clarification precisely because it seems to have this double significance. One signification, as we have seen, is the Torah's "pedagogical" function, where it restrains all-out forms of idolatry. The other is the Torah's "taxonomic" function – that is, its role in the cataloging of transgressions. Although commentators sometimes feel compelled to decide between them, these two roles are inextricably intertwined. The Torah could not serve a pedagogical role if it did not also play a taxonomic role in the naming of sins, especially idolatry. Instead of undifferentiated sinfulness swirling about in God's world, the Torah provided a means for identifying particular forms of sinfulness. That is, the Torah named sins.

Paul will restate the idea in his later letter to Christ-groups in Rome. There he claims that the whole world is accountable to God, in light of "the knowledge of sinfulness" that comes through the Torah (3:20). The Torah holds all accountable by bringing sinfulness to light, as a testament to the fact that all are under the power of Sin (3:9). Paul articulates much the same at two further points in Romans 4–5. In Rom 4:15, he uses the same noun that appears in the phrase under consideration in Gal 3:19 (*parabasis*, a violation of legal stipulations), with the meaning of the phrase being clearer in Romans: The Torah puts wrath into effect, since only when there are stipulations can violations of those stipulations become evident and initiatives against those violations become actionable. In Rom 5:13, Paul claims that sinfulness was not taken into account until the Torah came. The Torah revealed what transgression looks like, identifying offenses that would otherwise be unidentifiable by name.[21] Much the same is most

---

[21] The same point is evident also in Rom 7:7.

likely to be in play in Gal 3:19. What would otherwise be amorphous sinfulness becomes categorizable violations once the Torah's stipulations are articulated.

This line of thought provides a helpful backdrop for understanding Paul's claim of 3:22: "Scripture locked up all things under the power of Sin." That is to say, the divine voice within the Torah reveals that sinfulness cannot be explained without recourse to a cosmic power that engulfs "all things," ensuring that the effects of the power of Sin become recognizable within God's creation. Indeed, if it needed to be demonstrated that the power of Sin has enslaved all things within creation, the taxonomic Torah is the means for that demonstration. The devastating effectiveness of the power of Sin is illuminated in a way that was not evident apart from the giving of the Torah.

In this way, even the giving of the Torah serves an important role in God's defeat of Sin – not because the Torah offers life (it doesn't; 3:21) but because the divine voice within it categorizes the effects of Sin in order to offer an account sheet of the ways in which Sin's influence has infested all aspects of life. If we can personify Sin for a moment, we can imagine that its plan was to have its way without being recognized, with sins multiplying nebulously, unidentifiable, and without accountability or attribution. The divine voice within the given Torah is one way in which God has outsmarted the intention of Sin (in a sense) by introducing a taxonomy of sinfulness, transforming amorphous sinfulness into observable and actionable violations. The giving of the Torah, with the consequent "locking up of all things" in the column of Sin's overlordship, was God's way of exposing the power of Sin. By "locking all things up under the power of Sin," God ensured that Sin is no longer allowed to lurk in the dark recesses of the world, unrecognized, undiagnosed, and unacknowledged for the destruction it causes. God did not let Sin slither around in the background, manufacturing sinfulness in "all things" unimpeded, without accountability. Only the sovereign deity can unmask such a power. In this way, then, the Torah serves a function that is other than, but not independent of, what God was doing with the Abrahamic covenant. There is a sense of coordination of divine initiative in the utterance of the Abraham blessing and the articulation of the Torah, without any sense of divine schizophrenia.

The unmasking of the power of Sin, then, becomes the necessary backdrop for displaying the full extent of what God has done in the death and resurrection of Christ. This is not a new deity on the scene of history; this deity has already prepared the way for the influx of eschatological power by disclosing the cosmic enemy that is defeated in the eschatological sending of the Son. The articulation of the Torah was a means of exposing the otherwise clandestine cosmic antagonist. In a sense, the Torah was God's way of giving notice to the power of Sin that its days as the purported overlord of the created order were numbered – until "the fullness of time" (4:4), the coming of the one "to whom the promise had been made" (3:19), the coming of eschatological trust in the sovereign God (3:25).

THE CURSE ARTICULATED BY THE TORAH

This "locking all things under the power of Sin" did not pertain simply to the ethnic recipients of the Torah (for whom it functioned as a temporary pedagogue against the idolatry of the present evil age) but to the whole of humanity and, in fact, "all things." It is in this light that Paul's comments in 3:10 need to be considered. There Paul claims that a curse falls upon those for whom the works of the Torah form the basis of their confidence before God, those for whom the works of the Torah are key to their identity before God (citing Deut 27:26; compare Deut 29:20–21). Evidently this curse transpires because, as Paul now clearly views things in the light of Christ, all people are unable to keep the commands of the Torah for the purposes of generating eschatological life. And if the Torah's curse falls upon those who observe it or are eager to observe it, it must also fall upon those who do not even seek to observe it.[22] By simple logical extension, all people stand under the curse articulated by the Torah in one way or another. This follows closely along the logic of Gal 2:16, where Paul declares that "'no flesh' will be made righteous by works of the Torah" – a view that he and Peter both share (so Paul sees no need to spell out the argument further in 3:10 but simply assumes that the point is already in play). The scope of this agreed pronouncement includes both "Jews by birth" and "gentile sinners" (2:15). The curse of the Torah falls upon all humanity. As we will see when discussing Gal 3:13 in Chapter 6, the Torah's curse is rebuffed for those who are in Christ, because of what God has done in Christ – which we will consider more specifically in the following chapters.

---

[22] This last point is not articulated within 3:10–14, but it is probably an assumed feature of his discourse there. On the "omitted premise" of 3:10, see Das 2012; Hunn 2015.

CHAPTER 6

Participation in Christ as Power-Vortex

Jesus Christ "died for our sins," says Paul right at the start of the letter (1:4). It is folly to pretend that "our sins" have little to do with Paul's theological concerns. But it is also important to recognize why "our sins" are important in Paul's discourse. They serve as testimonies to a greater problem lying behind them: the power of Sin that has manufactured sinful relationships among "all things" (3:22). Grasping the full import of the claim that Jesus Christ died "for our sins" requires us to understand his death in relation to that all-encompassing power. Although they should not be downplayed, "our sins" are nonetheless not the ultimate problem; they are placeholders that invite fuller analysis of the problem that the death of Christ rectifies: God's triumph over the power of Sin.

This chapter explores the death and resurrection of Christ in relation to Sin. Here, I use the phrase "power-vortex" to discuss Paul's notion of participation in Christ, since that phrase captures the dramatic sense of being immersed in something so powerful that it produces a range of effects – effects in some sense destructive but also reconstructive.

THE DEATH OF JESUS CHRIST AND THE SOVEREIGNTY OF GOD

There is a reason why Paul's discourse in Galatians does not feature themes of the guilt, remorse, and repentance of the individual, or even divine forgiveness. Those things are no doubt in play theologically, and Paul probably would not dispute their importance. But they don't have a foothold in Paul's explicit discourse within Galatians because the heart of the problem lies at a much deeper level in Paul's theological analysis. Jesus Christ did not die simply to put into effect an ongoing cycle of repentance and forgiveness in a world dominated by the power of Sin. In that scenario, Sin would prove to be the ultimate sovereign, with the death of Jesus Christ being like a dose of occasional medicine taken by the repentant person to hold back the effects of Sin's cancerous reign. Quite differently, our sins testify to the purported overlordship of Sin; and in that regard, even Jews find in Christ that they too are sinners, and the Torah has not kept them from the overlordship of Sin (2:17). When the Torah itself (divinely given, albeit through mediators) cannot offer full protection from Sin, the depths of the desperate situation become soberingly evident.

For these reasons, it is important to keep in mind that Paul's full articulation in 1:4 moves from a statement about Christ's death "for our sins" to a purpose clause: "in order to deliver us from this present evil age." The need for forgiveness "for our sins" is implied in the first statement, but the problem God offsets in Christ is also, and indispensably, about liberation.[1] In Galatians, even while his discourse assumes the need for humans to be

---

[1] See B. Longenecker 2020c; 2020d.

forgiven for their sins/transgressions (1:4; 3:19), Paul's discursive stress is on deliverance. For Paul, the right relationships that are to be evidenced among Christ-followers bear witness to the fact that the enslaving influence of the power of Sin has now been shattered by the liberating death and resurrection of Jesus Christ. In a sense, Paul's discussions of issues that we might categorize as "atonement" or "ethics" or "corporate identity" are ultimately about the sovereignty of God. Is God in charge of this world when Sin seems to be the overlord of all things? The death and resurrection of Jesus Christ is the solitary testament to the exclusive sovereignty of God over the most entrenched force that conjures up the relational chaos that engulfs God's creation.

PARTICIPATION IN JESUS CHRIST

Instead of capitalizing on notions of guilt, repentance, and forgiveness, Paul's discourse foregrounds the participation of Christ-followers in what we might call "the Christ-event" – in particular, the death of Christ, which is salvifically available to Christ-followers because of the resurrection of Christ. Paul has several metaphors for signaling this participatory feature of Galatians: Christ-followers are "co-crucified with Christ" (2:19; see also 5:24; 6:14); they are "clothed with Christ" (3:27); they share in his "Sonship" (3:26; 4:1–7);[2] and just as Paul says that Christ lives "in me" (1:16; 2:20), so he says he labors (in labor pains) for Christ to be "formed" in and among the Galatians themselves (4:19). Christ-followers are conjoined with Christ in his death and, consequently, are blessed with the power of his resurrected life in their relationships with each other. Paul calls this "new

---

[2] On Paul's metaphor of adopted sonship, see Walters 2003; Heim 2017.

creation" (6:15).³ Far more than an endless spin cycle of sin-guilt-repentance-forgiveness, this discursive arena involves Christ-followers dying with Christ in order for Christ to come alive in and among them.

What should we call the "I am in Christ and Christ is in me" aspect of Paul's theology? Interpreters have tried to capture this rich theological nexus with various labels. In the early twentieth century, the term "mysticism" was suggested.[4] More recently, proposals have included terms like "interchange," "participationistic eschatology," and even "pneumatologically participatory martyrological eschatology."[5] These terms are attempts to capture Paul's understanding of redemption, in which people are liberated from the realm of the overlordship of Sin and relocated, through death and new life, in the realm of divine grace. Paul's conceptualization of Christ-followers in union with their Lord takes us into territory that is somewhat hard to map linguistically and requires specialized terminology. In essence, Paul depicts Christ-followers as being immersed in the death of Christ in order for the resurrected Christ to come alive within their lives.

In this arena of thought, Paul does not say the sort of thing that Christians in the twenty-first century often say: "Christ died for

---

[3] See Hubbard 2002:209–32. This interpretation takes "new creation" to be more anthropo-ecclesial (i.e., Christ-followers in transformed relationships with others) than cosmological (e.g., a new creational order), at least in the explicit discourse of Galatians. Moreover, Paul speaks of "new creation" when writing later to the Corinthians (2 Cor 5:17), and in that context the phrase does not have any explicit cosmological reference. Evidently Paul had not trained the Corinthian Christ-followers to think of the phrase in those terms, despite writing Galatians while he was with them (as seems likely, in 50 or 51).

[4] Schweitzer 1931.

[5] Respectively, Hooker 1985; Sanders 1977; D. Campbell 2005.

our sins so that we can be forgiven for our sins and live eternally." Paul would not dispute that, but it is not primarily how he articulates things in Galatians. Instead, his line of thinking is shaped more along these lines: "Christ died for our sins (which testify to the overlordship of Sin) so that we can die with him (thereby escaping the control of Sin) and find the power of his resurrected life coursing through our new life in relationship with God and with others by means of the Spirit." It isn't natural for us to say, "Christ loves you and died so that you too will die," but there is a hefty section of Paul's discourse that flows along those lines.

Notably, of course, Paul mentions the resurrection of Jesus Christ in only one place in Galatians, in the very first verse: God the Father "raised him from the dead" (1:1). We might think, then, that the resurrection is not very important to Paul's discourse in Galatians. But the resurrection of Jesus Christ is not inconsequential theological stuffing at the start of the letter that Paul drops as soon as he gets going. It is a central affirmation, even in Galatians – especially in Galatians. The whole of Paul's participationistic theology implies, requires, and builds on the resurrection of Jesus Christ. The resurrection of Jesus Christ empowers Paul's pointed claims about Christ-followers being clothed with Christ and sharing his Sonship, with Christ living in and being formed among his followers. Quite simply, Christ cannot come alive in his followers if he himself has not been raised. The fact that resurrection is mentioned only once is irrelevant to the theological interpretation of the letter; interpretation is more than just mathematics. In the same way that the power of Sin is mentioned only twice but is nonetheless the organizing principle around Paul's thought about what is wrong with "all things" in God's world (3:22; see also 2:17), so too the resurrection of Jesus Christ undergirds the participationistic discourse that is axial to Galatians.[6]

DEATH TO THE POWER OF SIN AND NEW IDENTITY FROM NOTHINGNESS

In order to probe the full mechanics of Paul's "participationism," it is important to foreground certain aspects of Jesus Christ's death and resurrection. In particular, for Paul's theological discourse to have its full effect, it is critical that the resurrection of Jesus Christ is recognized as the restoration of a life that had ceased to exist. This is an incredibly striking claim, no matter what century, no matter how familiar the notion of Christ's resurrection might be. When God the Father raised the Son to life, the resurrected life of the Son emerged from nothingness (compare Rom 4:24–25 in the context of 4:17). Astoundingly, Paul's discourse requires us to recognize that the Son willingly submitted to nonexistence in order to effect salvation for a world in the grip of Sin. The divine Son gave himself completely into the forces of annihilation, which tore through the identity of the divine Son.[7] The self-giving Son gave himself utterly into nonexistence: "Christ died" (2:21). Paul knows nothing about the crucified Son "staying" in the tomb until Easter, or finding a way out of death, or visiting the spirits of the deceased between his crucifixion and resurrection (in the "harrowing of hell"). Nor

---

[6] On the importance of the resurrection of Jesus Christ in Galatians, see Bryant 2001; Boakye 2017.

[7] These are the same forces that Paul attributes ultimately to the power of Sin. Compare Paul's verb "obliterate," *analoō*, in 5:15 when speaking about the moral character of life in spheres of life untouched by the Spirit of the self-giving Son.

is the Son a self-resurrecting deity.[8] Paul consistently speaks of the Son being raised by the Father.[9] For Paul, it seems, the Son of God was nonexistent between the late afternoon of what we call Good Friday and the morning of what we call Easter Sunday. Evidently the identity of the Son was held within the being of the Father (we must suppose) even when the Son himself had ceased to exist, in order for the Son to be resurrected to life once again, in lordship, empowered by the resurrecting power of the Father. The Son was "known by God" even when the Son himself did not exist.

All this is pertinent to Paul's participationistic discourse because Paul seems to imagine Christ-followers themselves as undergoing a similar process (as evidenced not least in his own autobiography of Gal 1-2).[10] When Christ-followers are crucified with Christ, they die – which is to say, they lose their identity as people who live in a world in which Sin is the overlord of all things. Their identity in that world collapses into nothingness. Sin no longer has an essential grip on those who die. The relational dysfunction that Sin manufactured for those alive in "the present evil age" no longer permeates and defines the relationality of the "dead" person. Only the sovereign God is able to bring life where there is nothingness. The power of Sin cannot do what the sovereign God does; it cannot reach into nothingness and find life there. The resurrection of Jesus Christ, then, testifies to the exclusive supremacy and dominion of God the Father. Nothing

---

[8] For this presentation of Jesus's identity, see John 10:18.
[9] See Rom 4:24-25; 6:4, 9; 7:4; 8:11, 34; 10:9; 1 Cor 6:14; 15:4 (*egēgertai* as passive, not "he rose," contra NRSV and CEB), 12-17, 20; 2 Cor 4:14; 5:15; Gal 1:1; Eph 1:20; Col 2:12; 1 Thess 1:10 (explaining what Paul means in 4:14); 2 Tim 2:8.
[10] On Paul's autobiography in Galatians 1-2, see Lyons 1985; Gaventa 1986; Barclay 2002.

but pure sovereignty can bring life where previously there was nothing. Sin promotes death in a sphere where God intended life; the power of God brings life out of the sphere where Sin promoted death.

Co-crucifixion with Christ strips the all-encompassing power of Sin of its veneer of sovereignty, severing in the process a person's enslavement to self-infatuation and self-promotion at the expense of others. No longer are Christ-followers (to be) trapped in the networks of dysfunctional relationality. Those who die with Christ are given life in a realm where the catastrophizing power of Sin no longer has overlordship. This is the realm of being in Christ, belonging to Christ, and being animated by the Spirit of the Son.[11] The death and resurrection of Christ is, then, a vortex into which identities are disassembled and reassembled. Disassembly happens when lives that have been shaped by the overlordship of Sin are extracted from the "present evil age" through death – through co-crucifixion with Christ. The death and resurrection of Christ is the pattern of transformation of Christ-followers. God the Father retained the imprint of the Son's identity during the period of the Son's nonexistence and then reconstructed the life of the Son in resurrection to lordship (itself an astounding gospel to proclaim on the urban streets of the Roman world and beyond); in the same way, God holds the identities of those who die with Christ (as Paul says, the Galatians are "known by God," 4:9)

---

[11] A number of scholars have recently argued, with some force, that many people in Paul's day thought that *pneuma* (here, "Spirit") had a material aspect (albeit "heavenly" material) and that Paul shares this view, with the Spirit (i.e., heavenly material) implanted in and uniting all those within the body of Christ. See Johnson Hodge 2007; Engberg-Pedersen 2010; Thiessen 2016:129–60; 2023:101–47.

and refashions them anew in the sphere of the Spirit's reconstructive power.

Of course, the identities of Christ-followers may well be consonant with their previous identities in many ways (just as Paul's identity had points of commonality before and after his encounter with Christ). Females, for instance, come alive as females in Christ, males as males in Christ, Jews as Jews in Christ, gentiles as gentiles in Christ, and on and on.[12] There is one primary way, however, in which their lives are different, and this difference makes all the difference to every aspect of life – that is, they are under new lordship. Whatever forms of identity are shared by the "I" under the identity influencers of the present evil age and the "I" who was crucified and now lives in Christ, those continuous strands of identity were held in the hands of God through the death of the "I," wherein God effects the discontinuous rupture of that identity from the grip of the power of Sin. When identity passes through the portal of Christ's death and into the sphere of Christ's resurrection, transformation is everything – "new creation" (6:15).

Of course, in Paul's view, not every form of identity is recreated by God as Christ comes alive in a Christ-follower. Here Paul's list of actions that display the proclivity for self-centered living are instructive and critical (5:19–21). If the Galatians had previously been devotees of pagan deities, that part of their identity does not

---

[12] It runs against the grain for us to say "enslaved persons, as enslaved persons in Christ"; but Paul, in effect, says as much in 1 Cor 7:21–24 (although see his important note in 7:21). The "household codes" of Col 3:18–4:1 and Eph 5:22–6:9 assume the same. Conversely, Paul makes sure that those who were free prior to becoming Christ-followers now think of themselves as enslaved to Christ (1 Cor 7:22). On Paul's discourse on behalf of the enslaved Onesimus, see B. Longenecker 2016b:158–59, 182–84, 189–90, 194–96.

get through the filter of the nonidolatrous death of Christ, being excluded by the fourth entry of Paul's list: "idolatry." There are forms of identity that Paul deemed to be incompatible with Christ coming alive within Christ-followers. In that regard, it is instructive to recall some of the entries in Paul's list of 5:19–21: acts of hostility, fighting, jealousy, acts of anger, acts of rivalry, acts of tribalism, acts of envy. Paul found these ways of living to run completely against the grain of the self-giving character of Jesus Christ. God does not resurrect those aspects of a person's identity that directly contravene the power of the Spirit of the self-giving Son.

Against this backdrop, Paul's comments in Gal 2:20 (or, in some versions, 2:19b–20) burst off the page: "I have been crucified with Christ and I no longer live, but Christ lives in me. And the life I now live in the enfleshed body I live by the trust that pertains to the Son of God, who loved me and gave himself for me."[13] For Paul, the "I" that is immersed in the present evil age has died. The "I" of the Christ-follower now lives as God brings Christ alive in the "I" by the Spirit of the Son. As a consequence, the prayer language of the Son (even in its Aramaic form) becomes the prayer language of Christ-followers, in whose hearts the Spirit cries out, "Abba, Father," just as the Son had done (Mark 14:36) in his unprecedented relationship to the Father. Here the mediated relationality of the Torah is of a different order to the relational intimacy of those in Christ, whose hearts are echo chambers of the nonidolatrous prayer address of Jesus Christ to the Father.[14]

---

[13] On the importance of this passage, see Gaventa 2014; Linebaugh 2020.
[14] On Paul's participationistic theology, see Dunn 1998:390–412; Hays 2008; C. Campbell 2012; Macaskill 2013; Thate, Vanhoozer, and C. Campbell 2014; Morgan 2020; Blackwell 2021; Snodgrass 2022.

THE TRUST THAT PERTAINS TO THE SON OF GOD

One phrase that Paul uses in 2:20 is heavily disputed, appearing also in 2:16 and 3:22. When discussing these verses, I have used the phrase "the trust that pertains to" Jesus Christ (2:16) or the Son of God (2:20). I have left this intentionally ambiguous. The word "trust" has traditionally been understood as something attributable to Christ-followers (their trust), with the Greek phrase *pistis Iēsou Christou* translated as "(our) trust in Jesus Christ." But the Greek term *pistis* (which can also mean "faithfulness") can be understood as something attributable to Jesus Christ himself, with the phrase translated as "(the) trust/faithfulness of Jesus Christ."

These are both viable interpretations of the Greek, and arguments can be made to show the legitimacy of either of them.[15] Both fit well within the larger contours of Paul's theological worldview. In Gal 2:16, for instance, Paul emphasizes the trust of Christ-followers: "We ourselves have trusted in Christ Jesus." And the trust of Christ-followers stands front and center in Galatians 3 (as well as a few occurrences in Gal 5–6). Obviously, then, that option works well. But Paul also highlights the trusting obedience of Jesus in other letters (e.g., Rom 5:12–21; Phil 2:6–8; etc.), and the motif of "the trust of Christ" may well be connoting something similar in Galatians.

For my part, I am inclined to think that "the trust of Jesus Christ" is the better interpretation of the phrase in 2:16, as well as in 3:22 and the similar construction in 2:20.[16] In particular, the

---

[15] For discussions of *pistis Christou*, see (among many others) Hays 2002; Dunn 2008; Stubbs 2008; Bird and Sprinkle 2009; Hooker 2016; Downs and Lappenga 2019.

[16] Making a decision on this matter requires accounting for data beyond Galatians, including Rom 3:25 (together with 3:22 and 26) and Phil 3:9; see also Eph 3:12.

phrase "the trust of Jesus Christ" seems to signal trust that God the Father is faithful and would raise him from the dead (see also Chapter 9). If Paul does not elaborate on this theme within Galatians, that might not be because this interpretation of the phrase is wrong but because, as Paul says in 2:15–16, both he and Peter agree that being seen as righteous before God is "through the trust/faithfulness of Jesus Christ" (if this interpretation is correct). Because they agree on that principle, Paul does not spend time discussing it. Instead, he discusses how Christ-followers relate to the trusting Christ Jesus, and that is through their own trust in Christ. Notice, though, how well this interpretation of the phrase sits within the immediate context of 2:20. Paul has asked in 2:17 whether participation in Christ renders the power of Sin to be sovereign, since even Jews (and not just gentiles) are now shown to be among the category of "sinners." The Christ who comes alive in Christ-followers is Paul's ultimate answer to that question, precisely because the one who comes alive in Christ-followers is the Christ who trusted faithfully in a trustworthy God; consequently, God looks upon those who trust in Christ and declares them "righteous" because Christ's trust comes alive in those who trust in Jesus Christ. "I live by the trust of Jesus Christ" (2:20). This leads to the conclusion of the text unit, already noted earlier but worth repeating: "For if righteousness could come through the Torah, then Christ died needlessly." This death, enshrouded in trust in God's faithful and life-giving power, is where Paul locates the transforming "grace of God" (2:21).

INSTEAD

Also in 2:20, Paul highlights the love of Jesus Christ ("who loved me"). Paul tethers this important claim to another essential theological feature: Christ died in the stead ("instead") of those who were under the destructive forces of Sin. One passage in the letter picks up on this theme in particular: "Christ redeemed us from the Torah's curse by becoming a curse for us" (3:13). Here, the "us" might be the people of Israel, but since everyone inevitably violates the Torah's taxonomy of sinfulness, the "us" of 3:13 most likely references all people. Paul cites Deut 21:23 to explain how Christ redeemed all from the curse rightfully pronounced by the Torah: "because it is written, 'Cursed is everyone who hangs on a tree.'" Other Jews had been crucified by Rome, of course, but Paul interprets this scriptural passage christologically, and exclusively so. This motif of cursing one who hangs on a tree provides Paul with the grounds for linking the Torah's curse to Jesus Christ himself, who absorbs the curse for those who die with him. Paul gives no scope for imagining that Jesus Christ (who himself was "born under the Torah"; 4:4) had actively transgressed the Torah's stipulations; Jesus's passive hanging on the tree is the only way Paul can imagine the Torah's curse to legitimately encompass even the messiah himself.[17]

It needs to be emphasized that this does not mean the Torah was "wrong" to curse Jesus Christ (with the consequent view that the Torah has always been in opposition to God). The Torah's curse was redemptively coordinated within the plan of God, with Jesus Christ becoming the substitute for sinners, as the rightful curse of the Torah against them was transferred to him.[18] But if the death of Christ is necessarily substitutionary, it is at the same time necessarily participatory, so that those who are crucified with Christ can participate in the eschatological life of the crucified

---

[17] See 2 Cor 5:21 for a similar train of thought.
[18] On substitutionary atonement in Paul, see Gathercole 2015.

Son. In that participation, they are freed from the curse articulated by the Torah that rightfully had applied to them when they were residents of "the present evil age." It is important to remember, again, that Paul envisages the Torah to have a divine origin, so its pronouncement against the "hanging messiah" was not a miscarriage of justice or an utter surprise to God, or any other permutation we might imagine. Instead, it was all part of God's sovereign and established plan to redeem humanity from the enslavement of Sin. In the sovereign plan of God, Christ died in the stead of those rightly cursed by the Torah.

At times in the history of interpretation, this "substitutionary" aspect of Paul's theologizing has been taken beyond the boundaries of responsible theological control.[19] Despite how it has been used by others beyond Paul, this substitutionary aspect is essential to Paul's own theological discourse in Galatians and beyond (Rom 8:1–3; 2 Cor 5:21; see also 1 Pet 2:24). In Galatians, it is intertwined with the "participatory" aspect that Paul develops so extensively. As such, the primary theological context for this substitutionary aspect of Paul's discourse emerges from Gal 1:4 and 2:20: "[Jesus Christ] gave himself for our sins ... [He] loved me and gave himself for me."

---

[19] Some interpreters took Jesus's substitutionary death to suggest that God the Father had to pay off the devil with the blood of Jesus Christ, or that God the Father is a viciously wrathful and sadistic deity. Sometimes this comes with the implication that this deity's followers should extend divine violence against anyone they deem to be anti-God. All of this needs to be repudiated as having no foothold in Paul's theological discourse.

CHAPTER 7

Decentering Identity Values

The world that the power of Sin oversees is one in which identities are valued and devalued in perpetual permutations. If we anthropomorphize the power of Sin, we can imagine that Sin really does not care which forms of identity are valued and which are devalued. As long as people have an incessant thirst for "status capture" in one form or another (and with that thirst comes covetous acquisitiveness and the disadvantageous denigration of others), the goals of the power of Sin are satisfied. Identities that Paul deems to be acceptable as "micro-identities" in Christ are, in the world dominated by the overlordship of Sin, raised to the level of "macro-identities." And when macro-identities proliferate numerously in an aggressively competitive and combative world, social chaos results.

Historians have recently cast fresh light on the phenomenon of socially constructed "ethnic hierarchies" of the ancient world.[1] These were hierarchies by which people-groups placed themselves at the top of an assumed scale of ethnic identities and relegated

---

[1] See especially Harland 2019; 2021; 2023. For discussion of this phenomenon within the Greco-Roman world, see Johnson 1989; Stanley 1996; Esler 2003:40–63; Cosgrove 2006. The term "ethnic hierarchies" is from Hagendoorn 1993.

other ethnicities to lower positions, or placed other ethnic identities in peripheral positions from the center of preferred ethnic identity – usually employing demeaning cultural stereotypes in the process.[2] These ethnic hierarchies, or "claims to civilizational priority,"[3] were rampant in Paul's world, with definitions of ethnic superiority and inferiority determined by who was constructing the ethnic hierarchy – always to gain some social advantage over people in other ethnic groups. The result was a world marked out by "social and cultural snobbishness," provoking oppositional forms of relationality.[4]

Many Jews of Paul's world had experienced the adverse effects of these ancient ethnic hierarchies. Like most ancient Jews living in the aftermath of the reign of Antiochus IV (175–164 BCE), Paul would have known this from the popular stories about Antiochus's pogroms against the Jewish people. Antiochus's military campaign resulted in the capture of the lands of various indigenous cultures and the enforced alignment of those cultures with his Hellenizing program. In this, the Jewish people were a particular target. Antiochus suppressed the observation of Jewish practices, requiring Jews to worship pagan deities (including himself) – even within the precincts of the Jerusalem temple. Jewish scriptural writings were burned, circumcision and Sabbath observance were forbidden, and Jews were forced to eat foods deemed by them to be impure. These initiatives were

---

[2] Kloppenborg (2019:13) notes that in Paul's world, "[e]thnic generalizations were ... common and served as caricatures of types of people."
[3] Harland 2023:317.
[4] See Rowlandson 2013:231 (noting in particular the "dissing" of the Egyptians) and Hall 1997:47. More broadly, see Jenkins 1994, Hall 1997, and Isaac 2004 on the "invention of racism in classical antiquity." My thanks to Reichert Zalameda for pointing me to these works.

intended to decimate Jewish identity within Antiochus's empire in order to give that empire a uniformity based on Hellenistic identities and values – demonstrating an extreme "ethnic hierarchy," with the goal of obliterating one ethnic identity altogether. Jews who did not cooperate with Antiochus's program were commonly slaughtered. Stories of those Jews (especially the Maccabean martyrs) who stood bravely opposed to the suppression of their ethnic identity circulated widely among Jews of Paul's day (see especially the books of 1–4 Maccabees).[5] Unsurprisingly, the names of the Maccabean heroes were among the most popular names of Jewish males in Judean culture when Christ-devotion was first getting a foothold.[6]

If Antiochus's program was exceptional, it was not without precedent, nor was it a thing of the past in the world of the early Christ-followers. A case in point is evident in a paragraph of the *Histories* written by the Roman historian Tacitus (56–120). Noting that Moses introduced "new religious practices" for the Jews to observe, Tacitus highlighted that these practices are "quite opposed to those of all other religions" (5.4) and characterized the Jews as an ethnic group that "feel[s] only hate and enmity" toward other nations, "sit[ting] apart at meals ... [and] adopting circumcision to distinguish themselves from other peoples by this difference" (5.5). Paul would have attributed Tacitus's exaggerated and stereotyped rhetoric ("hate and enmity") to the influence of the power of Sin, which itself manufactures "hate and enmity" among people of different identities, with misrepresentations and exaggerations being peddled as truths that people willingly consume.

---

[5] And, of course, these stories are the basis for the annual celebration of Hanukkah even today.
[6] See Ilan 2002; Bauckham 2017:67–92.

But apart from Paul's estimate, it is little wonder that many Jews of his day remained valiantly opposed to any attempt to flatten out the distinctives of their ethnic identity. They were well versed in how injustice is perpetuated as a necessary by-product of attempts to increase concentrations of power in particular hands. The Jews had experienced that in their recent history, and they told and retold those stories as part of their corporate identity. They were well aware of "ethnic hierarchies" that often worked to their disadvantage as an ethnic group.[7]

RENOUNCING THE PRIORITIZATION OF GENTILE IDENTITY

Paul seems to have been acutely aware of the evils that can be perpetuated when one form of identity is prioritized over another (a phenomenon evidenced in the social identities of various groups of Greco-Roman "associations" as well).[8] When Paul looked at what was happening in the Galatian assemblies, he saw precisely the same thing happening. One identity was valued over other forms of identity – the imposition of what he deemed to be an unhealthy "ethnic hierarchy." Without keeping the broader scope of Paul's discourse in view, however, a study of Galatians can inadvertently intimate that Paul was fundamentally

---

[7] At the same time, many Jews wanted to be recognized as integral members of their local settings, coexisting peacefully alongside the people of other ethnic groups while also having the right to observe the practices that made them distinctive within their societies (although, of course, there were exceptions). On the complexity of these dynamics, see Goodman 1998:3–14; L. Levine 1998:18–32; Barclay 1999; Collins 2000:1–25; Gruen 2002; Grabbe 2021:112–37.

[8] On hierarchies among associational groups, see Ascough 2022.

concerned to peripheralize Jewish identity in particular. That impression, however, would be a tragic misrepresentation of his interests. It is extremely important, then, to establish the context of Paul's discourse in Galatians by keeping an eye on other occasions of Paul's discourse.

Paul's letter to Christ-followers in Rome provides a helpful balance in this regard. In that letter, Paul is suspicious that gentile Christ-followers were susceptible to a privileging of non-Jewish forms of identity, with an inbuilt premise that Jewish identities were inferior to non-Jewish identities. "I am speaking to you gentiles," he says bluntly, noting that he speaks as the "apostle to the gentiles" (11:13). "Don't brag," as if they are better than Jews (11:18); "do not become proud" (11:20), as if God prefers other ethnic identities over Jewish identity. If gentile Christ-followers start down this road, they should not be surprised if they were to be "cut off" from God's grace (11:19–22) – precisely because, in Paul's view, divine grace falls upon identities that are wholly unworthy, with no human identity having "worth" that attracts divine grace. The whole of Rom 11:13–22 is framed in quite a serious theological register because Paul is concerned that an "ethnic hierarchy" could take hold within Christ-groups – a hierarchy in which one form of identity is being denigrated (Jewish) in order to raise the profile of other forms of identity (gentile) within communities that cherish divine grace. Paul speaks harshly in this context because this kind of manipulation runs directly contrary to his view of divine grace.

Moreover, in Rom 14:1–15:6, Paul defends the right of Jews to continue to observe the Torah even as Christ-followers, as one (and only one) legitimate identity in Christ. Paul was concerned that Jewish identity was being seen as a second-rate form of identity in Christ. Further down this road lies the theological atrocity of "replacement theology" that has so often found its way into later Christian discourse – with God's affections now solely favoring the gentiles, since the Jews are caricatured as heart-hardened Christ-killers deserving of eternal punishment. This was the furthest thing from Paul's intention.[9] So in Rom 14:1–15:7, Paul takes steps to ensure that Jewish identity is recognized as a legitimate identity within Christ-groups. This follows from his case in Romans 4, where he shows that Abraham is the father of both circumcised and uncircumcised Christ-believers (not simply one or the other). And in Romans 11 Paul can say that "with regard to election, they [ethnic Jews] are beloved, for the sake of their ancestors, for God's gifts and God's calling are irrevocable" (11:28–29). Consequently, when we see Paul working the other side of the street in Galatians, we must recognize that he does not simply patrol the one neighborhood and not the other. In Paul's view, all neighborhoods are vulnerable to precisely this corrosive influence.[10]

EXAMPLES OF UNHEALTHY IDENTITY PRIORITIZATION

What Paul saw in Galatian Christ-groups is what he saw happening all around him. In the world under Sin, the prioritization of a particular identity over other identities was everywhere. It was not a special characteristic of Judaism, but neither were Jews exempt from it.

To demonstrate the point, a few Jewish texts (together with a host of non-Jewish texts) articulate a worldview that comes close

---

[9] On the divergence of Paul's intention and later uses of Paul's letters, see Boyarin 1993; Barclay 1996.
[10] In Romans Paul articulates a temporal (or salvation-historical) priority of the Jewish people (1:16; 2:9; 11:13–24; 15:27). If there is a foothold for this in Galatians, it is in 4:4–5 and 6:16. See Chapter 9.

to the kind of thing Paul is concerned to extract from Christ-groups. The text of *Jubilees* (second century BCE) offers a highly interpreted version of the text of Genesis and the first twelve chapters of Exodus. It includes these words, purportedly from Abraham to Jacob (22.16): "Observe the commandments of Abraham, your father: Separate yourself from the nations, and do not eat with them. Do not do the things they do, and do not associate with them. For their works are unclean, and all their ways are a pollution and an abomination and uncleanness." A good reason is offered for this attitude toward the gentile nations – that is, they are immersed in idolatry (22.17–18):

> They offer their sacrifices to the dead and they worship evil spirits, and they eat over the graves, and all their works are vanity and nothingness ... How they err in saying to a piece of wood: "You are my god," and to a stone, "You are my Lord and my deliverer." As for you, my son Jacob, may the Most High God help you and may the God of heaven bless you and remove you from their uncleanness and from all their error.

Here Abraham, the "father" of the ethnic people of Israel, denigrates non-Jewish nations. They are inferior, not least because of their idolatry. As a consequence, "all their ways are a pollution and an abomination and uncleanness" and "all their works are vanity and nothingness."

The *Letter of Aristeas* (also second century BCE) depicts Moses as having separated Jews from other nations of the world. He fenced the people of Israel off from others (139, 142; compare Paul's analogy of the Torah as a pedagogue). The Torah served the role of

> impregnable ramparts and walls of iron, that [the people of Israel] might not mingle at all with any of the other nations, but remain pure in body and soul, free from all vain

imaginations ... Therefore lest we should be corrupted by any abomination, or our lives be perverted by evil communications, he [Moses] fenced us around on all sides by rules of purity.

The *Letter of Aristeas* was written as a defense of Jewish practice in a Hellenistic world of polytheistic idolatry. In that defense, it presents Jews as superior to "the other nations" in an obvious "ethnic hierarchy."[11]

In the first decade of the second century, a text was written that helps reveal the sort of thing that Paul might list as the influence of Sin on a *stoichei-ic* identity. In his apocalypse, the Jewish author of 4 Ezra seeks an explanation for the destruction of Jerusalem in 70 by the forces of Rome. In this excerpt from that important text, these words are spoken to God (6:55-56):

> All this I have spoken before you, O Lord, because you have said that you created this world for us [the ethnic people of Israel]. As for the other nations that have descended from Adam, you have said that they are nothing, and that they are like spittle, and you have compared their abundance to a drop from a bucket.

Here, a prioritizing of one identity results in the belittling of other identities, with all other nations being "nothing," "like spittle," and completely inconsequential to God. Many Jews held other views of the gentiles, including the notion that there could be, in fact, "righteous gentiles" among them.[12] But at times some Jews seem to have fallen into the trap of articulating their identity in terms of an ethnic hierarchy – just one of the many ethnic

---

[11] The author of Acts has Peter make a statement that draws heavily on a similar view: "You all realize that it is forbidden for a Jew to associate or visit with outsiders" (Acts 10:28).

[12] On "natural law proselytes" or "righteous gentiles," see Donaldson 1997:60-69, 230-36. See also Bockmuehl 2000:150-62; Novak 1983.

hierarchies that swirled around in the ancient world.[13] In these instances, ethnic identity has become (in Paul's terms) a *stoicheion*, an influence used by the power of Sin.

RENOUNCING THE PRIORITIZATION OF AN ETHNIC IDENTITY

In Galatians, Paul sought to rid the Galatian Christ-groups of the ancient (and all too modern) tendency to slip into an unhealthy "ethnic hierarchy." Of course, for a moment within Galatians Paul speaks as someone who approaches life in this fashion. In his discourse to Peter, Paul notes that he and Peter are "Jews by birth and not 'gentile sinners'" (2:15). But Paul proceeds to problematize this way of looking at the world (not least in 2:17). It comes with an implicit ranking of different forms of identity, with the denigration of gentiles as "sinners" opening the door to forms of relational hostility between people of different identities. This is why Paul sees Peter's behavior in Antioch as "condemned" (2:11). In Paul's view, Peter's act of "separating" himself from gentile Christ-followers implied that Jewish identity was a superior form of identity in Christ, implicitly compelling "gentiles to live like Jews" (2:14). This unnecessary "ethnic hierarchy" contravenes "the truth of the gospel" (2:14).

It does not surprise us, then, to see Sin foregrounded just a few verses later. In Paul's view, even "Jews by birth" become recognized in Christ as those in the grip of the power of Sin apart from

---

[13] Thiessen (2023:84) captures the point simply: "Many ancient Jews viewed non-Jews negatively." Some Jews viewed other Jews as defaulting on God's covenant with Israel – as in the case of the Qumran community on the shores of the Dead Sea, who saw themselves as "sons of light" and other Jews as "sons of darkness."

Christ – "sinners as we seek to be seen as righteous in Christ" (2:17). Only participation in the identity-transforming death of Christ redeems people from their otherwise inescapable enslavement to Sin's overlordship. Being baptized in Christ immerses Christ-followers in the absence of worth, in order that their worth might be found only as Christ himself comes alive in them. It is only when Christ is formed within the life patterns of Christ-followers that God recognizes anything worthy of the term "righteousness."

This context helps to explain Paul's discourse in Galatians 4:8–11, where Paul discusses the Galatians' situation in relation to the *stoicheia*. In Paul's theological calculus, if gentile Christ-followers adopted Torah observance, they would be reverting to a situation in which one form of human identity is prioritized – which is to say, they would be reverting to a *stoichei-ic* situation, even as they, as gentiles, had previously been under idolatrously configured *stoicheia*.[14] Placing themselves "under the Torah" would be equivalent to going back to life "under the *stoicheia*" because gentile Christ-followers would be subscribing to the belief that one micro-identity in Christ is to be a macro-identity salvifically conjoined to the death of Christ. To start prioritizing micro-identities as macro-identities is to play the "hostility game" manufactured by Sin.[15]

Against that is Paul's notion of divine grace, where no form of human identity, in and of itself, is worthy of divine grace. The only identity that God the Father rescues from the clutches of nonexistence is that of the Son. To insist that God's favor also requires a particular form of human identity is to misunderstand

---

[14] On Paul's charge that the Galatians are regressing, see Martin 2020.
[15] On Galatians and "social conflict," see Esler 1998.

completely the exclusively christological configuration of divine grace and is ultimately to move the gospel of God's grace back into the playground of the power of Sin. In Christ, the identity influencers that spawn particular legitimate identities (Jewish, Samaritan, Egyptian, Armenian, etc.) and that were once pawns in Sin's program are now freed – together with the identities they influenced, to be empowered by the Spirit of God.

THE PROLIFERATION OF LEGITIMATE IDENTITIES AND THE NONIDOLATROUS WORSHIP OF CHRIST-GROUPS

Paul was adamant that people's macro-identity in Christ is not overshadowed by any other form of identity. The only legitimate macro-identity is trust in Jesus Christ. But as long as that is the case, legitimate sub-identities are intended to flourish in Christ.[16] Paul did not want legitimate sub-identities to be renounced in Christ-groups; instead, he wanted those sub-identities to be affirmed in new ways along new lines of relationality in the power of God's grace.

---

[16] Of course, because he moves Jewish identity to the position of a legitimate micro-identity in Christ, he also says controversial things about that form of identity. We see this in Phil 3:5–8, for instance, where his Jewish identity is shockingly categorized under the label "excrement." He means this in relation to his macro-identity in Christ. (For a similar interpretation of this passage, using a different frame of reference, see Phillips Wilson 2023.) Because Paul seeks to ensure that Torah observance is no longer the absolute authority for crafting the identity of Jewish Christ-followers, we sometimes see adjustments in his understanding of how the Torah continues to be regulatory of Jewish micro-identity in Christ. Nonetheless, Paul is not sneaking his way toward the absolute abandonment of Torah observance among Jewish Christ-followers. That would run contrary to his view of the unity of all nations lifting their voices in praise to God.

This includes the sub-identity of Jews of the Torah. For Paul, Jews in Christ are no longer "under the Torah" in its pedagogical role of keeping idolatry at bay; the purest form of idolatry-free relationality is through participation with Christ. But in the nonidolatrous sphere of being in Christ, Jews can still observe the Torah. Although they are no longer to be "*under* the Torah" (which was their situation in the pre-Christ era), they are the ethnic group "*of* the Torah" – a term that, although not articulated by Paul as such, captures the sense that Jews may continue to observe the Torah even in Christ, although only as a micro-level form of identity.[17] Paul did not think that the differentiation between Jewish and non-Jewish identities was now to be set aside in Christ, in some amorphous, monochrome, ethnically undifferentiated corporate entity.

There is an underlying reason why this is important. For Paul, God seeks the praise of all the nations, collectively, in Christ. This theme, with its foothold in Gal 3:28, is developed more fully in Rom 15:7–13 (the capstone of his argument throughout the first fifteen chapters of that letter). All nations are joined together in Christ to offer nonidolatrous worship of Abraham's God.[18] Here, monotheism is not simply a belief in one God but the corporate worship of the one God: monolatry. For Paul, monolatry requires a recognition of the exclusive oneness of God (as articulated in Gal 3:20) conjoined to the oneness of the nonidolatrous people of that one God. In a sense, the theological sinews of Galatians can almost be reduced to "God is one ... [and] you are all one in Christ Jesus" through trust in Jesus Christ (3:20, 28).

---

[17] See also Phillips Wilson 2022.
[18] See Horrell 2005:182–89; B. Longenecker 2016a.

In Christ, legitimate forms of identity are preserved in the only idolatry-free context where all the nations are united in praise of God. The God who is worshipped in Christ-groups of all legitimate identities is the same God whom the Jews had long praised in a pedagogical context distinct from the other nations. In Christ, relationality with God is found in unprecedentedly intimate fashion, with all the nations (Jews and gentiles) coming together without the social discord that testified to the overlordship of the power of Sin prior to the coming of Jesus Christ. Paul's expectation sits well alongside the universalistic expectations held by some other Jews who believed that when God acts in ultimate eschatological power, all nations together will praise God – with Jewish voices of praise being joined by the praising voices of gentiles.[19] Paul affirms that in Christ, God has acted to remove the narcissism of small differences that curtailed that vision – differences that are small in relation to the transcendent God whom all are to worship. Consequently, when Paul says "neither circumcision nor uncircumcision" matters (5:6; 6:15), he means that they don't matter and are not important at the macro-level of Christ-followers and Christ-groups. There is a sense, of course, in which these identities do, in fact, matter, and they fully matter – as Christ-followers of diverse micro-identities gather to worship their Lord. In that context, these diverse identities are not utterly meaningless in Christ – just the opposite. Paul sees them as "meaning-full" only in Christ, where they are gathered in relationally productive ways, not least in their diverse but corporately united praise to God. This is new creation.

[19] See Donaldson 2007.

CHAPTER 8

The Slavery of Christ-Giving Love

Paul did not see Christ-devotion in individualistic terms. He did see it as involving individuals, of course, and as intensely personal. Paul could not have said, for instance, "God's Son loved me and gave himself for me" if he did not think Christ-devotion to be intensely personal. The Son of God loves people personally. And Christ-followers stand before God individually (e.g., Gal 5:5; 6:7–8). But Paul's emphasis on personal relationship does not filter into the individualistic categories that mark so much of the Western world today. In Paul's frame of reference, personal relationship with God does not equate to an individualistic piety, precisely since Paul understood life as relational.[1] Apart from relationships, personal identity is weak and insignificant. Identity is formed and found in relationships. And there are relationships of all kinds. Relationship with God is first and foremost; this is what Paul refers to as "being known by God" (4:9). But there are other relationships that need to be taken into account. Christ needs to be "formed among you" (*en hymin*), Paul says to the Galatians (4:19). The only thing that matters is "trust that continues to work in practical ways [*energoumenē*] through love" (5:6).

---

[1] See Eastman 2017.

TRUST WORKS

This kind of working trust does not become established within the hearts of Christ-followers without a practical outlet – a form of expression, a way of living in relation to God and others in renewed patterns of life. Christ-followers do not just love God in their hearts, as if that's all that matters while they wait for their souls to be transported to heaven. If Christ-followers are known by God and know God's love, Paul expects divine love to overspill into all of their relationships in the here and now. In this way, Christ himself is "formed" within those relationships, coming alive within them, so that people can see Christ in the embodied lives of Christ-followers.

What does that look like? It looks like the "other-centered" love of the Son of God. Other-centered lives within the community of Christ-followers mirror the self-giving of Jesus Christ who "loved ... and [therefore] gave." Paul held a deep conviction that trust works, works itself out, in dynamic outward expression. The out-working of trust is "other-centered" love within Christ-groups. This is the "ethical" product of Paul's participationistic theology. To make the point, we might imagine a situation in which a Christ-follower is asked, "Who are you, fundamentally?" Paul would be content if the Christ-follower responded, "I am seen in my relationships with others, where I hope you'll see Christ himself, empowering a life lived for the enrichment of others."

Paul does not imagine this to be "salvation by works." His participationistic discourse prevents that interpretation. The Spirit of Christ animates the good that transpires within the lives of Christ-followers, in conformity with the patterns of Christ's own self-giving life and as Christ-followers keep in step with the Spirit. The power of the Spirit does not simply make people nice;

nor does it simply give them a "Christian" ticket to ensure that their souls go to heaven when they die. The Spirit necessarily empowers forms of living that testify to the lordship of Christ. In this way, the relational world of Christ-followers evidences God's sovereignty over the power of Sin. Christ-groups are proleptic corporate enclaves of "the kingdom of God" (5:21) in advance of the fulfillment of the "hope of righteousness" that Christ-followers await (5:5).

ENSLAVED TO OTHERS

The tough thing about relationality within communities of Christ-followers is that those communities are intended to be diverse. Benevolent regard for others flows more easily, we might observe, when people are united around shared points of identity. It is easy to love yourself and, by extension, to love people who share common and cherished features of your own identity. Conversely, care for the other meets with resistance as identity differences increase in number and in significance.

That is why Paul has so much work to do when it comes to ensuring that groups comprising many different identities require active forms of love to oil the machinery of the group's inner workings. That kind of thing does not arise easily or naturally. Consequently, Paul insists on the necessity of living by the Spirit. Corporate relationality is kept healthy as the Spirit interweaves "other-regard" among the diverse membership of Christ-groups. A diverse group that lives by the Spirit serves as the testament to the distinctiveness of what it means to be "clothed with Christ." When functioning properly, diverse Christ-groups are the exhibit of divine power, precisely because the forms of relationality within them go beyond "love for one's own people" into "love for those who are not (otherwise) one's own people."[2] Seen in a different light, those who are not one's own people become one's own people in Christ: "You are all one in Christ Jesus" (3:28). This is the proof, the display, of the eschatological power of the Spirit. If Christ-groups in Galatia want to protect the Spirit's presence in their midst in order to retain their eschatological blessings, prioritizing one form of identity will not accomplish that. Instead, the Galatians need to allow the Spirit to instill forms of "other-regard" in groups that do not prioritize any particular form of identity. In that way, the fruit of the Spirit is the proleptic manifestation of the eschatological defeat of the power of Sin.

It should come as no surprise, then, that there is such a heavy dose of discussion about corporate ethos in Paul's letter to the Galatians (especially in chapters 5 and 6). Paul imagined that only in patterns of other-regarding relationality can communities arise in testimony against the overlordship of Sin – communities of diverse Christ-followers whose members are enslaved to each other by the power of the Spirit. And in that regard, Paul even imagines that what the Spirit is doing among them might overspill in their engagement with others beyond Christ-groups as well (6:10; compare 1 Thess 5:15; 2 Cor 9:13; Rom 12:20–21).[3]

OPPOSITION, VOLITION, AND PROCESS

Although Sin is not an overlord in Christ-groups, Paul knows that enlivening a healthy corporate ethos is not all saccharine and

---

[2] Here I am borrowing from Matt 5:46–47: "If you love those who love you, what reward do you have? Even the tax collectors do that. And if you greet only your own people, what are you doing more than others? Even pagans do that."

[3] See B. Longenecker 2010.

simple. In fact, when discussing the power of the Spirit within corporate relationships, Paul contrasts the Spirit with what he calls *sarx*, which especially in Galatians 5 seems to refer to "the propensity for self-centered living" (often translated simply as "flesh"; see esp. 5:13, 16–17, 19, 24; 6:8).[4] In 5:17 Paul notes that "the propensity for self-centered living stands in opposition to the Spirit, and the Spirit stands in opposition to the propensity for self-centered living, and the two are in opposition to each other." Although Paul is convinced that living consistently in step with the Spirit offsets self-centered living, he is aware that self-centered living can all too easily transpire even within Christ-groups. He knows that the lives of Christ-followers don't fully conform to the cruciform patterning of the Spirit's guidance.[5] He knows that Christ-like identity, or Christ coming alive among Christ-followers, is not automatically

---

[4] Some scholars see *sarx* in Galatians as a cosmic power (see de Boer 2011:335–39, where the claim is asserted but not proven). This view is unlikely. Paul claims that those in Christ have crucified (an active verb) the *sarx*, with its passions and desires (5:24); it is not at all clear how Christ-followers themselves can be said to crucify a cosmic power. (Contrast the active sense of 5:24 with the passive "have been crucified" in 2:19–20 and 6:14 – that is, God has put Paul to death in Paul's connection to the power of Sin, by means of co-crucifixion with Christ.) Moreover, Paul exhorts the Galatians not to sow "to the *sarx* of one's own self" (6:8), which is not the language expected when referencing a cosmic power (the equivalent would be the nonsensical phrase, "your own cosmic power of Sin"). Instead, in 5:24 Christ-followers are said to crucify their propensity for self-centered living – something Paul can only imagine as they live by the power of the Spirit. They are not enslaved to *sarx* (unlike an enslaving cosmic power). Paul knows of the propensity for self-centered living that those in Christ all too often choose to enact (see 6:1) "in the enfleshed body" (2:20), imitating patterns of life in a world dominated by the power of Sin – patterns that are at war with the Spirit's own influence (5:17).

[5] Much the same is evident in Paul's discussion of the Spirit in contrast to *sarx* in Romans 8, where all talk of the power of Sin that saturated Paul's discourse in Romans 6–7 (see also 5:21) drops away, foregrounding *sarx* instead (see 8:3–13).

conjured up in full by the Spirit, with completely transformative results. So Paul encourages the Galatians to consider what they "sow" – whether they choose to sow to (that is, to live lives characterized by) the *sarx* or the Spirit; only sowing to the Spirit is in line with "eternal life" (6:7–10). And one manifestation of the fruit of the Spirit is "self-control" (5:23).

Other passages in the Pauline corpus enlarge on the point somewhat. For instance, in 1 Cor 9:26–27 Paul uses athletic images of strenuous effort to talk about his diligence in enslaving his body (*sōma*). In Phil 3:10 Paul talks of the necessity of Christ-followers "being conformed to" Christ's death, but he immediately adds this phrase: "It's not that I have already reached this goal or have already been perfected," and "I do not imagine that I myself have reached this [goal]" (Phil 3:12–13). Earlier he encouraged the Philippians to "work out your salvation with fear and trembling" (2:12) while also noting that "it is God who is at work in you, enabling you both to will and to work for his good pleasure" (2:13; see also 1 Thess 2:13).

When God reconstructs identity in co-crucifixion with Christ, the result is not immediate perfection but immediate process – process within a fresh corporate context with new forms of supportive relationality emerging from the transforming power of the Spirit (e.g., 1 Thess 3:12–13). This is the context in which the final clause of Gal 5:17 is best recognized: Because the Spirit and "the propensity for self-centered living" (*sarx*) are in opposition, this means that "you [plural] shouldn't do whatever you want to do" (CEB) but, instead, you should continually offer yourselves to the Spirit's leading. As long as Christ-followers are "in the enfleshed body" (2:20), they see the machinations of Sin all around them and can choose, as free agents released from that power, to adopt strategies that replicate the strategies of that power. Actions and attitudes that Sin populates in "this present evil age" can be repopulated, as illegitimate intruders, within the lives of Christ-followers. Consequently Paul exhorts the Galatians (who were "called to freedom") not to allow their freedom to become "an opportunity" to exert the human "propensity for self-centered living" (5:13). The more they lean into the Spirit's power through their exclusive trust in Jesus Christ (as their macro-identity), the less they open themselves to the social cancers that can transpire, illegitimately, even among members of Christ-groups as they negotiate embodied life in "the present evil age."

It seems, then, that Paul expects Christ-followers to experience a transformation of their volition in this process of putting on Christ within their corporate context. To be "guided by the Spirit" (5:16) and "led by the Spirit" (5:18) and to "live by the Spirit" (5:25) requires Christ-followers choosing to "keep in step with the Spirit's guidance" (5:25) and thereby "sowing to the Spirit" (6:8). Divine empowerment is not a package given to Christ-followers independently of their relationship to God. Instead, enlivened by the Spirit at work within their volition, Christ-followers become conduits of the Spirit's transforming power in their relationships with others.

THE CORPORATE CONTEXT OF SELF-GIVING LOVE

Paul's comments in 4:12b–15 are interesting in this regard, since they seem to imply the Spirit's own formation of the volition of the Galatians. These verses focus on the welcome the Galatians extended to Paul when he first arrived. Paul's point, however, is not simply that the Galatians were initially nice to him; the passage has much more theological heft than that. The Galatians' initial reception of him ran against the cultural canons of common sense in the ancient world. This is because Paul was physically ailing and a stranger to them. In the ancient Mediterranean world (and even today in many cultures), that combination would make people extremely wary of him. Such a person could easily be a wielder of "the evil eye" (compare 3:1) – a phenomenon in which a person was thought to be able to manipulate the resources of someone else in order to acquire those resources at the other person's expense.[6] In this light, Paul, a stranger with a physical ailment, could be suspected of being able and willing to cast an evil glance on others in the expectation of acquiring some of their health to shore up his failing body. According to the cultural canons of his day, Paul was a potential danger to the Galatians' well-being. In that situation, the culturally recognized response would be for them to keep the stranger away, to shun him, and to spit (together with other gestures that we still have in our canon of gestures today). So when Paul says, "You did me no wrong [when I came to you]," he isn't just complimenting them nicely. Highlighting their exceptional behavior, Paul is making a theological point by commenting on their spiritual character. They "welcomed" him (4:14). In fact, says Paul, "you would have dug out your eyes and given them to me" (4:15). Instead of spitting at Paul (4:13, *ekptyō*, usually undertranslated as "reject" or "despise"), their extraordinary choice to welcome him demonstrated that the Spirit was already at work among them, at the level of their volition, and bringing out patterns of life that reflected even the self-giving of Jesus. Paul does not mention the Spirit in this passage, but his discourse in Galatians would suggest that he credits the Galatians' stunning actions to the Spirit's initial influence (compare 3:1–5). Paul wants the Galatians to see their reception of him as evidence

---

[6] On this, see B. Longenecker 1999; Oakes 2015:100–3.

of the Spirit's role in offsetting self-centered living even at the outset. The Spirit was, even in those early days, preparing their hearts for the cry of the Abba prayer of the self-giving Son, as they placed themselves in danger (according to cultural codes of security and insecurity) in order to benefit someone in need.

If the Galatians had made themselves vulnerable to Paul in his time of need, that was not to be a one-time demonstration of the Spirit's working. Christ-followers are not simply to look back on the Christ-likeness of their past with self-satisfied content, seeing it as a proof of their identity as Christ-followers, as if it were their identity badge, their security, their trophy. In each of Paul's exhortations to "be guided by," "be led by," and "keep in step with" the Spirit, the verbs he uses are in the present tense, which is probably intended to convey a continuative sense – "continue to be guided," "continue to be led," and "continue to keep in step." The same is true of other stipulations Paul gives: "continue to be enslaved to each other through love" (5:13); "continue to carry the burdens of each other" (6:2). So too, the only thing that matters is "trust that continues to work in practical ways through love" (5:6). Everywhere Paul exhorts the continuance of Spirit-inspired self-giving in concrete, hands-dirty, practical ways.

The fruit of the Spirit is critical to all this. Paul describes that fruit collectively as "love, joy, peace, patience, kindness, goodness, faithfulness, gentleness, and self-control" (5:22–23). These items on Paul's list of the fruit of the Spirit are indicative (rather than exhaustive) of the kind of character of life that should define the ethos of all Christ-groups.[7] Paul is not suggesting that Christ-

---

[7] On the fruit of the Spirit, see Dörnyei 2022. Note that the "fruit [singular] of the Spirit" is different from the "gifts [plural] of the Spirit" that Paul recounts in Romans 12 and 1 Corinthians 12, since Christ-followers do not receive all the gifts of the Spirit.

followers are meant to be known as sweet-tempered, friendly, agreeable people; Jesus Christ did not die simply to produce charming people. Instead, these qualities are the Spirit-induced qualities of life that foster the corporate life of Christ-followers as they transcend the corrosive relationality of self-centered living that marks out "the present evil age" all around them. The fruit of the Spirit is to characterize the eschatological character of every Christ-group. The "household of trust" (6:10) is the corporate context in which "each person should test their own actions" (6:4), with healthy Christ-groups fostering the development of Christ-likeness in the lives of every Christ-follower.

In this way, other-centered living does not equate to self-abuse, self-loathing, self-negation, or self-disrespect. Christ-likeness is not drudgery divine. In Paul's list of the fruit of the Spirit, "love" is followed by items that set self-giving love in a flourishing and healthy corporate context. Notice, for instance, "joy," or "kindness," or "goodness," or "gentleness," or "self-control." These do not describe the ethos of a group of self-loathing zombies for God. Instead, self-giving love operates in and from (what we might call) the healthy self within the context of other-centeredness shared by all members within a flourishing community of fulfillment and joy.[8]

And for Paul, "the healthy self" is the Christ-in-me self empowered by the promised Spirit (3:14) – the Christ who has been made known as the one who lived and died "for" others (2:20; 3:13). Just as Christ gave himself, and gave himself as the gift, so also participation in his transforming death becomes the power-vortex of new relational connections of Christ-giving, even Christ-gifting, as Christ comes alive within the networked

---

[8] On Paul's vision of human flourishing in Christ, see Jipp 2023.

relational connectivity of Christ-followers. In an important sense, other-centeredness (or "for-ness") is not so much "self-less-ness" as it is "Christ-full-ness."

This Christ-giving/Christ-gifting ethos is to permeate all instantiations of "new creation." As a consequence, it will characterize the lives of all members of the community, with each instance of "Christ-full other-centeredness" being met in return by other instances from elsewhere within the community. As all members contribute Christ-full-ness, they will be enriching the resources of the Christ-gifted community.

In this way, supporting others does not mean letting others get ahead while you fall behind; it means cultivating the relational prosperity of the community, which itself benefits all those within it who themselves are conduits of Christ-full-ness.[9] At every point, Paul's discourse assumes this inter-involvement and intertwined responsiveness among members of Christ-groups. In that setting, the giving of oneself (or better, perhaps, the giving of Christ's self) for the well-being of others encounters other forms of self-giving (or Christ-giving) that originate from elsewhere within the community, with the directionality of self-giving/Christ-giving nonprescribed and not determined by the directionality of previous gifts. This is not self-interestedness, and it is certainly not self-loathing.[10] It is relational abundance. It is people

---

[9] Compare Phil 2:4: "Let each of you look not to your own interests, but to the interests of others." Here, the key is the term "each of you" (not "the most gullible of you"), with each one doing this in relation to the others. Compare similar statements in the Pauline corpus, which also need to be read in this context, such as 1 Cor 10:24, 33; 13:5. Paul even talks of his own efforts for the sake of the gospel as part of his interest in being a "co-sharer" in the gospel's fruitfulness (1 Cor 9:23).

[10] If it were, Paul could not say, "love your neighbor as yourself" (5:14), in which he assumes a healthy form of self-regard. Presumably the basis for a

thriving in noncompetitive communities of abundant mutual support and relational productivity. Quite simply, the act of giving evokes blessing (see 2 Cor 9:7; Acts 20:35) in the Christ-like, Christ-given, Christ-full communities that Paul has in mind. This is how the summary of the entire Torah, "Love your neighbor as you love yourself" (Lev 19:18), is fulfilled within Christ-giving groups (Gal 5:14).

The Galatians' own experience testifies to this same conviction that acts of giving evoke divine blessing. When Paul recounts how the Galatians first accepted him despite the dangers (according to cultural values of their day) of accepting an ill stranger in their midst, he says that the Galatians received *makarismos* (4:15). In Paul's letters beyond Galatians, this Greek word appears only in Romans 4. There it refers to the "blessedness" that God bestows on those loved by God (Rom 4:6, 9).[11] This sense is rarely captured by translations and commentators of Gal 4:15, however. Usually their interpretations suggest that Paul is talking about the relationship between the Galatians and Paul rather than the Galatians and God. So the word is translated as "the great attitude you had" toward me (CEB), or "the good will you felt" toward me (NRSV), or "your blessing of me" (NIV). But there is no good reason for thinking that Paul uses the term any differently in Gal 4:15 than in Romans 4, where it refers to a blessedness that derives from God. In making themselves vulnerable to the needs of others (i.e., Paul), the Galatians were being moved by the Spirit and blessed by God. This is just one example of what we see in various

---

healthy self-regard emerges from the fact that the Son of God had loved Paul and all sinners even in their sinfulness (Gal 2:20; Rom 5:8).

[11] Compare Jesus's use of the term's adjective *makarios* in the phrase "Blessed are the . . ." (Matt 5:3–10 and elsewhere).

places throughout the Pauline corpus (and the New Testament). The life of the Christ-follower is not to be characterized by onerous self-effacement, being used and abused by all, becoming the doormat to be walked on by people who are all too eager to take advantage of others. Paul imagines the lives of Christ-followers to be enriched in exhilarating relationships of mutual Christ-full other-centeredness, in which other-regard results in an abundant corporate life that testifies to the experiential novelties of healthy relationships as indications of divine blessedness. In a world dominated by social Darwinism, Paul sees the authentic Christ-group as the exciting display of the dawning of "the kingdom of God" (5:21). All this emerges from their cruciform location in Christ, in which their corporate identity and (thus) their individual identities are nurtured by the power of the Spirit of the Son – what might be called "resurrectional cruciformity" or "resurrection suffused cruciformity."[12]

And so, in the inevitable instances when a Christ-follower shatters the self-giving ethos of a Christ-group, the renewal of the ethos is to be a corporate enterprise. "If any one (among you) is caught in some sin, you who live by the Spirit should restore that person in a gentleness of spirit" (6:1). Paul warns, however, that the Christ-followers who take the initiative in this act of renewal need nonetheless to "be on guard" to ensure that they themselves "are not tempted." This seems to be a warning against thinking too highly of themselves (see 6:3; see also 2 Cor 2:11), enjoying the moment too much, as if they were somehow the self-appointed guardians of the group. Ethical watchdogs can easily become self-important, an attitude that opens the door to the self-

---

[12] Gorman 2019:74.

centered self-infatuation and moral pageantry that runs contrary to the identity of those in Christ.

In Galatians, Paul's discourse about right relationships is interwoven with reflections on the ethos of Christ-groups – their corporate atmosphere and formative culture. Christ-groups are to be cultures where Christ-like regard for the other is nurtured, for the well-being of all in mutual relatedness and blessedness. Paul is concerned to promote not just the right way to think about one's relationship with God; he is concerned to ensure that right-thinking translates into right-living, in the process of birthing Christ in and among Christ-followers. In short, Christ comes alive most evidently in the corporate life of Christ-followers as they learn, each in their own way, how to live "in Christ" and, therefore, in Christ-full-ness, by the empowering Spirit.[13] Paul might well have said to Christ-followers of his day, and no doubt ours as well, "Imagine the stories that can emerge from Christ-full communities set free from the idolatry of self-infatuation by the power of the Spirit."

---

[13] For discussions of the ethics of Galatians, see Barclay 1988; 2014; O'Donovan 2014; Rabens 2014; L. Williams 2023.

CHAPTER 9

The Hope of Righteousness and the Faithfulness of God

At this point, we have the resources fully in hand to discern what Paul means by "righteousness" in his letter to the Galatians. Paul does not offer a paragraph in Galatians on the meaning of "righteousness." It seems that the Galatians knew what Paul was talking about when he uses the term. For us, filling that term with content requires textual spadework throughout the letter to make connections and fill in blanks. His conceptualization of righteousness merges with other important features of this theologizing – in particular, his understanding of the faithfulness of God, including divine faithfulness to "the Israel of God" (6:16).

RIGHTEOUSNESS AND THE SOVEREIGNTY OF GOD

One passage in Galatians arguably gives the overarching context for interpreting the term "righteousness" in this letter: 5:4-6, and in particular 5:5. There Paul refers to "the hope of righteousness." This is curious, since that phrase moves "righteousness" temporally forward, in a sense, into the future, where it has never been placed previously within the letter – or at least not explicitly so. If situating the term "righteousness" within this temporal context is new to the letter's discourse, it also seems to frame what has been assumed all the way through that earlier discourse – although it is also important to note at the outset that Paul does not simply leave the term in a future register, as we'll see.[1]

In Jewish tradition in particular and in the Greco-Roman world in general, the term "righteousness" (with its adjective "righteous") derives from a courtroom setting.[2] "Righteous" is the pronouncement that people hoped to hear from a judge presiding over their case, as the judge ultimately "reckons" their status. When a judge determines that someone is "righteous," that person is established as being "in the right" in the relationships that were under consideration. When situating "righteousness" as a prospective hope in 5:5, Paul temporally elongates the perspective of his discourse to ground it ultimately in the eschatological courtroom, with God as the eschatological judge pronouncing who is in the right.

The future orientation of "the hope of righteousness" in 5:5 supplies the context for interpreting earlier references to the noun ("righteousness," 2:20; 3:6, 21), adjective ("righteous," 3:11), and verb (2:16–17 [four times]; 3:8, 11, 24; 5:4) – with the verbal sense best captured in the translation "to declare or see someone as righteous" (often translated as "to justify") or, in the passive, "to be declared or seen to be righteous." So in 3:11 Paul's phrase "No one is seen to be righteous before God" (see 2:16) seems to draw on the same courtroom metaphor, with a pronouncement about a person's standing being articulated by God in the role of the divine judge.[3] So too in 3:6, Abraham was "reckoned" righteous

---

[1] On Gal 5:5 in relation to the fuller context of Galatians, see Kwon 2004.
[2] See Ps 7:8–9; 9:4, 7; 11:7; 17:1–7, 15; 18:20–24; 143:2; Mic 7:9; Isa 43:9, 26; 50:8; 53:11. Also Deut 25:1. See Prothro 2016a. On Paul's theology of "justification" in general, see Prothro 2018; 2023.
[3] Compare 5:10.

because of his trust in God – a divine reckoning from a God who makes pronouncements.

Of course, in Paul's proclamation the divine declaration of being "righteous" derives from divine grace (2:21), channeled solely in relation to what God has done in Christ, for those whose identity before God rests solely in Christ. In 5:4, Paul restates his point, with the warning that adding Torah observance to trust in Christ results in being "cut off from Christ" – or, as Paul says ominously, "You have fallen from grace." Since Paul continues to address the Galatians as "brothers (and sisters)" in Christ from start to finish (1:2 and 6:18, with eight other occurrences throughout the letter),[4] it seems that Paul has not yet given up hope for the Galatians. But being cut off from Christ is a real prospect, nonetheless. Paul imagines that Christ-followers can, in a sense, lose their way in relation to God. Paul probably is not suggesting that God's declaration of righteousness is changeable, as if one day God declares someone to be righteous in Christ and the next day God revokes God's previous pronouncement. It would seem instead that the divine pronouncement of righteousness is eternally articulated solely in relation to manifestations of trust in God's promissory action (as with Abraham long ago) – now made clear in what God has done in Christ. What changes is not God's pronouncement; what changes is how people are aligned to that eternally stable pronouncement of righteousness.

Of course, for Paul, God is more than a judicial pronouncement-maker. God has taken salvific initiatives, sending the Son and the Spirit, to ensure that the eschatological pronouncement "righteous" applies to those in Christ. Paul's language of righteousness often transposes into the language of (eschatological)

---

[4] Gal 1:11; 3:15; 4:12, 28, 31; 5:11, 13; 6:1.

life. In 2:15–21, Paul's discourse is framed in terms of righteousness at the beginning and end (2:16–17, 21) but in terms of life (and its opposite, death) in between (2:19–20). In 3:21 Paul notes that "if a collection of instructions had been given that was able to generate [eschatological] life, then righteousness would indeed have come by the Torah," placing righteousness and eschatological life together. In this light, Paul's citation of Hab 2:4 (*ho dikaios ek pisteōs zēsetai* in Gal 3:11) might be read not simply as stating a principle (i.e., "the righteous will live on the basis of trust") but more as a promise: "The one seen as righteous by trust will live."[5] That is to say, those in Christ are seen to be righteous by their status-vacuous trust in Christ and are therefore promised the life of the eschatological kingdom (5:21). Where righteousness interfaces with eschatological life, the Spirit is there. Paul weaves the Spirit into his retelling of the story of Abraham (4:29), linking the blessing of Abraham to the giving of the promised Spirit to those of trust (3:14). In contrast to the curse (3:10, 13) and death (implied), the story of Abraham's trust, seen as righteousness, unfolds into the blessing of the promised Spirit (3:14) and "life" (3:11).[6]

---

[5] De Boer (2011:350–51) suggests that the same is true of the citation of Lev 18:5 in Gal 5:14, in which the whole law is fulfilled in the eschatological promise, "You will [in the eschatological age] love your neighbor as yourself." This is possible, but see Oakes 2015:171.

[6] There is discussion as to whether eschatological life infuses Paul's notion of "righteousness" itself or whether the declaration of righteousness is conceptually distinct from the giving of eschatological life. Blackwell (2021) thinks they are co-infused. Prothro (2018:154) thinks they are closely related but distinct. Prothro (2018:149–54) also demonstrates that Martyn's proposal (that Paul transfers the *dikai-* word group from a legal sense of judicial pronouncement to a military/liberative sense of "rectification," as in Martyn 1997) is unconvincing. Further, he shows that "righteousness" is not a cipher exclusively for "to be a true member of God's family" (141–54).

But if righteousness is rooted in the eschatological pronouncement of God (5:5), Paul also sees it, together with eschatological life, as something experienced in the present by those who trust solely in Christ. Those pronounced righteous in Christ experience something of that eschatological life as they are united with Christ, who himself was restored to life by God the Father. Those in Christ already participate in Christ's Sonship, already enjoy the blessings of the Spirit, already experience something of the eternal life that ultimately awaits them. Paul believed that eschatological life is resourced by the Spirit already, in eschatological moments of Christ-full-ness exhibited by the small groups of Christ-followers that were increasingly taking hold around the Mediterranean basin of his world. In those groups, Christ-followers in all their cultural diversities were already relieved of their enslavement to the power of Sin and were already joined together in Christ Jesus in the worship of the one God, in joyful enslavement to each other, and in the hope of (the eschatological pronouncement of) righteousness. Because the power of Sin had stood in the way of all this, those small and novel Christ-groups were microcosms of the sovereignty of God – prototypes of the kingdom of God in the time before the return of Jesus Christ. Their corporate lives, empowered by the Spirit, testified to the sovereignty of the God who enacts divine sovereignty in and through Christ.

This is why the dining practices of early Christ-followers mattered to Paul (as in 2:11–14) and why the idea that gentiles should be circumcised flew in the face of "truth of the gospel" (as in 2:1–10 and throughout). The identity hierarchy that the Galatians were tempted to buy into runs directly counter to God's pronouncement of righteousness. God does not see trust in Christ as righteousness only if it is matched by some other form of identity as well. Trust in Jesus Christ, nurtured by the Spirit and devoid of pretense regarding the merit of all other forms of identity, aligns Christ-followers with the pronouncement of righteousness.

As Christ-followers choose to walk in step with the Spirit, they see Christ-likeness brought alive within them in a corporate nest of Christ-like relationships, and that experience brings joy – one manifestation of the fruit of the Spirit. That experience of joy then fosters the choice to live in step with the Spirit in further instances. Christ-followers increasingly learn of the blessings of choosing to walk by the Spirit, who brings Christ alive within them, by which they are seen to be righteous in the eyes of God. Paul seems to think that trust in Jesus Christ, properly nurtured by the Spirit, prompts the choice to walk by the Spirit. Therein lies "the hope of righteousness."

THE FAITHFULNESS OF GOD

It is important to note what Paul's discourse assumes from start to finish: God is faithful.[7] This conviction was not under debate in Galatia, so Paul does not address the matter in a paragraph of explicit explanation. But discerning the theological convictions that support Paul's explicit discourse is often just as important as understanding that discourse itself. Paul elaborates this conviction explicitly in other letters.[8] In Galatians, the underlying conviction that God is faithful holds Paul's discourse together.

---

[7] For fuller articulation of this section and the section on "the Israel of God" (later in this chapter), see B. Longenecker 2023.

[8] See for instance 1 Thess 5:24; 1 Cor 1:9; 10:13; 2 Cor 1:18; Phil 1:6; Rom 3:4–5; 15:8. To exaggerate slightly, the whole of Romans, and in particular Romans 9–11, is framed by this conviction. See further B. Longenecker 2023:233–37.

For instance, Paul could not have spoken of eagerly awaiting the hope of righteousness "through the Spirit" if he was not supremely confident that the Spirit would continue to guide Christ-followers and bring Christ alive within them in the interim.[9] God will faithfully provide the Spirit, and the Spirit will faithfully empower those in Christ. They do not need the Torah as a pedagogue to get them to that blessed future pronouncement; they have the faithful Spirit. Moreover, in Christ, God is shown to be faithful to that divine word spoken to Abraham: "All the gentiles will be blessed in you" (3:8, citing Gen 12:3). Abraham's trust rested precisely on the conviction that God's promissory word will be fulfilled – much like Christ-followers trust in God's promissory word regarding "the hope of righteousness."

Perhaps the ultimate expression of divine faithfulness is an intra-divine phenomenon – exhibited between the Father and the Son. The opening verse of Galatians assumes this character of divine faithfulness in the simple phrase, "God the Father ... raised him [Jesus Christ] from the dead" (1:1). God's faithfulness fills the implied narrative behind the discourse of this verse. God did not leave Jesus Christ in the realm of nonexistence. In the resurrection of Jesus Christ, divine faithfulness interlocks inextricably with divine sovereignty. Moreover, as I proposed briefly in Chapter 6, the phrase "the trust that pertains to Jesus Christ" may actually refer to the trust that Jesus Christ himself exhibited in the faithfulness of God the Father. Jesus Christ went willingly and

---

[9] Downs and Lappenga (2019) propose that the *pistis* of Jesus Christ refers to Christ's faithfulness to Christ-followers in the time before the arrival of the kingdom of God. In my view, while this is not theologically incorrect, in Paul's preferred discourse that role belongs to the Spirit, while the trust of Jesus Christ is aligned differently – that is, in relation to the faithfulness of God.

faithfully into nonexistence (i.e., he "gave himself"; 1:4; 2:20) precisely because he knew God the Father to be faithful (in this case, the Father's faithful commitment to the life of the Son). The resurrection of Jesus Christ is the ultimate testimony of the faithfulness of God, upon which the certainty of Christ-followers rests. The faithfulness of God holds all of Paul's discourse in Galatians together. If it does not get explicit discussion within the text, God's faithfulness is a theological conviction that lies "just beneath the surface" of Paul's discourse.

One other passage deserves careful consideration. In 4:4-5 Paul gives the story of salvation in the briefest of terms. The core of that story lies in this divine initiative: "God sent God's Son, born of a woman, born under the Torah, to redeem those under the Torah, that we could receive adoption as sons" (and daughters, we might want to say). It is certainly notable that in a letter that makes Jewish identity tangential to what matters in Christ, these verses highlight the Jewish identity of Jesus Christ ("born under the Torah," 4:4), with the redemption of the Jewish people as one of the objectives of that ethnically embedded incarnation ("to redeem those under the Torah," 4:5). This, I submit, is a story about divine faithfulness – in fact, faithfulness to the Jewish people.

This is not some alien form of theologizing that lands temporarily and artificially in Galatians. Paul's discourse about the Torah as the pedagogue of the Jewish people provides the context for its interpretation. Long ago the Torah had been established among the ethnic people of Israel to serve as their protective (as well as a confining) temporary pedagogue. The Torah was mediated through angels, which simultaneously connotes both a positive and a negative aspect – the negative being its mediated character (in contrast to the intimacy of the Abba cry), the positive being its divine origins "higher than" the angels. Paul's discourse in 4:4-5 fills out the situation further. Jesus Christ became incarnate under the Torah – unsurprisingly, since this was the only group whose ethnic charter denounces idolatry. The purpose was, in the first instance, to redeem those under the Torah. In this light, the establishment of the pedagogical Torah among the ethnic people of Israel was not an end in itself. It was a means for displaying God's faithfulness in a historical frame, reinforcing this aspect of the character of the deity whose good news Paul proclaimed.

God did not simply show up in human garb to redeem the world de novo, unencumbered by past involvements. The incarnated humanity of the Son was specifically Jewish for the purpose of demonstrating the faithfulness of God. The giving of the pedagogue had nothing to do with God favoring one particular ethnic group whose identity had greater value in the eyes of God than any other ethnic group. The Torah was established among a particular people-group so that they might become a display of the redemptive faithfulness of God "in the fulfillment of time" (4:4). Gentile Christ-followers can confidently trust in Christ because God in Christ has demonstrated divine fidelity. The history of Israel is of critical importance in this regard, even in Galatians, not because salvation history is to the fore in that text (it isn't) but because God's dealings with those under the pedagogical Torah demonstrate something about the character of the God that Paul has invited gentiles to worship. Divine trustworthiness is seen in the incarnation of Jesus Christ – "under the Torah in order to redeem those under the Torah" in the first instance, as divine faithfulness is proclaimed throughout the world in an invitation to all nations subsequently.[10]

---

[10] The two *hina* clauses of this verse need to be seen not as saying much the same thing (as is usually done) but as saying two different things that work

An elaborate discourse about God's commitment to ethnic Israel does not germinate within the soils of Galatians. It is only in Romans (particularly Romans 9–11) that the soils are right for that. But even Galatians has a foothold for that later discussion, with the establishment of the Torah among the Jewish people as a protective (and constraining) temporary protector (3:19 and 24–25), providing the historical context for the demonstration of God's faithfulness, as implied in the curt narrative of 4:4–5. If there is any "salvation-historical linearity" in Galatians, it does not pertain to the ongoing history of a particular people-group. Instead, it pertains solely to God and God's temporally expansive initiatives – in the past in terms of the Abrahamic promise and the protecting Torah, and "in the fulfillment of time" in terms of the divine sending and resurrection of the Son, together with the sending of the Spirit into the hearts of Christ-followers. These divine initiatives emerge from the eternally faithful character of God, as demonstrated ultimately in the death and resurrection of Jesus Christ, certifying God's faithfulness to a historic people-group as a welcome testimony of divine constancy to and for all those in Jesus Christ.

THE ETHNIC PEOPLE OF ISRAEL

What does this suggest about the ethnic people of Israel? Some interpreters argue that Paul's theological discourse is exclusively concerned with and articulated for the desperate situation of

together. The first clause (regarding "those under the Torah") expresses a complementary purpose to the primary purpose (regarding the full rights of sonship), with the first clause expressing an essential purpose that is integrally associated with, allied to, and enmeshed within this primary purpose.

gentiles, without any real implication that the Jewish people are to be involved in God's redemptive activity in Christ. The Jews, after all, have been given the Torah in a special covenant with them. The Mosaic covenant is for them; Jesus Christ is for the gentiles.[11]

This interesting proposal (sometimes called the "two ways" interpretation) has ebbed and flowed over the past few generations. To its credit, this view rightly tries to avoid a disastrous misuse of Paul's letters (especially Galatians) when tied to an anti-Jewish or anti-Semitic cause. Paul would be horrified to see how his text would later be put to use. But on the other hand, he might just as much be aghast at the thought that the good news pertained only to gentiles. When Paul says that "all things are under the power of Sin" (3:22), he does not add "except for the Jews," nor does he say, "but Jews have the Torah, so they're okay." He says just the opposite, as we have seen, in 4:4–5: Jesus Christ "was born under the Torah to redeem those under the Torah."[12] In 3:28, it is unlikely that the grouping of "Jew" and "gentile" as "one in Christ Jesus" simply gestures to an exceptional situation where a few Jews have decided (though unnecessarily, in the "two ways" view) to trust in Jesus Christ. The claims of 3:28 go directly to Paul's theological vision of new forms of intimate relationality

---

[11] Some (but not all) interpreters within "the radical new perspective" (or the so-called Paul within Judaism approach) adopt this view. For early representatives of this view, see Gaston 1987; Gager 2000; Nanos 2002. Boccaccini (2020) proposes that Paul held "three ways" to salvation. Thiessen (2023:149–57), who consistently offers stimulating "radical new perspective" readings, argues against a two ways (or, for that matter, three ways) interpretation of Paul.

[12] The significance of this passage is notably underappreciated by interpreters of virtually all interpretative camps. It is currently, in my view, the most neglected text in the study of Galatians.

in Christ-groups, with Jews and gentiles joining together in Christ, as those who trust in Christ, in the worship of God.

Galatians makes it clear that this is not discourse for the benefit of gentiles alone. It is, of course, true that since Paul thought of himself as the apostle to the gentiles, he was particularly interested in thinking through the implications of what the death and resurrection of Jesus Christ mean for gentile Christ-followers, to whom the Galatian letter seems (primarily?) addressed. But in doing so, he also took account of the significant implications the Christ-event has for understanding God's covenant with the ethnic people of Israel. After all, he saw his mission to the gentiles as intermeshed with Peter's mission to the Jews (2:1–10), in a two-pronged missional focus that included the Jewish people.

It is not surprising, then, that when he recounts his speech to Peter in 2:15–21, Paul highlights that he and Peter shared some fundamental theological convictions. Noting that both he and Peter were, in fact, Jews from birth (2:15; see also 2 Cor 11:22; Rom 11:1; Phil 3:5), Paul claims that they agreed that "a person is not seen as righteous [i.e., in the sight of God] by the works of the Torah but through the trust that pertains to Jesus Christ," because "by the works of the Torah no one will be seen as righteous" (2:15–16, a pronouncement pertaining to "all flesh," *pasa sarx*). Peter and Paul also agreed that "we [Jews] are ourselves found to be sinners as we seek to be seen as righteous in Christ" (2:17). This is not simply theology for gentiles. Both Peter and Paul recognize that they, as Jews, are in need of trust in Christ in order to be righteous before God. This is why Christ loved Paul the Jew and gave himself for him, since Torah observance does not result in being seen as righteous by God (2:20–21). Christ's death here is for a Jew in a salvific deficit – evidently a particular case that displays a universal. The Torah's own wish, it seems, is for Jews to die to the Torah (as their macro-identity before God), at least if that is what Paul is suggesting in 2:19: "I died to the Torah through the Torah." The Torah's own program revises its significance in the coming of the eschatological age.[13] Paul is not saying that this is only true for gentiles who might decide to observe the Torah; he is depicting the Torah in this fashion without ethnic qualifications of any kind – that is, its revised significance pertains to the people of Israel. And although Paul's discourse in 4:21–31 is primarily intended to place Jerusalem-based Christ-groups in the context of enslavement, it is difficult to disentangle that group from any group whose identity prioritizes the giving of the Torah on Mount Sinai (4:25) – that is, 4:21–31 is pregnant with implications for Jews who are not Christ-followers and who, in Paul's view, are consequently enslaved "under the Torah."[14]

Paul thought that all people, both gentiles and Jews, were in deficient relationships to God except through the grace in Christ that set them right with God. Paul did not imagine that the divinely sent "messiah" was not, in fact, the messiah for the people of Israel, who are not in need of a messiah. Instead, Paul

---

[13] This might be because, as Paul presents it, the principle of the Torah is that of "doing" (as in Lev 18:5, cited in Gal 3:12).

[14] Martyn (1997b:205) underplays this point but in the end is forced to accept that "Judaism stands somewhere in the *background* [of 4:21–31]" (emphasis in the original). See also Barclay 2001; Eastman 2010:388; Byrne 2014; Marcus 2017:114–15. Thiessen (2016:73–101) offers a stimulating reading of Gal 4:21–31, arguing that Paul opposed gentiles adopting Torah observance simply because (as in one tradition within Judaism; see *Jubilees*) adult gentiles can never be true Jews, who are circumcised on the eighth day (that is, Paul had an "essentialist" or "primordialist" view of Jewish identity; see Matlock 2012; Fredriksen 2017:128–30). But if this was at the forefront of Paul's mind, it did not make it onto his papyrus very well; instead, Paul seems primarily to have taken different discursive routes in Galatians.

continued to imagine Israel's messiah to be the savior of the people of Israel, even while he (Paul) took the gospel to the gentile nations.[15] In Galatians Paul does not suggest that the only problem of nonbelieving fellow Jews is their lack of trust in Jesus the messiah; instead, he claims that Jesus the messiah was sent to redeem those "under the Torah" from their situation "under Sin" (3:22), with all the ramifications of that claim that we have explored in this book.

It is true that Paul did not imagine himself to have abandoned the God who was committed in ongoing faithfulness to the ethnic people of Israel. It is true that Paul wanted gentile Christ-followers to look a lot more "Jewish" than they had looked when they were "pagans."[16] It is true that Paul did not intend for the coming of the messiah to undermine the ethnic practices of the people of Israel (who can observe Torah as a legitimate and necessary micro-identity in Christ). It is true that Paul often shows signs of unshakable indebtedness to the traditions and concerns evidenced in large swaths of his ancestral heritage. It is true that Paul's discourse falls within the tremendously vibrant diversity of covenantal Judaism (or Judaisms) of his day. But it is also true that, as a consequence of the coming of the messiah, Paul rethought and reconceptualized his worldview and his practice. Thinking backward from what God has done in Christ, Paul came to understand all people, even his beloved kinspeople in Judaism, to be under the power of Sin. In his discourse, even the ethnic

---

[15] Although I translate the Greek *Iēsous Christos* as "Jesus Christ" instead of "Jesus the messiah," the resonances of the latter should not be excluded from Paul's use of *Christos* (see Novenson 2012), even if they are not often weight-bearing in his explicit discourse.

[16] See Fredriksen 2010.

people of Israel are shown to be in need of God's redemptive efforts in Christ – in whom alone, according to Paul, there is the hope of righteousness for all people-groups.

THE ISRAEL OF GOD

With this in view, consideration needs to be given to Paul's comments in 6:16, where he refers to "the Israel of God." The phrase is difficult to interpret with precision because there are, in a sense, so many moving parts in the verse, and it isn't perfectly clear which parts work most closely together. But although we can never be certain, some options are better than others.

Just prior to 6:16, Paul reaffirms that diverse identities of circumcised life and uncircumcised life are to be seen only as micro-identities in Christ: "Being circumcised doesn't count for anything, just as not being circumcised doesn't count for anything; the only thing that matters is new creation" (a slightly expansive translation of 6:15). The ideas in 6:16 are connected to this pronouncement (by means of the Greek *kai*, "and"), but in what way? There are four main components of 6:16:

1. The pronouncement of "peace upon" a particular group;
2. The pronouncement of "mercy upon" a particular group;
3. A group identified as "those who keep in step with this rule" (i.e., the rule articulated in 6:15 about new creation transcending the importance of all other identities);
4. A group identified as "the Israel of God."

It is fairly clear that #1 and #3 go together, with God's peace falling upon those who keep in step with the "new creation" message of the gospel. What isn't clear is how #2 and #4 are to be understood in relation to this. There are three main options:[17]

- In option A, #4 explains #3, so that those who keep in step with the gospel are collectively identified as "the Israel of God." In this option, #1 and #2 work together to explain the blessings enjoyed by this single group. A slightly expansive translation would read, "Peace and mercy upon those who keep in step with this rule – that is, upon (those who are) the (eschatological) Israel of God."

- In option B, #4 is somewhat differentiated from #3, with "the Israel of God" being Jewish Christ-followers who have not yet adopted the rule articulated in 6:15 (such as the new teachers themselves) and with the term "the Israel of God" probably being their own preferred self-designation. In this option, #1 works with #3, and #2 works with #4. A slightly expansive translation would read, "Peace upon those who keep in step with this rule, and mercy even upon (those who call themselves) 'the Israel of God.'"

- In option C, #4 is completely differentiated from #3, with "the Israel of God" being Jews who do not have trust in Jesus Christ; as in option B, #1 works with #3, and #2 works with #4, with #4 being a different group than in option B. A slightly expansive translation would read, "Peace upon those who keep in step with this rule, and mercy indeed upon the Israel of God (in their continuing disbelief)."

What are we to make of these options?

---

[17] There is variation even within the individual options. For instance, options B and C present "peace" and "mercy" as two distinct blessings; it is possible that they should appear together as "peace and mercy upon . . . and upon . . . ."

Righteousness and the Faithfulness of God 157

Option A makes sense in a letter where Paul has redefined traditional concepts christologically (like "the progeny of Abraham"). Perhaps he is simply reconceptualizing the term "the Israel of God" so that it refers not to the ethnic people of Israel but to Christ-followers, both Jews and gentiles. But the Greek text of 6:16 throws up some difficulties for this interpretation, which scholars have to sit lightly to when adopting this interpretation.[18]

Option B allows the letter to be framed with an eye to the new teachers, with the opening curse formulas of 1:6–9 balanced by a blessing upon them (and others like them) in 6:16. Unlike option A, there is nothing in the Greek construction to preclude an interpretation of this kind. Nonetheless, it is not readily apparent that a blessing of this kind fits the rhetorical context of the letter. Not only has Paul pronounced divine displeasure (i.e., curses) upon them but he clearly also wants the Galatians to expel the new teachers from their midst (4:30). For Paul to pronounce a blessing on them at the close of the letter might send confusing mixed messages about the new teachers in a setting where Paul cannot let up on the pressure against them.

Option C benefits from the fact that most (and probably all) occurrences of the word "Israel" in Paul's letters refer to the ethnic people of Israel. And Paul regularly uses the word "mercy" to

---

[18] So, for instance, although Moo (2013:402) holds to this view, he does so while admitting that "the syntactical evidence favors interpreting 'the Israel of God' as an entity separate from 'those who follow this rule.'" The view that "those who follow this rule" are identified as "the Israel of God" is weakened by its reliance on the extremely rare "epexegetical *kai*" to explain the *kai* of the final phrase, *kai epi ton Israēl tou theou*. (Moo [2013:402] concedes that *kai* "does not often function epexegetically.") Without an explicative or "epexegetical *kai*" in play, the verse clearly has two referents.

reference God's grace in a situation of disobedience. In that light, peace is upon those who obediently keep in step with the rule of 6:15, while mercy is called upon or pleaded for in relation to the Jews who have not put their trust in Jesus Christ. This interpretation makes sense, is in line with Paul's Greek construction, and resonates well with Paul's terminology elsewhere in the Pauline corpus. But is it likely? After all, Paul has repeatedly urged gentile Christ-followers not to adopt Torah observance, so why would he, at the very end of the letter, include a blessing upon Torah-observant Jews?[19]

This is the common criticism of option C. But the criticism has very little force. It assumes that Paul could not have countenanced complexity or conveyed intricacies. But Paul's very letter repeatedly speaks against such assumptions. Moreover, Paul has already portrayed his mission to the gentiles as intricately linked to the mission to the Jews (2:6–9); why would it be surprising for him to ask for God's mercy upon the Jews at the end of the letter? The new teachers were probably encouraging gentile Christ-followers to adopt circumcision (and full Torah observance?) precisely to benefit the mission to the Jews. Paul's plea for mercy upon the Israel of God indicates that he too affirms that mission; nothing he has said in Galatians undermines that mission. Option C fits the Galatian exigency perfectly.[20]

Further, as we have seen, Paul has already shown the sending of God's Son to have been for the purpose, in the first instance, of

---

[19] This view has become mantric. Two of the many representatives are Moo 2013:403; Wright 2021:370, 377. I once held it too (B. Longenecker 1998:87–88).

[20] See especially Bachmann 2008:101–23; Eastman 2010; Novenson 2014:37–38; Barclay 2015:418–21, 445; Osten-Sacken 2019:313–16; B. Longenecker 2023.

redeeming those under the Torah (4:5). Why would Paul not plead for God's mercy upon them at the end of the letter, in the hope that more Jews would come to put their trust in Christ – in "the hope of righteousness" and in greater fulfillment of that purpose? They are the Israel of God, chosen to be the historical people through whom God has displayed God's faithfulness. It is wholly in keeping with Paul's discourse in Galatians for him to offer a final plea for divine mercy to be showered on the people God has used to display divine faithfulness and sovereignty. The gospel that Paul takes to the gentiles is reliant precisely on that display.[21]

---

[21] Here again, Paul is shown to be wholly "within Judaism." On the hope for the restoration of Israel within Jewish traditions, see Staples 2021.

PART III

Positioning the Theology of Galatians

In this section of this book, attention will be given to making connections. Chapter 10 considers some of the ways that Galatians interfaces with other parts of the New Testament. Selected moments in the interpretation of the text are then overviewed in Chapter 11. Some brief comments regarding how Galatians might be seen to resource theological conversations in twenty-first-century contexts appear in Chapter 12, concluding the book.

CHAPTER 10

Galatians and the New Testament

Of the twenty-seven texts of the New Testament, Galatians was one of the earliest to be written. This chapter canvases some of the ways it correlates with the theological discourse of other New Testament texts. The exercise could be repeated and expanded significantly, of course. Here only some starting points are offered for consideration.

GALATIANS AND ROMANS ON TORAH AND ISRAEL

What we see in Galatians is raw, empowered Paulinism in its most concentrated form – at least with regard to issues of righteousness and Torah observance. The other letter that deals extensively with those issues is Romans, a letter that is meticulous and deliberate in its theological discourse. Galatians draws its power from the urgency of the moment, in which the Galatians are in dire trouble, in Paul's eyes. Romans is more of a calling card, laying out some of the distinctives of Paul's theological discourse in a way that allows the Roman Christ-followers to get to know what he stands for – precisely because he has a controversial reputation and wants to go to Spain with their support of his ministry.

That controversial reputation may well have something to do with the reception of Galatians itself among certain sectors of the early Christ-movement. Letters like Galatians were circulated between communities and beyond the communities to which they were first written.[1] Consequently, Paul's reputation as someone with a contentious presentation of the good news may also have spread between communities.

In that regard, Romans looks at times like a further development of some of the things Paul touched on in Galatians, placing somewhat similar discourse in a somewhat different theological setting. In Romans, Paul addresses at length some of the same issues he addresses in Galatians, but with its sixteen chapters to the six of Galatians, it comes across as a bit more measured. Comparisons between the two letters are easily made regarding the Torah and the people of Israel.[2]

In the later letter we hear, "Is the Torah sin? Absolutely not" (Rom 7:7). The Torah brings about knowledge of sin (7:7; compare 3:20; 4:15; 5:13; and the taxonomy of sinfulness in Gal 3:22), but the Torah itself is "holy" (7:12), "good" (7:13, 16), and "spiritual" (7:14), and its commands are "holy, righteous, and good" (7:12). It is, in fact, "the Torah of God" (7:22, 25). In Romans Paul makes no mention of the Torah's mediation through angels at the hand of a mediator – although Moses is the attributed author of Lev 18:5 (see Gal 3:12) concerning "righteousness that comes from the Torah" (Rom 10:5).

In Romans there is no sense that the Torah served as the pedagogue of the people of Israel for a predetermined period, 430 years after Abraham and up to the time of Christ, although there is the claim that Christ is the "*telos* of the Torah with regard

---

[1] See D. Smith 2020.
[2] Martyn (1997b:37–46) presents Romans as "one of the earliest interpretations of Galatians" on precisely these two issues.

to righteousness" (10:4) – where *telos* probably has more of a sense of "end" than simply "goal." Unlike Romans, Galatians has no remnant theology (11:1–5) and gives no indication that God has hardened parts of ethnic Israel according to God's own good purposes (9:19–23; 11:7, 25). The people of ethnic Israel have a theological priority in Romans, especially chapters 9–11, which significantly expand the relatively few comments about ethnic Israel in Galatians (especially 4:5 and 6:16). In Romans, "salvation" for "everyone who has trust in God" is explicitly glossed as being for "the Jew first, and also the Greek" (Rom 1:16; see also 2:9 [twice]). In fact, gentile Christ-followers are participating in the "spiritual blessings" enjoyed initially by the Jewish people (15:27, evidently referencing the faithfulness of God demonstrated historically in relation to that people-group), just as gentile Christ-followers are engrafted as unnatural branches into an olive tree of grace in which the ethnic people of Israel are naturally embedded (11:17–24). In Galatians, Paul agrees that a Petrine mission to unbelieving Jews is an appropriate strategy (2:7–8); in Romans, he hopes his own mission to the gentiles might make some Jews jealous so that they place their trust in Christ (11:11–14). In Romans, Paul asserts that the ethnic people of Israel will eventually be saved by trust in Christ – that is, both parts will be saved, both the remnant (11:1–6) and the part that God has temporarily hardened in order to allow gentiles to enter (11:7–25).[3] As a consequence, God is shown to be faithful to his word to ethnic Israel (11:1, 26–29), with Christ having become "a servant of the circumcised" in order to prove "the trustworthiness

---

[3] Many questions remain in relation to Paul's claim that "all Israel will be saved" (Rom 11:26). It is exegetically tortuous to read this as saying that the church, as the new Israel, will be saved.

of God" (15:8; see also Gal 4:4–5). In Romans, Paul makes clear that Abraham is the father of the ethnic people of Israel (4:9–12, 16) – a point not articulated in Galatians. Paul describes himself as "a descendant of Abraham" when referencing his Jewish identity (11:1) and notes that Jesus Christ himself was a descendant of the patriarchs of ethnic Israel (Abraham, Isaac, and Jacob; 9:5), with the messiah's ministry itself being a confirmation of "the promises made to the patriarchs" (15:8) and with ethnic Israel being "elect" and "loved for the sake of the patriarchs" (11:28). And in Romans Paul has far more discursive space to explain the legitimacy of Jewish Christ-followers observing Torah as part of their cultural identity (14:1–15:6) – something that is not out of line with Galatians but which was not required in the urgency of the Galatian situation.

GALATIANS AND THE CANONICAL PAULINE CORPUS

The christological focus that we see throughout the whole of Galatians is arguably the spine that runs throughout the whole of the Pauline corpus – both the texts where his authorship is undisputed and those where it is disputed.[4] And throughout his letters Paul consistently probes what it means to be followers of Christ. In that regard, Paul's theological discourse regularly highlights the self-giving of Christ as the basis for the appearance and extension of "Christ-full-ness" within Christ assemblies. Unsurprisingly, then, even discourse about the importance of

---

[4] There is agreement that Paul wrote 1 Thessalonians, Galatians, 1 Corinthians, 2 Corinthians, Romans, Philippians, and Philemon (in the most probable sequential order). There is disagreement on whether Paul wrote 2 Thessalonians, Colossians, Ephesians, 2 Timothy, 1 Timothy, and Titus (in the order of likelihood regarding Paul's authorship).

financial care for those in desperate need (as in Gal 2:10; 6:9–20) appears consistently throughout the Pauline letters, whether disputed or undisputed.[5]

Discourse about the Spirit that is so prominent in Galatians also (and unsurprisingly) has a strong foothold across almost the whole of the corpus of the Pauline letters. Divine love "has been poured into our hearts through the Holy Spirit that has been given to us" (Rom 5:5) – an assurance that Paul develops significantly in Romans 8.[6] This is the Spirit who brings life (Rom 8:2, 6; see also 7:6), the Spirit who ensures that "the righteous requirement of the Torah" is fulfilled in the Christ-like lives of "those who walk according to the Spirit" (Rom 8:4; compare being "led by God's Spirit" in 8:14). The contrast between the Spirit and the *sarx* ("the flesh") that we see in Galatians reappears in Rom 8:6–13. So too does the contrast of enslavement and sonship through the Spirit (8:14–15) – including the cry of sonship "Abba, Father" (8:15)

---

[5] Beyond Galatians, see Rom 12:13–16 (see also 12:8); 1 Cor 11:17–34; 16:1–4; 2 Cor 8–9 (see esp. 9:13); 1 Thess 5:14; 2 Thess 3:6–13; Eph 4:28; 1 Tim 5:3–16; Titus 3:14. On "the poor" in Gal 2:10 as the local poor wherever Christ-groups are founded, see B. Longenecker 2010:189–206. Typically "the poor" of 2:10 is interpreted as a reference to impoverished Christ-followers in Jerusalem. In this interpretation, the Jerusalem leaders instruct Paul to raise funds for their impoverished community. For this interpretation to be compelling, however, the Galatians would have needed to know that "the poor" was an established term referring to Jerusalem Christ-groups or members within them, since Paul does nothing to explain that in the letter. But the evidence for this is nonexistent, and a fuller spread of data suggests the opposite. See B. Longenecker 2010:157–82; 2020b. Of course, later Paul undertakes an initiative to support the poor in Jerusalem, but this is a development (with a specific target) of the more general principle articulated in Gal 2:10. See B. Longenecker 2010:184–89, 338–44. For a study of this verse in relation to Paul's apocalyptic discourse, see B. Longenecker 2018a.

[6] See B. Longenecker 2014 for a polyvalent interpretation of "the love of God" in Rom 5:5.

that Paul referenced in Galatians (4:6). In Rom 8:9–11, Paul places Christ-followers in the Spirit and the Spirit in them. The Spirit is "the first crop of the eschatological harvest" in God's work toward the redemption of creation (8:23), so that the Spirit assists Christ-followers, knowing their hearts and articulating their needs in their prayer life before God (8:26–27). Beyond the references cited here, there are seven further references to the Spirit in Romans alone. To canvas the Spirit in Paul's other letters would take us too far into the woods of almost all of those texts. But the primary emphasis throughout the Pauline corpus is on the Spirit's steadfast involvement in the lives of Christ-followers in the time before the return of Jesus Christ.

"God is one," says Paul in Gal 3:20, affirming the central tenet of Jewish monotheism. This monotheistic deity is spoken of as God the Father who sent God's Son, Jesus Christ the Lord, and who sends the Spirit of the Son (4:4–6). The same affirmation, "God is one," appears in Rom 3:30, where it is used to support the point that this deity relates to people of all nations through trust in Christ. In 1 Corinthians we see an astounding reworking of the Jewish Shema, prayed twice a day by Jews of Paul's day: "Hear, O Israel, the Lord our God, the Lord is one" – the words of Deut 6:4. Paul takes the two nouns, "God" and "Lord," and gives them two referents: God is further identified as "God the Father" and "Lord" is further identified as "the Lord Jesus Christ." In this way, Paul ends up with a christologically focused reformulation of his ancestral traditions: "There is one God, the Father, from whom all things come and for whom we live; and there is one Lord, Jesus Christ, through whom all things come and through whom we live" (1 Cor 8:6). Theological formulations of this kind became the resources for later Christian theologians as they sought ways to articulate the theological nuances of one God in three persons: the

Father, the Son, and the Spirit – with the Spirit being "the Spirit of God" or even "the Spirit of the Son."[7] Along with this reworked confession of the Shema, it is also possible (but not probable) that Paul addressed Jesus Christ as "God" in Rom 9:5.[8]

In Galatians, Paul frequently depicts people as being "under" various phenomenon – not only "under the Torah" but also "under the *stoicheia*" and, along different lines, "under the power of Sin." This "power of Sin" is also featured in Rom 5:12–21 and Rom 7:7–25, where it is said to enter the world, influence people within it, and reign as one of the overlords of an enslaving system that God shatters in Christ. This is what Paul calls being "under the power of Sin" in Rom 3:9. In Romans 6, Paul makes it clear that Christ-followers are freed from this power, even if they might unfortunately continue to yield themselves to its patterning of life.[9]

In Rom 5:12–21, this power is coupled with "the power of Death," another reigning overlord and one that takes center stage in 1 Corinthians 15. In that chapter, the power of Death (not simply human deaths, but an overarching power whose talons are evidenced in the deaths of all people) is "the final enemy" of God (1 Cor 15:26). These overarching powers have their first foothold

---

[7] The ecumenical councils of Nicaea (325), Constantinople (381), and Ephesus (431) are notable for this, but individual theologians (in particular, Tertullian) had already been hard at work crafting a view that corresponded with later Trinitarian formulations.

[8] Rom 9:5 is best interpreted without a christological reference: "The one who is over all things is God, who is blessed forever. Amen." Compare 2 Cor 1:3; 11:31; Rom 1:25.

[9] The person who speaks in Rom 7:7–25 is "sold as an enslaved person under the power of Sin" (7:14). This description, together with various other indicators, suggests that Paul is not speaking of himself but is using "speech in character" to depict a particular person (a Jewish person in an "Adamic" situation) outside the sphere of grace in Christ. See B. Longenecker 2005:88–93.

in the extant Pauline corpus in Galatians (the power of Sin in 2:17 and 3:22). Not a world away is Paul's relatively loose construct of "principalities and powers" – what Eph 6:12 calls "the cosmos grabbers" (*kosmokratores*), referring to the way they are clutching at God's creation in efforts to tear it away from God's control.

Although in Romans 5 it is clear that the power of Sin entered this world through the transgression of Adam, it is not clear whether Paul thought that power existed prior to the transgression of Adam. In no extant text does Paul give explicit consideration to the ontological origins of these superhuman powers. Nor does Paul discuss their relationship to the figure he refers to as "Satan" in some letters other than Galatians (e.g., 1 Thess 2:18; 1 Cor 5:5; 7:5; 2 Cor 2:12; 11:14; 12:7; Rom 16:20).

We have seen several passages in which Pauline letters display the sovereignty of God in relation to the created order and the powers at work to undermine God's sovereignty (see also Col 1:15–20). In Galatians, Paul's discourse speaks of "new creation" (6:15), a term that gestures primarily toward the creation of new patterns of relationship within Christ-groups rather than being a cosmological reference regarding the restoration of the created order. It is even possible to read Galatians as if the cosmic order is left under the domination of the power of Sin while Christ-followers sneak out with their Lord into some arena where their relationships are set in order, apart from the created order. This is the way some "gnosticizing" Christ-followers of the second and third centuries probably read some of Paul's discourse. Paul himself would have contested this interpretation vigorously, declaring it a misunderstanding of his intentions.[10] Nonetheless,

---

[10] So too he would have challenged the view that in Galatians "[t]he sending out of the Son" has "no impact on the cosmos" (Perriman 2023:329). At the

there is little in Galatians to counter that misunderstanding directly.

Paul's letter to the Galatians foregrounds a suprahuman dimension of life (being "under" the power of Sin and other phenomena) and regularly focuses on interpersonal and intergroup relations as inventories of the identity of people and people-groups. Ephesians builds on both of these things with its reference to the "hostility" that had once existed between Jews and gentiles, prior to their incorporation into Christ: Jesus Christ "is our peace; he has made both groups into one group, and by means of his [broken] body he has broken down the wall of hostile division that divided us" (Eph 2:14). Similarly, the great mystery of God that Ephesians proclaims is not a world away from what we see in Galatians: "The gentiles have become fellow heirs, members of the same body, and sharers in the promise in Christ Jesus" (Eph 3:6). In this union of people who were formerly separated by the wall of hostility, we see God's purpose to "make known to the rulers and authorities in the heavenly places the wisdom of God in its right variety, through the assembly" of those in Christ (Eph 3:10).

In one of his "capstone" verses in Galatians, Paul writes, "There is neither Jew nor Greek; there is neither enslaved nor free; nor is there male and female, for you are all one in Christ Jesus" (3:28, CEB). The Corinthians received instruction along much the same lines, as did the Colossians, although with one notable difference: The reference to "male and female" is left out in letters that

---

very least, Paul would have said that it impacted the cosmos in declaring the sovereignty of God rather than the sovereignty of Sin and in creating a sphere of power that prefigures the ultimate manifestation of "the kingdom of God" (5:21).

postdate Galatians. In 1 Cor 12:13, Paul talks about Christ-followers being baptized by one Spirit into one body, "whether Jew or Greek, whether slave or free." The list of identities is expanded in Colossians, but even so, the phrase "male and female" does not appear there either – the reference is to Greeks and Jews, circumcised and uncircumcised, barbarian, Scythian, enslaved and free (Col 3:11). This might just be an insignificant variation, but probably there is more going on. Some Christ-followers in Corinth seem to have thought that gendered identities were erased in Christ, as if people could rise into spiritual states and leave behind their gendered identities. Paul took pains to insist that differentiated identities still exist in Christ; the creator God does not redeem his people into a spiritual androgyny. Paul thought there was confusion on this matter among the Corinthians (esp. 1 Cor 11:1–16). It seems likely, then, that he felt the need to drop the phrase "not male and female" when writing to the Corinthians. Probably the same aversion to unnecessarily causing confusion explains the omission of the phrase from Colossians as well.

Whether Paul or someone writing in his name, the author of Colossians contrasted being influenced by "the *stoicheia* of the world" (*ta stoicheia tou kosmou*) with the proper formation of Christian identity. Christ-followers can be "taken captive" by fundamental identity influencers that run contrary to Christian identity as those who have died with Christ (Col 2:8, 20).

GALATIANS AND NEW TESTAMENT TEXTS BEYOND THE PAULINE CORPUS

The author of 2 Peter, writing long after Galatians was written, affirmed the "wisdom" of Paul but added this proviso: "Some things he says in his letters are hard to understand" (3:16). It is possible that some of the later texts of the New Testament seek to take account of the difficulty in understanding Paul. For instance, the Acts of the Apostles spends more than half of its twenty-eight chapters featuring the ministry of Paul. But when we hear from Paul in that narrative, it is hard to find his tenacious preference for "participationistic" forms of theological discourse that is so evident in Galatians and other letters. Perhaps that aspect of Paul's theological discourse, as central and indispensable as it was to Paul's thinking, was considered too complex for the author's purposes.[11]

But the same author has other tendencies that run along lines different from those preferred by Paul. Nowhere, for instance, is Paul referred to as an "apostle" of the early Christian mission – a term that Paul used regularly as his calling card, displaying it prominently in most of his extant letters (except the Thessalonian letters, Philippians, and Philemon) and perhaps most prominently in Galatians. For the author of Acts, Paul is an "apostle" but only in the sense of being "the one who is sent" by the church based in Antioch (14:4, 14, where Barnabas is presented in similar terms).

Would Paul and the author of the letter of James have seen eye to eye? The issue is frequently debated. Paul would agree with the author of James that "faith is dead if it does not produce actions [*erga*]" (Jas 2:17). Paul would agree that it is illegitimate for Christ-followers to say that they "have faith without it being evident in their actions [*erga*]" (Jas 2:14), or for someone to say,

---

[11] While Acts is often a helpful source for reconstructing Paul's ministry, there are times when it is difficult to reconcile things we see in Paul's letters and what we find in Acts.

"You have faith and I have actions [*erga*]," to which the rightful response is, "Show me your faith apart from your actions [*ergōn*], and I will show you my faith by my actions [*ergōn*]" (Jas 2:18).[12] But Paul might want to quibble with the way the author of James reads the Abraham narrative of Genesis. It is a "foolish person" (2:20), says James, who tries to read the Abraham narrative as if it testifies solely to the sufficiency of faith. "Isn't it true that our father Abraham was seen as righteous by actions [*ergōn*] when he offered his son Isaac on the altar? You can see that faith was active with his actions [*synērgei tois ergois*], and faith was brought to completion [*eteleiōthē*] by actions [*ergōn*]" (Jas 2:21–22, a point reinforced in 2:24–26). Paul might question the wisdom of reading the Abraham story in quite this way (with Gen 15 being read in relation to Gen 22); it might just give a hostage to fortune. And the same is true for the way James makes the case in 2:24: Is it really wise to say that "a person is seen as righteous by actions and not by faith alone"?

The author of James, for his part, probably knows that some Christ-followers have proven themselves "foolish" by assuming, as some in the Corinthian community seem to have assumed, that Paul's gospel means that "all things are lawful for me" (1 Cor 6:12 [twice] and 10:23 [twice]) and that, because God is gracious to sinners, the more we sin the more we prove God to be magnificently gracious (Rom 3:7–8). As Paul notes, "some people accuse us of holding to this view" (Rom 3:8). Early Christ-followers like Paul and James were trying to find ways to articulate the necessity of trust being evidenced in lifestyle; some articulated the issue

---

[12] For an irenic reading of Paul and James, see Kamell 2014. Quite differently, see Hengel 1987 (the German title translates as "The Letter of James as Polemic against Paul").

along one form of discourse, others along other forms. Each form of articulation made important contributions to the emerging Christ-movement; each also was open to misinterpretation. The author of 2 Peter recognized this for the letters of Paul (i.e., "people who are ignorant and others who are unstable" distort Paul's letters; 2 Pet 3:16); Paul might say that the same could be true with regard to the letter of James.

In the end, Paul and James would both heartily endorse the claim that what matters is "trust continually working in practical ways through love" (Gal 5:6) or that Christ-followers should "demonstrate by their good lifestyle that their actions [*erga*] emerge from the humility that comes from wisdom" (Jas 3:13).

CHAPTER 11

The Afterlife of Galatians

This chapter tracks some moments in the reception history of Galatians.[1] This survey will inevitably fall short of being comprehensive, being more of a thumbnail sketch.[2] Our discussion features seven foci: (1) Jews, Christians, and church authorities in the early centuries; (2) Luther and the medieval church; (3) Judaism and grace; (4) God's apocalyptic invasion; (5) racial justice; (6) gender and power; and (7) Jewish and Muslim interpreters.[3]

JEWS, CHRISTIANS, AND CHURCH AUTHORITIES
IN THE EARLY CENTURIES

In the year 180, some Christians from the town Scillium in the northern region of Africa were brought to trial before the Roman

---

[1] For a survey of key interpreters of Galatians, see Riches 2013. See also Levy 2001; Pollmann and Elliott 2014.
[2] Missing, for instance, is the impact of Galatians on the arts. The 2017 film *Blade Runner 2049*, for example, includes mention of "the Galatians syndrome." This seems to reference an imbalanced relationality – in a world where identity domination is orchestrated by one group (humans) over another ("replicants").
[3] In this overview, it is convenient to adopt the language of "Christian" (instead of "Christ-follower") and "faith" (instead of "trust"), since these are the terms that were predominantly used by the interpreters discussed here.

governor. They were given the choice of either being killed as Christians or offering sacrifices in honor of the Roman deities and the emperor. The governor saw that they had brought a box to the trial. When he asked what the box contained, he was told, "Books and letters of Paul, a just man" (*Acts mart. Scillit.* 12). Evidently, when faced with the prospect of impending martyrdom, these late second-century Christians cherished these epistles of Paul.

Not everyone had such high regard for Paul's letters as the Christians of Scillium. Around the same time that those Christians were cherishing Paul's text, Jewish teachers were challenging some of the more radical statements that Paul articulated in Galatians. They argued that "the offspring of Abraham" refers to the ethnic people of Israel (not to a single referent in the first instance, as in Gal 3:16) and denounced Paul's claim that "the law is not unto life" (Gal 3:21).[4]

Christian theologians, conversely, adopted Paul's discourse and put it to new use in defining the Christian church over and against Jews.[5] One of the earliest texts upon which Galatians exerted significant influence is the text known as 5 Ezra (found in 2 Esdras 1–2), probably dated to the 140s. The author of that text attempted to show that God has abandoned his favor for the ethnic people of Israel, with God's affections transferring now to a new people-group: those in the Christian church. The author's supersessionistic "replacement theology" was fed by a number of texts. Among them was Paul's depiction of two women in Gal 4:21–31 – one enslaved (the Jerusalem that is below, with her

---

[4] See Rosen-Zvi 2017.
[5] On Paul's theology in the early centuries of its reception by Christian theologians, see Pervo 2010; Bird and Dodson 2011; Blackwell 2011; 2015; 2016; White 2014; Oliver and Boccaccini 2018; Schröter, Butticaz, and Dettwiler 2018; Aageson 2023.

children, linked to Mount Sinai) and one free (the Jerusalem that is above, with her children, linked to the Spirit). Meanwhile, in his *Dialogue with Trypho* (Trypho being a representative non-believing Jew), Justin Martyr explains Jewish unbelief using quotations from the New Testament gospels, the Old Testament, and Paul's letters (including Galatians). Like the author of 5 Ezra, Justin locates Jewish unbelief as a deviation from the ways of the God who revealed himself to Abraham, Isaac, and Jacob.[6] Tertullian saw Galatians as "the most decisive against Judaism" (*Marc.* 5.2).

Around the same time (esp. around 160–170), the extremely popular teacher Marcion adopted Galatians as a key text for his brand of Christianity. For Marcion (whose influence extended well beyond his lifetime), there was no reason to imagine the deity of ethnic Israel and the deity revealed in Christ Jesus to be one and the same; instead, these are two completely different deities. The God who had entered into a covenant with the people of Israel was the creator deity, who was morally deficient (prone to war, etc.). The God of salvation sent Jesus Christ to save people from the creator deity and from that deity's creation. Christians who link Jesus Christ to the creator deity have compromised Paul's theological precision. Marcion moved Galatians to the front of the Pauline corpus, signaling that everything in that corpus needs to be read through the lens of Galatians. But it was a highly edited version of Galatians that Marcion advocated, imagining that the text had been corrupted in places by those who wanted to align Jesus Christ with the deity of the Jewish people. So he removed any parts that could be interpreted in that light, enabling him to demonstrate that the cross of Christ saves

---

[6] See Werline 1999.

us from the despotic creator and the tyranny of the Torah of the Jewish people.[7]

Gnosticizing Valentinian Christians of the second and third centuries (following the interpretative approach of Valentinus) saw Paul's reference to "those who are spiritual" in Gal 6:1 as a reference to themselves, seeing themselves as being on a higher order of enlightenment than other Christians. They were free in Christ (e.g., Gal 5:1) and were not to be held back by other Christians who were enslaved to an inferior Christian gospel – just as Paul was free and had not allowed himself to be held back. In Paul's autobiography of Galatians 1–2, Valentinian Christians found precedent for forms of authority that originated directly from God apart from ecclesiastical authority (e.g., 1:1, 12, 17; 2:2). Valentinian Christians have died to the cosmos (6:14), a cosmos created by a lesser deity, in contrast to the saving deity of Jesus Christ, who was crucified in order to destroy the physical body of the lesser deity (who also gave the Torah to the Jews).[8] Valentinian Christians saw themselves (in contrast to other Christians) as embodying the progeny of Abraham (3:16, 19, 29), the new creation (6:15), and the Israel of God (6:16).[9]

Meanwhile, those charged with episcopal oversight of Christian churches often appealed to Paul as an established "apostle," with the bishops of the church deriving their authority from apostles such as him. When Ignatius of Antioch argued for the necessity of Christians falling in line with their legitimate bishops, he referenced Paul as being "approved" within the lineage of episcopal

---

[7] For a reconstruction of Marcion's probable text of Galatians, see BeDuhn 2013:229–33. On Marcion and the Jewish scriptures, see Davis 2021.
[8] On Valentinian interpretations of Galatians, see Pagels 1975:101–14.
[9] Along similar lines, see the second- or third-century *Books of Jeu* 1.3.5, as discussed in B. Longenecker 2015:93–100.

authority (Ign. *Eph.* 12), just as he could refer to both Peter and Paul as "apostles" (Ign. *Rom.* 4.3).[10]

But if this line of reasoning didn't work well with Christians in gnosticizing circles, neither did it work well with Jewish Christians of the second century, some of whom were derisory toward Paul. For instance, the second-century text known as the *Pseudo-Clementine Homilies* tells stories about Clement of Rome, who was purportedly converted to Christianity by Peter's influence. In that account, Paul is depicted in unremitting negative terms. In one part of that text (*Epistle of Peter to James 2*), Paul's gentile converts are said to reject Peter's teaching and, instead, adopt "certain lawless and trifling preaching of the man who is my [Peter's] enemy." Proof that this enemy, Paul, is wrong to argue for "the dissolution of the Torah" is drawn from Matt 5:18, where Jesus states that not a letter or stroke of a letter in the Torah will be erased until heaven and earth pass away. Moreover, Peter is shown to represent truth within the church, while Simon Magus represents evil within the church (2.17–18). This is the same Simon Magus who was depicted in the Acts of the Apostles as seeking personal profit from peddling the power of the Holy Spirit and being rebuked by Peter for seeking unauthorized use of power (Acts 8:9–24). In the *Pseudo-Clementine Homilies*, Simon Magus is a stand-in for Paul himself – here rebuked by Peter, in sharp contrast to Paul's rebuke of Peter in Gal 2:11–14. Paul is called "a false prophet" who came "from some deceiver"; his "deeds are those of a hater," and he himself is "an enemy," even "death" itself. In 17.13–19 Peter disputes Simon Magus's (i.e., Paul's) claim to be called to apostleship by the risen Christ – essentially

---

[10] In most of the patristic literature, references simply to "the apostle" almost inevitably refer to Paul.

undermining Paul's claims in Galatians 1 (esp. 1:1, 12, 15–17). No one can claim to be an apostle and yet criticize Peter, the one upon whom Jesus said he would build his church. To criticize Peter is to criticize Jesus Christ. Peter followed Jesus Christ during his earthly ministry, unlike the criticizer, who twists an alleged vision of the resurrected Christ into claims of apostolic privilege. Here we see a section of the Christian church distancing itself from Paul, reframing his self-presentation in Galatians so that he is shown to be a dangerous charlatan and sorcerer who has misled vast sections of the Christian church away from its proper Jewish heritage.

This view of Paul is not a world away from that of Porphyry, a Roman philosopher of the third century (c. 234–305) and a critic of Christianity. In *Against the Christians*, Porphyry argued that the Christian religion was not legitimate because, under the influence of Paul especially but others as well, it had severed its connection to the Jewish way of life and was therefore a newcomer (and consequently not to be trusted).[11] Similar in this regard are the Ebionites, a group of Christians who retained their Jewish identity and are known to us from the second through fourth centuries. They repudiated Paul. Whereas Marcion thought Paul was the only true apostle of the Christian faith and upheld Luke's Gospel as falling in line with Paul, the Ebionites used only the Gospel of Matthew and denounced Paul as an apostate.[12]

The issue of Paul's authority in relation to the Jerusalem apostles (such as Peter) had other permutations as well. When recounting the Jerusalem incident in Gal 2:1–10, Paul claimed that he and Barnabas "did not submit to them [the "false

---

[11] See Wilken 1984:197–98.   [12] On the Ebionites, see Bauckham 2003.

believers" who were secretly brought into the meeting] for a single moment" (2:5). But some interpreters and scribes knew of manuscripts in which the word "not" had been omitted in the process of transmission. Tertullian, for instance, claimed that Paul did, in fact, submit to leaders in Jerusalem. Tertullian (basing his view on this faulty manuscript tradition) imagined that Paul submitted to people in Jerusalem but only as a temporary strategy, until such time as Paul's gospel could be approved by the Jerusalem apostles later in the episode (*Marc.* 5.3.3; see also Irenaeus, *Haer.* 3.13.3; and others). Along different lines, Jerome (c. 345–420) thought that when Paul says in Gal 2:11, "I opposed him [Peter] to his face," he was using a Greek phrase that simply means "in appearance" – that is, Peter and Paul were acting out an imaginary dispute in order to teach others on the basis of that dispute (*Epist.* 112.3.4–11). That, unfortunately, is not a strong interpretation of the Greek (*kata prosōpon*), which connotes a public dispute involving confrontation based on significantly different points of view rather than feigned contrivance. But Jerome preferred to put an irenic spin on their motivation, in order to see these two apostolic figures acting in harmony to educate the church together.

LUTHER AND THE MEDIEVAL CHURCH

In the sixteenth century, Erasmus of Rotterdam (1466–1536) adopted Jerome's view that Peter and Paul had been working together in Antioch, rather than being at loggerheads with each other. This was an important model for Erasmus, who wanted to keep harmony in the church even while the winds of ecclesiastical reformation were beginning to blow. However, his contemporary, Martin Luther (1483–1546), tirelessly fanned the flames of reformation, together with others. Luther saw himself much like a Paul to the church's Peter, speaking truth vociferously against ecclesiastical power gone wrong. Galatians was especially important to Luther. "I have betrothed myself to it," he once noted. He taught Galatians on several occasions at the university in Wittenberg (Germany). To recognize the force of his reading of Galatians, it is important to recognize also how "Augustinian" readings of Paul's letters had influenced the medieval church, against which Luther was reacting.

Prior to his conversion to Christianity at the age of thirty-two, Augustine (354–430) had lived a life that he later deemed to be hedonistic and sinful. After converting to Christianity, he became a foremost theologian of significant influence. He directly attacked the views of another theologian, Pelagius (c. 354–418). For Pelagius, human nature is essentially good and without any stain of "original sin," so human beings are quite able to choose the good and decide to follow God because their volition is free to do so. Augustine disagreed with all this. He stressed that human beings are immersed in sinfulness, being wholly reliant on God's salvific grace, without any previous merit or goodness attracting God's attention. Even trust is a gift from God. After receiving divine grace, however, good works are essential, thought Augustine, if the Christian is to have access to eternal life. By the trust of the Christian, God's grace enables human nature to be healed of its brokenness and to progress in the habits of faith, as evidenced in the good works of Christians. God supplies those who trust in Jesus Christ with the ability to will the good, and in the act of willing to do the good, the Christian produces good works that demonstrate the effects of God's grace. In this way, righteousness is imparted within Christians, becoming a part of their own identity as they live a life of good works. God does not simply declare sinners to be righteous in Christ; God's grace enables them to become righteous in Christ. Christians should perform the habits of faith, with their works being appreciated by God as the prerequisites for enjoying eternal life.

Augustine read Gal 5:6 in this light. What matters is "trust working through love" – a claim that couples with the words of James, "faith without works is dead" (Jas 2:17; see also 2:20, 26). Augustine read Gal 3:21–22 to demonstrate that the Torah reveals the truth that human beings are sinners, although the Torah cannot change their will to do good because it cannot empower them to do so. Only righteousness infused within the Christian by grace empowers the improvement of the Christian. In living by the Spirit, they make progress by increasing their good works, which God rewards with eternal life. Since those good works can only flow from a previous gift of grace, when God crowns the merits of the Christian, God is only crowning God's own gift.[13]

This Augustinian framework had significant influence on important theologians such as Peter Lombard (1100–1160) and Thomas Aquinas (1225–1274). Aquinas, for instance, emphasized that divine grace perfects human nature. He saw this in Gal 2:19–20. For Paul to be crucified with Christ involves Christ acting on the soul of Paul, which in turn impacts the life Paul lived in the flesh/body. The Spirit of Christ changes the soul of the Christian, who undertakes acts of charity as a consequence of that change. Divine grace is met by the cooperative efforts of the person changed by grace, whose good works are the basis by which the Christian comes to be deserving of eternal life. Like Augustine, Aquinas highlighted Gal 5:6. He took from it that love is not intrinsic to faith but needs to be added to faith in order to

---

[13] On Augustine, see Levering 2013; Dubbelman 2020.

ensure the maturation of faith; that is, love needs to form faith ("faith formed in love"; *Summa theologiae* II-II Q. 4.4).

There were many points on which Luther was in agreement with Augustine and Augustinian interpreters of Paul. Despite the strengths of Augustine's own interpretations, however, an Augustinian perspective had allowed certain phenomena to take hold in the medieval church that Luther increasingly came to see as theologically problematic – in particular, the sense that righteousness could be imparted in the life of the Christian. Most insidious to Luther was the medieval practice of "indulgences." Buying indulgences (through a donation to the church or charitable work in its name) enabled Christians to offset the effect of their sins. Consequently, they would spend less time in purgatory before entering the blessings of heaven (so that one's experience of salvation could be shaped by the size of one's bank account).[14] Whereas Augustinian interpretations saw righteousness as imparted within the Christian, Luther saw righteousness as always external and foreign to the Christian. Righteousness is not infused within the Christian, as a new resource to draw on in the process of healing the human nature and undertaking good works; instead, Christ's righteousness is always alien to the Christian, who is always a sinner before God, except by way of the righteousness of Christ, which God sees and reckons to the believer. Whereas Augustinian interpretations saw trust as needing to be coupled to a believer's own righteousness, Luther saw trust itself as becoming manifest in righteousness – not "imparted" righteousness but, as the believer is joined in union with Christ, Christ's own "imputed" righteousness that is activated in sinners by faith. Faith does not need love to be added to it in order to

---

[14] On the economic dimension of Luther's theology, see Torvend 2008.

make faith complete and "formed"; Gal 5:6 simply means that God-given faith strides forward due to an inner potency that inevitably results in loving actions.[15]

JUDAISM AND GRACE

Luther interpreted Galatians as Paul's defense of liberative grace over against what he thought to be the enslaving legalism of the medieval church. In this, he saw himself to be giving voice to Paul's chastisement of the legalistic "works righteousness" of "Judaism." What Luther saw to be unhealthy in the medieval church he projected onto Judaism. He saw the Jews as confined in an arid, moribund religion in which they seek to strong-arm God into awarding salvation through good works.

This caricature, deeply entrenched in many centuries of Christian discourse and widespread in the study of the New Testament, was overturned in 1977. In *Paul and Palestinian Judaism*, E. P. Sanders argued that it has been a convenience of Christian scholarship to follow Luther's example of equating Christianity with grace and "Judaism" with "legalism."[16] Sanders problematized that convenience by illustrating how vast tracts of Judaism were animated by a profound awareness of divine grace upon the people of Israel, who were chosen by God to observe the Torah as part of their response to God's gracious covenant with them. Sanders called this "covenantal nomism" – a term devised

---

[15] Alongside Luther were other Reformers, such as Philip Melanchthon (1497–1560) and John Calvin (1509–1564). On the reception of Paul among the Reformers, see Chester 2017. Also Westerholm 2003; D. Campbell 2009:247–83. On Luther's engagement with Galatians in particular, see Hagen 1993; Hafemann 2014; Wengert 2014; Ngien 2023.

[16] For a precursor to Sanders 1977, see Sanders 1973.

to keep Jewish observance of the Torah ("nomism") within a context of covenantal relationship and divine grace.

There had been precedents to Sanders's argument, especially among Jewish scholars who had long argued that, if Paul presented Early Judaism as legalistic, he was either misinformed or disingenuous.[17] But if other voices had already begun to chisel away at the "legalistic" monolith, ultimately it was Sanders's effort that shifted the scholarly agenda. His argument, poked and prodded by others, has now been shown to have certain flaws or to require much greater nuancing (see the discussion of John Barclay later in this section). But his central argument in its most basic form has generally withstood the test of time regarding the covenantal character of vast swaths of Judaism in Paul's day. Even scholars with a robust "Lutheran" interpretation of Paul's theology frequently recognize that Luther's understanding of Judaism was skewed in its main emphases.[18]

From this development, the following question naturally arose: How are we to understand Paul (especially his letters to Galatia and Rome) against the backdrop of this new perspective on Judaism? Sanders himself offered some reflections on this over the course of his academic career, but his early assessment rang out loudly and clearly: For Paul, "the only thing wrong with Judaism was that it was not Christianity."[19] To state things in this way was, for James Dunn, wholly inadequate. Dunn thought this formulation to be unrefined, as if Paul's articulation of "Christianity" could be divorced from engaging with the broader context of Early Judaism. For Dunn, there had to be more nuance to Paul's discourse than Sanders allowed, since Dunn saw Paul's

---

[17] See, for instance, Schoeps 1959.   [18] Westerholm 2003.
[19] Sanders 1977:552.

discourse to have more traction within the Judaism of his day than Sanders seemed to be proposing.[20]

Whereas Luther thought the problem that Paul attacked was a theology that prioritized the necessity of "works" in general, Dunn reformulated things so that what Paul addressed was a theology that prioritized the necessity of "works of the Torah" – that is, works that were central features of Jewish identity in the Mosaic Torah (as in Gal 2:16; 3:2, 5, 10).[21] According to Dunn, the issue that Paul addressed in Galatians was not human "works" per se but practices that demonstrated Jewish obedience to God's covenant with them. Instead of the problem being works righteousness, Paul was countering the prioritization of an ethnic identity. Dunn thought his interpretation (which he named "the new perspective on Paul") gave Galatians its radical, pointed, and prophetic edge: "What Paul protested against" was a particular form of "assessing human worth," an insidious assessment of identity-calculation that went to a "more fundamental" issue "than the question of [human] ability to perform good works" – that fundamental issue being "the assumption that the way people are constituted by birth" determines their worth before God.[22] Galatians demonstrates that divine grace erodes people's certainty that divine favor is channeled in relation to particular forms of identity over other

---

[20] See his collection of essays in Dunn 2005. See also Hooker 1982.
[21] Thomas 2020 argues that the "church fathers" read Paul in precisely this light.
[22] Dunn 1993b:142–43. Dunn was careful to note that perhaps only some (but not necessarily all) first-century Jews adopted this characteristic and that it is not essential to Jewish identity in all times and places (Dunn 1990:249–50; 1993a:172). Sanders's follow-up to his 1977 work (Sanders 1983) is very much in line with Dunn's interpretation, although this similarity is frequently overlooked in overviews of scholarship; see, for instance, Sanders 1983:154–60.

forms of identity. That age-old trick, in which God is aligned with particular forms of power, is precisely what Paul opposed in the agenda of the new teachers at Galatia. Dunn thought Galatians was powerfully prophetic and that it addresses a core feature of the human condition.[23] The Swedish bishop Krister Stendahl had said much the same in his influential work of 1976, finding Paul's discourse about justification to have been "triggered by the issues of divisions and identities in a pluralistic and torn world."[24] As we will see, many people living in oppressive contexts would likely agree with Stendahl and Dunn on the profoundly liberative potential of Galatians for addressing deeply entrenched systems of injustice.

Despite Dunn's own perception of Galatians as radically liberative, others saw his work as relatively flat theologically, giving us a Paul who did little more than reinterpret "covenantal nomism" to include gentiles in the mix. Whereas Dunn thought Sanders's Paul was an anomaly "outwith" Early Judaism (as the Scot in Dunn would say it), some thought Dunn's Paul was too indistinct within Early Judaism. Dunn could speak of "the covenant purpose of God now [having] reached its climax in Christ Jesus,"[25] with that climax having world-altering implications for individuals, communities, and society. But Dunn's focus was so much on relationships between Jews and gentiles in Christ that he tended to neglect the way Paul's discussion frames that issue in terms of the human condition more fundamentally and the failure of the Torah to address that condition.[26] For some critics, what Dunn ends up with is a salvation-historical scheme in which

---

[23] See Dunn 2005:32–36.   [24] Stendahl 1976:40.   [25] Dunn 1990:202.
[26] Dunn sometimes did justice to that dimension of Paul's discourse. See for instance his discussion of "the flesh" (*sarx*) in Dunn 1994:70.

gentiles are simply inserted into Israel's covenant relationship; in this, Paul was simply correcting a misunderstanding about covenant identity. But Paul's critique of the Torah's inability to give life goes much deeper than a misunderstanding.[27] Late in his career, Dunn claimed that his advocacy of "the new perspective" was never intended to dislodge more traditional (or "Lutheran") interpretations of Paul's discourse.[28] In his early contributions, however, Dunn seemed to juxtapose these approaches as an either-or rather than a both-and. If he had been more nuanced early on, the debate might have been much different and potentially more productive.[29]

Along with Dunn and as early as 1978, N. T. (Tom) Wright was at the forefront of rethinking Paul's discourse in the wake of Sanders's description of Judaism as "covenantal nomism." Over the years, Wright has refined his interpretation, with the most nuanced presentation of his ideas embodied in his magnum opus *Paul and the Faithfulness of God* in 2013. Wright's interpretation is much more firmly narratival than Dunn's. For Wright, God's faithfulness to Israel is shown ultimately in Christ Jesus, who undertook Israel's own God-given assignment, living out Israel's predicament and embodying Israel's role as the light to the nations. The glory of God had been absent from Israel in exile until the messiah Jesus took Israel's exilic curse upon himself in his death. God always intended to deal with the sins of the world in this way, piling them up on Israel, in whose position Jesus stood, being the faithful Israelite through whom the divine plan singularly flows. Consequently, God is reassembling "Israel" (in a sense)

---

[27] Dunn responded to the criticism in Dunn 2005:26–33.
[28] See Dunn 2005:29–30, 33; 2014.
[29] B. Longenecker 1998 is an early attempt to avoid the either-or.

by incorporating Jews and gentiles into the resurrected messiah. Paul's discourse is thoroughly Jewish as well as thoroughly revisionist in the light of the coming of the messiah. Galatians plays an early part in that vision, bringing Jews and gentiles together in the messiah as the worldwide family of Abraham, an embodiment of God's transformation of new creation. The salvation history overseen by God in the past has now been radically transformed in light of Christ, with retrospective christological insight reframing what God was doing in the past in view of the eschatological coming of the messiah.

In an important development of Sanders's work, John Barclay's *Paul and the Gift* (2015) demonstrated that while grace may have undergirded most Jewish discourse in Early Judaism (as Sanders showed), it is not everywhere the same (as Sanders did not show).[30] Barclay illustrated that the conversations about divine grace and human action were being carried out in Early Judaism, with different "perfections" affecting the way the two were seen to be related. A text like Galatians is very much a part of that diversity of conversation within the Judaism of Paul's day, although radically so. In Galatians, Paul is shown to contest against the claim that a particular form of human worth can count as something of value in God's sight. Here Paul's discourse of grace differs from most other discourses of grace, or gift, since gifts were responsibly given only to recipients who were already worthy in some fashion. Paul's discourse of God's incongruous grace is applicable both to the issue of Jews and gentiles in Christ and to claims of preferential human status or identity in general, with the social relationships of those in Christ being the location where divine grace is embodied, expressed, and performed.

---

[30] See also the abbreviated version in Barclay 2020.

GOD'S APOCALYPTIC INVASION

One of Dunn's critics was J. Louis Martyn.[31] Martyn considered Dunn's view of Galatians to be a domestication of Paul's "apocalyptic" discourse, being closer to the new teachers' "salvation-historical" gospel than to Paul's apocalyptic gospel. For Martyn, it is as if Dunn started with covenantal nomism and simply added a dose of christology to the mix. In Martyn's view, Galatians shatters any attempt to add Christ to any preexisting formulation, since God in Christ is not containable within any previously established scheme. With humanity being "under" various cosmic forces, Paul's participationistic discourse exhibits an apocalyptic register in which God rescues people from suprahuman forces that have enslaved humanity. Paul's focus was on how God has taken the initiative in Christ to invade the cosmos, breaking into the nonsalvific histories of the world to rescue people from their various forms of bondage and to rectify the cosmos. The issue in Galatians is less about confrontation between people-groups (i.e., Jews and gentiles) and more about confrontation between God and anti-God forces. For Martyn, the Torah is in opposition to the will of God (being given by angels) from which the apocalyptic invasion of God in Jesus Christ rescues Christians.

Several scholars are heavily indebted to Martyn's interpretation of Galatians – including Martinus de Boer, Douglas Campbell, Beverly Roberts Gaventa, and (to a slightly lesser extent) Susan Eastman.[32] But there was a time (albeit short-lived) when things looked like they might go along different lines. In his 1980 book

---

[31] See Martyn 1991.
[32] For a survey of apocalyptic interpreters of Paul, see Davies 2022. For a survey of apocalyptic interpretations of Galatians, see B. Longenecker 2023.

Paul the Apostle: The Triumph of God in Life and Thought, J. Christiaan Beker argued that Paul's letters always display two characteristics: (1) They are situationally contingent, with each letter being a word on target for a particular situation, and (2) the situational discourses of those letters are always fed through an "apocalyptic" matrix about the eschatological triumph of God, which gives them coherence. Martyn, however, was not convinced that you could have it both ways, at least not when Galatians is in the mix. For Beker, "apocalyptic" discourse is oriented toward the future rectification of the cosmos. For Martyn, that description might work for texts like 1 Thessalonians, 1 Corinthians, or Romans but does not work for Galatians. In Galatians, the apocalyptic character of Paul's thought is centered not on the future but on God's past invasion of the cosmos – the cosmos-shattering cross of Christ. Martyn's point was effectively lodged. Whereas Beker had to see Galatians as an exception that problematized his presentation of Paul's future-oriented "apocalyptic" theology, Martyn highlighted the cross-orientation of Galatians as the heart of Paul's "apocalyptic" worldview.

It is notable also that in Beker's reconstruction of Paul's theology, God's faithfulness to the ethnic people of Israel is at the core of everything "apocalyptic"; if God could be shown to be unfaithful in his commitment to ethnic Israel, the whole apocalyptic scheme would collapse.[33] For Beker, God's faithfulness will be revealed in the future. Beker made this case largely on the basis of Paul's discourse in Romans – not least Romans 11. Martyn, in effect, posed the question to Beker, "Where do you see that future-oriented faithfulness to Israel in Galatians? Galatians is devoid of salvation-historical commitments, except God's promise to

---

[33] Beker 1986; 1990:21-22.

Abraham."[34] Beker had no comeback. And so, for many years since, the apocalyptic approach to Paul shifted from Beker's lane (in a sense) to Martyn's.

RACIAL JUSTICE

The approaches outlined in the previous sections overlap with the interpretations of those who see Galatians as fertile soil for challenging the ecclesiastical and cultural impediments to racial justice. Despite their suppression in the "Jim Crow South" of the United States, some people of African descent raised their voice against certain forms of North American Christianity.[35] William J. Seymour (1870–1922), a Black charismatic minister, likened the prejudices against Black people within many American churches to Peter's "prejudices" against gentiles in Gal 2:11–14. He called on American churches to embrace Paul's call to stand firm in the truth of the gospel, referencing also Gal 3:28 (with its uniting of enslaved and free) as an egalitarian manifesto. Galatians 3:28 was a primary text in the prophetic voices of other Black ministers as well, such as Charles Harrison Mason (1864–1961) and Martin Luther King Jr. (1929–1968). King coupled that verse with Paul's emphasis on "new creation" in 6:15, although he also noted that the new patterns of behavior that the gospel calls Christians to embody will inevitably result in "the marks of Jesus" being pressed into their bodies by their persecutors – referencing Paul's experience of persecution in Gal 6:17 and foreshadowing King's own assassination in 1968. For Reverdy Cassius Ransom (1861–1959), an African Methodist Episcopal pastor, Paul's call to do good to

---

[34] See Martyn 1982.
[35] The following two paragraphs draw material from Bowens 2020.

all in the household of trust (Gal 6:10) served as an indictment against segregationist churches in America.

Just as Seymour spoke of his "love" for "white brethren and sisters," so too a nineteenth-century Black man known only as Charlie testified to his Christian love for his former enslaver. When his former enslaver met with him some thirty years after their enslaver-slave relationship had ended, the enslaver apologized for his earlier brutality. Charlie responded as follows: "I have forgiven you ... I love you as though you never hit me a lick, for the God I serve is a God of love, and I can't go to his kingdom with hate in my heart." Trying to live a life worthy of Paul's gospel, Charlie explained how he had left the past behind: "I had felt the power of God and tasted his love, and this had killed all the spirit of hate in my heart ... Whenever a man has been killed dead and made alive in Christ Jesus [referencing Gal 2:19–20], he no longer feels like he did when he was a servant of the devil."

These interpretative initiatives have been carried forward by Black interpreters of Galatians in the early twenty-first century. For instance, in *No Longer Slaves: Galatians and African American Experience* (2002), Brad Ronnell Braxton reads Galatians through the experiences of Americans of African descent, demonstrating the striking relevance of Paul's argument for Christian engagement with racial bias in twenty-first-century America. Paul's charge that love of neighbor is linked to a healthy respect of one's own self (5:14) connotes that Americans of African descent should be affirming their Blackness and telling their own stories, both individually and communally, as a starting point in the implementation of Paul's corporate vision.[36] Paul's

---

[36] Braxton 2002:8–20, 32–34, 59–64, 105–9.

own sense of apostolic authority (Gal 1–2) confirms the sense in African American communities that validation does not come from structures organized by people with other skin colors and cultures but ultimately from God. Galatians affirms the celebration of one's own cultural heritage while also affirming that of others, in unity that comes from being in Jesus Christ. More recent is Esau McCaulley's *Reading while Black: African American Biblical Interpretation as an Exercise in Hope* (2020). Although it is not a work on Galatians in particular, McCaulley notes the liberative potential of Gal 3:28 (highlighting its unpopularity among enslavers) and reads "the present evil age" (1:4) to include the enslavement and economic exploitation of Paul's world, propped up by spiritual forces of evil. While Galatians is not a call for Christians to establish God's kingdom on earth, it is a call for discernment of the spiritual forces that are manifest within the structures of cultures.[37]

GENDER AND POWER

In a similar way to interpretations foregrounding race and identity, feminist, postcolonial, and womanist engagements with Galatians in the late twentieth and early twenty-first centuries have also offered readings of Galatians with regard to gender and colonialist constructs of identity.[38] The content of Gal 3:28 is often seen to offer the basis for fostering female agency among those in Christ (together with Paul's emphasis on freedom from

---

[37] For their earlier work in New Testament studies, see Braxton 2000; McCaulley 2019. Wan 2023 points out the limitations of Gal 3:28 as a social program of liberation.

[38] The impetus for this derives especially from Schüssler Fiorenza 1983.

the restraints of the *stoicheia* in 4:3, 9).[39] Moreover, whereas the new teachers direct the Galatians' focus androcentrically on circumcision, Paul fragments that focus, thereby opening space for female agency within Christ-groups.[40] If some features of Galatians offer glimpses of innovative relationships along gender lines, it is nonetheless recognized that Paul was often constrained by his historical context, with his own situational discourses critiqued at times in light of the ideal vision of his gospel.

The view that Paul's theology is ultimately liberative for women is not some late development in the history of interpretation. It has early expressions in a second-century text like *Acts of Paul and Thecla* and in second-century Montanism, both of which recognized Paul's theology to involve radical freedom for women.[41] It is also prefigured in the experiences of Black women centuries after the second century.[42] In the nineteenth century, the free Black woman Zilpha Elaw (1790–1800s [death date unknown]) had a powerful preaching ministry. Having felt called by God, she saw Paul's own apostolic legitimacy as paving the way for preaching ministries like hers – those that run contrary to the expectations of others but are empowered by God nonetheless. A near contemporary of Elaw, Julia Foote (1823–1901) was a Black woman deacon. In her autobiography, the union with Christ evident in Gal 2:19–20 suggests transformation beyond

---

[39] Eisenbaum 2001.
[40] Wiley 2005. But see the cautions against a latent anti-Judaism in this approach in A. Levine 2006:73.
[41] On women and gender in the apocryphal Acts (including the *Acts of Paul and Thecla*), see Hylen 2015; Streete 2021; on Montanism, see Trevett 1996.
[42] The rest of this paragraph draws on Bowens 2020 and Andrews 1986. See also Foote 1879. As Bowens makes clear, not all African Americans have found the Pauline corpus to be liberative.

cultural identities. Combined with her own personal commission from God (as in Gal 1) and Paul's words in Gal 3:28, Foote saw herself in Pauline terms in her influential preaching ministry. One of her sermons led to the conversion of a renowned enslaver; after the event she describes the situation in Paul's words: She had birthed Christ within him (compare Gal 4:19).

Further along this trajectory of liberative readings, postcolonial readings of Galatians depict Paul as one who stands against the discourse of power used to fortify the prospects of the powerful.[43] For Paul, the power of the cross comes face-to-face with the power of empire – especially the Roman imperial order and its underlying ideology. Those who controlled the power structures of the world tried to eject Jesus Christ from their spheres of influence; God's resurrection of Jesus Christ signals the illegitimacy of oppressive power conglomerations of the world. Even imperialist definitions of gender are at stake. So in Galatians, Paul's own body is demasculinized by weakness (4:12) and marked by emasculating stripes of vulnerability (6:17); God's calling stopped Paul in his tracks – the tracks of one blindly following the course of (male) domination (1:13–14) – so Paul can even liken himself to a mother giving birth (4:19; see also Paul's image of himself as a nursing mother in 1 Thess 2:7). Paul's discourse and actions strike against the gendered assumptions of power, as defined by the imperialism of the Roman world.

Postcolonial readings are close siblings to transgender and womanist readings of Galatians. In transgender interpretations, Paul's wish that the new teachers would castrate themselves in 5:12 is taken to illustrate a nonbinary potential in relation to

---

[43] See Lopez 2008; Niang 2009; Kahl 2010; Bedford 2016; Harker 2018.

sexual differentiation. The same is true for Paul's negation of the "male and female" binary in 3:28, and Paul's mothering imagery in 4:19 is seen not simply as a feminized metaphor but as holding transgender potential.[44] Much like feminist and postcolonial readings, womanist readings locate issues of gender equality within their broader contexts of racial and class-based oppression. In this, the experiences of Black women in the struggle for justice often serve as the arbitrator for what can ethically be said about Paul's discourse. At times, Galatians fares well in this enterprise, with Gal 3:28 being seen as a "counter-terror rhetoric" of cultural and political challenge.[45] At other times, even if there are aspects of Galatians that foster female agency, there is also a perceived need to push back against the form of Paul's discourse. His use of an enslaved woman (Hagar) as an example of fleshly existence to be despised (Gal 4:21–31) is seen as an instance of an empowered person (legally free and male) buying into culturally oppressive stereotypes unreflectively and potentially harmfully. And Paul's rejection of circumcision as a phenomenon of "the flesh" or the body has been compared to the rhetoric of the ruling authorities of any age who seek to control the bodies of others (especially those of Black women).[46] Rhetorical strategies that belittle others (as in Paul's charge that the Galatians are "foolish" in 3:1 or his "castrate themselves" of 5:12) are called out as rhetorically demeaning and ethically egregious.[47] The very practice of "othering" people as opponents, as Paul does of the new teachers, is vilified.[48] Interpretations of this kind are less interested in the content of

---

[44] See Marchal 2020:68–112.　[45] See Parker 2018; 2021; M. Smith 2020.
[46] See Kaalund 2021; Gabrielle 2023.　[47] Kaalund 2020:36–37.
[48] See Yarbro Collins 2023:15.

Paul's discourse than in the kinds of power relationships that his discourse builds on and the extent to which that discourse engenders the human flourishing of all.[49]

Meanwhile, Kathy Ehrensperger has argued that evaluations of Paul's discourse need to take full account of its historical context. Paul clearly intended to influence Christians, of course, but not as a dominating tyrant seeking to control the powerless – a model evident in imperialistic structures of the day. The very fact that Christ-groups were voluntary in nature prevents us from seeing Paul in that light. Instead, Paul's discourse is more along the lines of a nurturing parent. All good parents use discourse (sometimes strenuously pronounced discourse) to steer their children, and those power relationships are always asymmetrical. But the ethical question about asymmetry is whether parents are rearing children to help them emerge from that asymmetry and flourish beyond it. Asymmetry is only domination when it is established in fixed, stabilized hierarchies that are intended to be permanently ongoing. Paul's ministry in general, including his discourse in Galatians, does not conform to domination. Instead, we more often see relationships of trust between Paul and the Christ-groups that he helped to found. The fact that he established Christ-groups and then moved on, without establishing proxy leaders subservient to him, suggests as much. When writing subsequent letters occasioned by issues within those assemblies, Paul sought to guide them in order to empower them (with the Spirit, we might say with reference to Galatians) and remove himself from their indigenous forms of development.[50]

---

[49] Yarbro Collins 2023. [50] See Ehrensperger 2004; 2009; 2022.

JEWISH AND MUSLIM INTERPRETERS

How has Paul been received by Jews in the last century or so, especially with regard to his discussions of Jews and belief in Christ? The Jewish scholar Hyam Maccoby gave voice to the view that Paul was a charlatan, mixing together a hodge-podge of religious convictions that had little to do with Judaism and seeking then to disguise his roguish invention with a dose of quotations from the Torah but taken out of context (as in his quotations of scripture in Galatians).[51] Other Jewish scholars have been more appreciative of what they think Paul was doing – apart from its messianic and soteriological aspect.[52] Claude Montefiore commended Paul for finding a way to introduce an alternative (albeit flawed) form of universalism into the first-century Jewish discourse. For Hans-Joachim Schoeps, modern Judaism was to be reformed in the spirit of Paul himself, even if Paul's own solution was unacceptable and heretical, not least in misrepresenting the Judaism of his own day. Richard Rubenstein commended "Paul's dream of a united mankind in which tribal and creedal differences would finally be obliterated," finding Paul's gospel to be "consistent with a compelling strain in Jewish thought that has persisted from the days of the prophets to our own time." Jacob Taubes saw Paul as a Jew whose gospel was politically explosive in its revolutionary aspects. Rabbi Nancy Fuchs-Kreimer (currently with the Reconstructionist Rabbinical College) has applauded Paul's attempt to overcome the domestication of God within Second Temple Judaism by

---

[51] See especially Maccoby 1998.
[52] Gager 2015 argues that this was also true for many Jews in the early centuries of the Christian era.

postulating a God who acted in surprisingly fresh ways, even in relation to the Torah.[53]

Similarly, Daniel Boyarin presents Paul as "a Jewish cultural critic" whose "critique is important and valid for Jews today" and whose questions "about culture are important and valid for everyone today."[54] Boyarin notes that there is a supersessionist dimension in Paul's thinking, but he also insists that "Paul's [supersessionistic] doctrine is not anti-Judaic" in itself, maintaining that "Paul's discourse [is] indigenously Jewish" in the ancient world, where supersessionistic postures were adopted by Jews in disagreement with other Jews. But that does not mean, cautions Boyarin, that Paul's indigenously Jewish discourse is therefore unproblematic. Although Paul never intended for anti-Semitism to emerge from his depiction of the Jews as Abraham's descendants "according to the flesh" (with Christians being descendants "according to the Spirit"), Paul's discourse in Galatians did have this unhealthy payoff, with Paul's theology being ultimately inimical to Jewish identity.[55]

Since the 1970s, however, some have seen Paul in much different terms altogether and without a shred of supersessionism. Pamela Eisenbaum makes the point poignantly in the title of her 2009 book, *Paul Was Not a Christian* – since he lived and died as a Jew at a time when there was no such thing as Christianity. Eisenbaum adopted the view that Paul's theology of justification by trust in Christ addressed gentiles only; Paul had no expectation that Jews needed to adopt faith in Jesus Christ. The ethnic people of Israel

---

[53] On these and other examples of Jewish scholars finding merit in Paul's project, see especially Langton 2005a. On Paul in Jewish-Christian relations, see Langton 2005b.
[54] Boyarin 1994:2–3.
[55] See, for instance, Boyarin 1993:69–70.

have their covenant and the gentiles have Jesus Christ.[56] This "two ways" interpretation, frequently credited to Lloyd Gaston and John Gager, tended to be viewed as a respectable but unconvincing attempt to make Paul more polite, more acceptable to modern sensitivities, especially in a post-Holocaust situation – after six million Jews (and others) had been hideously slaughtered as a result of an incipient anti-Semitism that thrived in certain sectors of "Christianized" Europe. But with Boyarin and others showing just how dangerous Paul's theology could be to Jewish identity, this controversial "two ways" interpretation began to gain special attraction and has some advocates among Pauline interpreters.

Meanwhile, a recent attempt to interpret Galatians "through Muslim eyes" represents a fresh development in the interpretation of Galatians. In 2018 Shabbir Akhtar published his interpretation of Galatians. The tone of his work is irenic and respectful, but Akhtar helpfully lays bare where Paul's letter oversteps the boundaries of acceptability from a Muslim perspective. So, for instance, regarding Paul's advocacy of trust in Christ, Akhtar simply notes that "Islam dismisses it as blasphemous mythology." Or with regard to the "hope of righteousness" in Gal 5:6, Akhtar notes, "[U]nlike Muslims, Christians can feel secure, through the grace of God in Christ, against incurring God's wrath and just judgement. Muslims dismiss this attitude as a presumptuous denial of the awe in which human beings should stand as they contemplate God's mysterious majesty and judgement."[57] Paul would have largely endorsed Akhtar's first sentence and seen the second as an opportunity for further discussion of the "mysterious majesty" of God in Christ.

---

[56] Gaston 1987; Gager 2000.   [57] Akhtar 2018:89 and 161 respectively.

CHAPTER 12

What Paul Might Say

The Christ-following new teachers of Galatia knew scripture. In Paul's view, they did not understand the gospel, and consequently they did not navigate scripture in accordance with the gospel. Paul claimed to understand the gospel, and so he knew how to read scripture in its light. Therein lies the letter Paul sent to the Galatians. But what might he say today?

If Paul were alive in the twenty-first century, his theological analysis of the fundamental problem in "this present evil age" would probably not be much different from that evidenced in his first-century letter to the Galatians. Perhaps he would adjust his discourse only to elaborate further on the extent to which the power of Sin has manufactured discord within our world, which seems at times to have taken our world to the brink of utter chaos – socially, culturally, politically, materially, environmentally, and technologically. Trajectories that Paul could only imagine in his world have since been elongated to "perfection" in an age where "hate your enemy" is backed by firepower at every level of society in a manner that Paul could not even have begun to imagine. The "identity influencers conscripted by the power of Sin," Paul would suggest, "have been working overtime to enslave people to the delusional importance of their own micro-identities." The successes of the power of Sin are advertised everywhere in our world, as relational dysfunction seems increasingly to take on almost a life of its own, without any sense of how it might be stopped in its tracks. Even Christ-devotion is frequently used to advance forms of political power. "To the Christians, I become a Christian, in order to win some of them," he might say (in a contemporary spin on 1 Cor 9:19–23).[1] "What a dangerous, tribalistic, idolatrous world the power of Sin has constructed," Paul might say to us, in shocked dismay.

Similarly, if Paul were alive in the twenty-first century, he would probably affirm that his theological vision of life lived "in Christ" is as important now as it was in the first century. "Christ-full living among Christ-followers is itself the embodied proclamation of divine power for a world out of joint," Paul would encourage us, with impassioned fervor and urgency. But he would also warn Christ-followers today to be vigilant against the ever-present tendency to place aspects of themselves into their definitions of what God cherishes as righteousness. In that regard, "righteousness" does not bend favorably toward particular national identities, or toward specific political parties, or toward privileged races, or toward certain cultures. Christ-followers today will need to be attentive to the insights of Christ-followers beyond their own cultural settings, in communications geared to learn from each other where they might be in danger of embedding

---

[1] For example, I've recently seen a man in a heated dispute with his neighbor (in a different US state than the one I live in) shout down his adversary with these words: "I've been justified by God, so I can kick the fucking shit out of you!" This is an individual episode of what can manifest itself when one form of micro-identity (in this case, the identity of one particular man) is aligned with God's favor – a phenomenon that (as history and current events have demonstrated over and over) is alive and well at all levels of human interaction, including much so-called Christian discourse and practice.

(even unknowingly) their own identities in the definition of what trust in Christ is to look like. This process of discernment will be as hard to accommodate as Christ-groups accommodating multiple identities in first-century Galatia. Nonetheless, it is a task urgently required of Christ-followers of the twenty-first century, perhaps in fulfillment of Paul's exhortation, "through love, become enslaved to one another" (Gal 5:13) – being attentive to the needs and insights of other Christ-followers beyond the situatedness of oneself, one's group, and one's own localized influences.

As much as we might warm to his radical vision of new creation, we might nonetheless have the nagging sense that Paul simply replicates precisely what he denounces. Could it be that by privileging one form of identity (i.e., exclusive Christ-devotion) as a macro-identity, Paul simply plays the power game that he attributes to Sin? One of the consequences of postmodern culturalization is that we have honed our expertise in deconstructing forms of foundational thinking. It is satisfying, in a sense, to dismantle ideological constructions. And perhaps Paul's can be dismissed in a single swipe with critiques of this kind while decrying Christian exceptionalism. Doesn't the pattern of his theological discourse simply map directly onto patterns of discourse that he excoriates?

Paul would be the first to agree that his discourse wields power. He calls it "the proclamation that elicits trust" (3:2, 5), and in that proclamation lies the transforming power of new creation. So power, yes. And Paul may well address the force of the question by resorting to autobiography. "I have seen God's Son, Jesus Christ, exalted as Lord. And I have seen the Spirit of the resurrected Son acting in power within communities of Christ-followers. The Philippians. The Thessalonians. The Galatians. The

Corinthians. Lives are transformed," he would say, "by a power that is only attributable to the working of the divine Spirit of the Son" (referring us to Gal 3:5 for starters). So Paul would probably be unapologetic about prioritizing the exclusivity of Christ-devotion alone. "I prioritize participation with Christ because therein lies our access to the divine life – the divine life made intimately accessible. I should be cursed if I failed to make this known. It is the good news of divine blessing," Paul would assure us, with unwavering, exceptional confidence.

APPENDIX

Did Galatians Accomplish Paul's Purpose?

Although we can never be sure, it would seem that Paul's letter did what he hoped it would do. If this letter was written in 50 or 51 (as seems likely), Paul wrote another letter to the Galatians a few years later, speaking to them in a manner that indicates his apostolic authority was still intact at that point. This is the impression given by 1 Corinthians, a letter written in 54 (a standard proposal for that letter's date). When speaking in that letter about the collection of money that he is raising for the Jerusalem Christ-followers, Paul says this: "Concerning the collection of money [*logeia*] for God's people [in Jerusalem], I expect you to do what I have directed the churches in Galatia to do" (1 Cor 16:1).[1] From this single verse we can glean that, even during his stay in Ephesus (from about 52 to 55), Paul is still in touch with the Christ-groups of Galatia, and he is still giving them directions – articulating stipulations about the collection of money that he was raising among Christ-groups he had founded in order to signify their unity with Christ-groups in the Roman province of Judea. Evidently, Paul's first letter to the Galatians did what Paul had hoped it would do. The Galatians did not abandon Paul's leadership and theological vision. Three or four years after

---

[1] On Paul's collection, see Downs 2016.

the letter was delivered, the Galatian communities were still vibrant enough for him to expect their participation in his collection efforts. Paul's view might have been that the Galatians had, indeed, listened to what scripture says, "driving out" the new teachers (recalling his words in 4:30) and affirming the good news that he had presented.

Our curiosity is piqued, however, when we turn to Paul's comments about the collection in Romans. In that letter dating from the year 57 (most likely), Paul mentions that Christ-followers from Macedonia (i.e., Philippi, Thessalonica) and Achaia (i.e., Corinth) are contributing to the collection funds, but he does not mention Galatian participation. This might well be significant. If the Galatians were still onboard with the collection at that point (two or three years after mentioning them in 1 Cor 16:1), we would expect Paul to mention that to show Roman Christ-groups the extent of support for his collection. It would not have been prudent to neglect mentioning a whole geographical area of Christ-groups that supported his mission, especially when Paul writes to Roman Christ-groups in order to lay the foundation for a future mission to Spain, with the support (including financial support) of the Roman Christ-followers.

Are there other options to explain Paul's failure to mention Galatian support when writing Romans? Perhaps the Galatian Christ-groups had fallen apart in the mid 50s (because of financial hardships). It is hard to imagine all those communities disbanding, however. Since Galatian Christ-groups were probably still in existence when Paul wrote Romans, perhaps Paul didn't mention their support because they had already collected their contribution and sent it to Jerusalem. But it is still somewhat curious that Paul didn't mention that. If Paul had known about the Galatians already sending support to Jerusalem in their own entourage of members, wouldn't he have found a way to signal their support in that manner?

Other options? Perhaps the Galatians dropped out of Paul's orbit of apostolic authority between the writing of 1 Corinthians and the writing of Romans. What would have prompted that? Perhaps it was the collection itself. The Corinthian letters might provide some clues in this regard. In 1 Cor 16:1, Paul calls the collection a *logeia* (in Greek), which does not really suggest a voluntary collection but more of a mandatory requirement.[2] The next year, when discussing the collection again in two full chapters (2 Cor 8–9), Paul never once uses that term; instead, he repeatedly points out the voluntary nature of the collection. This shift in the way Paul characterizes the collection probably indicates that the Corinthians had reacted badly toward the notion that they were required to participate. We know that after Paul wrote 1 Corinthians, his relationship with the Corinthians took a nosedive (as indicated repeatedly in 2 Corinthians). It is just possible that the Galatians had much the same reaction, perhaps pertaining to the idea that they were virtually required to do such a thing (as a *logeia*). Paul had founded Galatian Christ-groups in the late 40s; he wrote them a scorching letter in 50 or 51; then around 53 he wrote to them again, directing them to participate in a collection of funds. Perhaps the Galatian Christ-groups decided that they were not going to participate; it might just have been a stretch too far.[3] The Corinthians seem to have been restored to good relations with Paul again by 56 or 57 (when Paul wrote

---

[2] See Esler 2022.

[3] The other option, but far less likely, is that Galatians dates to the mid-50s and represents the breakdown in the relationship. But Paul's collection efforts problematize this possibility. It would mean that Paul wrote the polemic of Gal 4:21–31 (Jerusalem in slavery) in the midst of the collection effort for "the

Romans); by contrast, it seems likely that the Galatians decided not to participate in Paul's collection, although we cannot tell what their motivation might have been or whether they considered themselves to have broken away from the orbit of Paul's apostleship as a consequence.

The fact that the Galatians were still in Paul's "camp" when Paul wrote 1 Corinthians in 54 seems to indicate that the Galatians stuck with Paul after receiving his letter in 50 or 51. Notice, however, just how significant it is that Paul undertook a collection for Christ-followers in Jerusalem after his sharp polemic in Gal 4:21–31 about the present-day Jerusalem being enslaved, like Hagar and her children. That polemic was targeted against the new teachers in particular, but it seems to assume that more than the new teachers were among those "enslaved." Probably the Christ-groups in Jerusalem are included in the indictment; beyond them might lie non-Christ-following Jews as well, since Paul credits their leaders with persecution of the Christ-movement (as in 1 Thess 2:14–16). For Paul to write such harsh polemic in his letter to the Galatians in 50/51 and then to make strenuous efforts to raise money on behalf of Christ-groups in Jerusalem as early as 53 is quite a notable development.[4] Evidently by the time Paul began his collection efforts he wanted

---

poor among the saints in Jerusalem" (Rom 15:26). All things are possible, but this is extremely unlikely.

[4] Perhaps the lack of participation by the Galatians in Paul's collection (if that is what happened) is explained by their understandable perplexity about where Paul stood with regard to Christ-groups in Jerusalem. We might imagine them to have said something along these lines: "First he tells us that Christ-followers in Jerusalem are enmeshed in slavery, then he instructs us to commit money to them in a collection he is taking on their behalf. Following him in this development just doesn't make enough sense."

it to be known that his discourse in Galatians regarding the Jerusalem Christ-groups was not the final word on the subject.

Perhaps, then, it was Paul's discourse in Galatians that was the anomaly in this ongoing relationship with Jerusalem Christ-followers. Although there were tensions in Paul's relationship with Jerusalem-based apostles, we should avoid overplaying those tensions. When writing to the Corinthians in 54, for instance, Paul mentions Peter (or "Cephas") four times, and never is there a note of animosity against him (1 Cor 1:12; 3:22; 9:5; 15:5); the same is true for his one mention of James (15:7). Perhaps, then, Galatians is the outlier in its depiction of certain apostolic tensions.

Suggestions for Further Reading

Of the more substantial commentaries published in recent years, see especially deSilva 2018; de Boer 2011; and Moo 2013. See also (in chronological order) Schreiner 2010; Das 2014; Oakes 2015; Keener 2018; 2019; and Wright 2021. Commentaries with slightly older publication dates that still repay close attention include (in chronological order) R. Longenecker 1990; Dunn 1993a; Martyn 1997a; Witherington 1998; and Hays 2000. For commentary for a general readership from a Roman Catholic perspective, see Vanhoye and Williamson 2019, and from a Protestant perspective, see S. Williams 1997.

For theological engagements with Galatians (in English) that aren't in commentary format, see Barrett 1985; Dunn 1993b; Martyn 1997b; Bachmann 2008; Congdon 2008; Das 2014; Elliott *et al.* 2014; Barclay 2015:331–446; 2020:38–74; Oakes and Boakye 2021; and Eastman 2022.

For close analysis of the Greek text of Galatians, see deSilva 2014.

Bibliography

Aageson, James W. 2023. *After Paul: The Apostle's Legacy in Early Christianity*. Waco, TX: Baylor University Press.

Abasciano, Brian J. 2007. "Diamonds in the Rough: A Reply to Christopher Stanley concerning the Reader Competency of Paul's Original Audiences." *Novum Testamentum* 49: 153–83.

Akhtar, Shabbir. 2018. *The New Testament in Muslim Eyes: Paul's Letter to the Galatians*. New York: Routledge.

Andrews, William M., editor. 1986. *Sisters of the Spirit: Three Black Women's Autobiographies of the Nineteenth Century*. Bloomington: Indiana University Press.

Ascough, Richard W. 2022. "Defining Community-Ethos in Light of the 'Other': Recruitment Rhetoric among Greco-Roman Associations." Pages 191–207 in *Early Christ-Groups and Greco-Roman Associations: Organizational Models and Social Practices*. Waco, TX: Baylor University Press.

Bachmann, Michael. 2008. *Anti-Judaism in Galatians? Exegetical Studies on a Polemical Letter and on Paul's Theology*. Translated by Robert L. Brawley. Grand Rapids, MI: Eerdmans.

——— 2021. "Die 'Opponenten' des Paulus im (heilsgeschichtlich profilierten) Galaterbrief: Alte und neue Zugänge."

Zeitschrift für die neutestamentliche Wissenschaft 112: 145–79.

Barclay, John M. G. 1988. *Obeying the Truth: A Study of Paul's Ethics in Galatians.* Edinburgh: T&T Clark.

———. 1993. "Conflict in Thessalonica." *Catholic Biblical Quarterly* 55: 512–30.

———. 1996. "'Do We Undermine the Law?': A Study of Romans 14.1–15.6." Pages 287–308 in *Paul and the Mosaic Law.* Edited by James D. G. Dunn. Tübingen: Mohr Siebeck.

———. 1999. *Jews in the Mediterranean Diaspora from Alexander to Trajan (323 BCE–117 CE).* Berkeley: University of California Press.

———. 2001. "Review of J. Louis Martyn, *Galatians: A New Translation with Introduction and Commentary.*" *Review of Biblical Literature,* November 26, 2001.

———. 2002. "Paul's Story: Autobiography as Testimony." Pages 133–56 in *Narrative Dynamics in Paul: A Critical Assessment.* Edited by Bruce W. Longenecker. Louisville, KY: Westminster John Knox Press.

———. 2011. *Pauline Churches and Diaspora Jews.* Grand Rapids, MI: Eerdmans.

———. 2014. "Grace and the Countercultural Reckoning of Worth: Community Construction in Galatians 5–6." Pages 306–17 in Elliott et al. 2014.

———. 2015. *Paul and the Gift.* Grand Rapids, MI: Eerdmans.

———. 2020. *Paul and the Power of Grace.* Grand Rapids, MI: Eerdmans.

Barrett, C. K. 1985. *Freedom and Obligation: A Study in Paul's Letter to the Galatians.* Louisville, KY: Westminster John Knox Press.

Bauckham, Richard J. 2003. "The Origin of the Ebionites." Pages 162–81 in *The Image of the Judaeo-Christians in Ancient*

Jewish and Christian Literature. Edited by Peter J. Tomson and Doris Lambers-Petry. Tübingen: Mohr Siebeck.

2017. *Jesus and the Eyewitnesses: The Gospels as Eyewitness Testimony*. Second edition. Grand Rapids, MI: Eerdmans.

Bedford, Nancy Elizabeth. 2016. *Galatians*. Louisville, KY: Westminster John Knox Press.

BeDuhn, Jason D. 2013. *The First New Testament: Marcion's Scriptural Canon*. Salem, OR: Polebridge Press.

Beker, J. Christiaan. 1980. *Paul the Apostle: The Triumph of God in Life and Thought*. Minneapolis, MN: Fortress Press.

1986. "The Faithfulness of God and the Priority of Israel in Paul's Letter to the Romans." *Harvard Theological Review* 79: 10–16.

1990. *The Triumph of God: The Essence of Paul's Thought*. Minneapolis, MN: Fortress Press.

Belleville, Linda L. 1986. "'Under Law': Structural Analysis and the Pauline Concept of Law in Galatians 3:21–4:11." *Journal for the Study of the New Testament* 26: 53–78.

Bird, Michael F. and Joseph R. Dodson, editors. 2011. *Paul and the Second Century: The Legacy of Paul's Life, Letters, and Teaching*. London: T&T Clark.

Bird, Michael F. and Preston M. Sprinkle, editors. 2009. *The Faith of Jesus Christ: Exegetical, Biblical, and Theological Studies*. Milton Keynes: Paternoster.

Blackwell, Benjamin C. 2011. "Paul and Irenaeus." Pages 190–206 in Bird and Dodson 2011.

2015. "Two Early Perspectives on Participation in Paul: Irenaeus and Clement of Alexandria." Pages 331–55 in *"In Christ" in Paul: Explorations in Paul's Theological Vision of Union and Participation*. Edited by Kevin J. Vanhoozer,

Constantine R. Campbell, and Michael J. Thate. Tübingen: Mohr Siebeck.

2016. *Christosis: Engaging Paul's Soteriology with His Patristic Interpreters.* Grand Rapids, MI: Eerdmans. Originally published as *Christosis: Pauline Soteriology in Light of Deification in Irenaeus and Cyril of Alexandria.* Tübingen: Mohr Siebeck, 2011.

2021. "The Holy Spirit, Justification, and Participation in the Divine Life in Galatians." Pages 123–43 in *Cruciform Scripture: Cross, Participation, and Mission.* Edited by Christopher W. Skinner, Nijay K. Gupta, Andy Johnson, and Drew J. Strait. Grand Rapids, MI: Eerdmans.

Boakye, Andrew K. 2017. *Death and Life: Resurrection, Restoration and Rectification in Paul's Letter to the Galatians.* Eugene, OR: Wipf & Stock.

Boccaccini, Gabriele. 2020. *Paul's Three Paths to Salvation.* Grand Rapids, MI: Eerdmans.

Bockmuehl, Markus. 2000. *Jewish Law in Gentile Churches: Halakhah and the Beginning of Christian Public Ethics.* Edinburgh: T&T Clark.

Bowens, Lisa M. 2020. *African American Readings of Paul: Reception, Resistance, and Transformation.* Grand Rapids, MI: Eerdmans.

Boyarin, Daniel. 1993. "Was Paul an 'Anti-Semite'?: A Reading of Galatians 3–4." *Union Seminary Quarterly Review* 47: 47–80.

1994. *A Radical Jew: Paul and the Politics of Identity.* Berkeley: University of California Press.

2012. *The Jewish Gospels: The Story of the Jewish Christ.* New York: The New Press.

Braxton, Brad Ronnell. 2000. *The Tyranny of Resolution: 1 Corinthians 7:17–24*. Atlanta, GA: Society of Biblical Literature.

———. 2002. *No Longer Slaves: Galatians and African American Experience*. Collegeville, MN: Liturgical Press.

Brewer, Eric J. 2022. "Suspicion, Integration, and Roman Attitudes toward Associations." Pages 33–48 in *Greco-Roman Associations, Deities, and Early Christianity*. Edited by Bruce W. Longenecker. Waco, TX: Baylor University Press.

———. 2025. "*Akoē Pisteōs* (Gal. 3:2–5) and Martin Luther's Place in Pauline Scholarship." *Journal of Theological Studies*, forthcoming.

Bryant, Robert A. 2001. *The Risen Crucified Christ in Galatians*. Atlanta, GA: Society of Biblical Literature.

Byrne, Brendan. 2014. "Jerusalems Above and Below: A Critique of J. L. Martyn's Interpretation of the Hagar–Sarah Allegory in Gal 4.21–5.1." *New Testament Studies* 60: 215–31.

Calvert-Koyzis, Nancy. 2004. *Paul, Monotheism and the People of God: The Significance of Abraham Traditions for Early Judaism and Christianity*. New York: T&T Clark.

Campbell, Constantine R. 2012. *Paul and Union with Christ: An Exegetical and Theological Study*. Grand Rapids, MI: Zondervan.

Campbell, Douglas A. 2005. *The Quest for Paul's Gospel: A Suggested Strategy*. New York: T&T Clark.

———. 2009. *The Deliverance of God: An Apocalyptic Rereading of Justification in Paul*. Grand Rapids, MI: Eerdmans.

Carter, T. L. 2005. *Paul and the Power of Sin: Redefining "Beyond the Pale."* Cambridge: Cambridge University Press.

Chester, Stephen J. 2017. *Reading Paul with the Reformers: Reconciling Old and New Perspectives*. Grand Rapids, MI: Eerdmans.

Collins, John J. 2000. *Between Athens and Jerusalem: Jewish Identity in the Hellenistic Diaspora*. Second edition. Grand Rapids, MI: Eerdmans.

Congdon, David W. 2008. "The Trinitarian Shape of πίστις: A Theological Exegesis of Galatians." *Journal of Theological Interpretation* 2: 231–58.

Cosgrove, Charles H. 1988. *The Cross and the Spirit: A Study in the Argument and Theology of Galatians*. Mercer, GA: Mercer University Press.

⸺ 2006. "Did Paul Value Ethnicity?" *Catholic Biblical Quarterly* 68: 268–90.

Coşkun, Altay. 2022. "Pauline Churches in the Galatike Chora: A New Plea for Their Location in North Galatia." Pages 323–64 in *Galatian Victories and Other Studies into the Agency and Identity of the Galatians in the Hellenistic and Early Roman Periods*. Edited by Altay Coşkun. Leuven: Peeters.

Das, A. Andrew. 2012. "Galatians 3:10: A 'Newer Perspective' on an Omitted Premise." Pages 203–23 in *Unity and Diversity in the Gospels and Paul*. Edited by Christopher W. Skinner and Kelly R. Iverson. Atlanta, GA: Society of Biblical Literature.

⸺ 2014. *Galatians*. St Louis, MO: Concordia Publishing.

Davies, Jamie. 2022. *The Apocalyptic Paul: Retrospect and Prospect*. Eugene, OR: Cascade.

Davis, Philip Andrew. 2021. "Marcion's Gospel and Its Use of the Jewish Scriptures." *Zeitschrift für die neutestamentliche Wissenschaft* 112: 105–29.

de Boer, Martinus C. 2007. "The Meaning of the Phrase τὰ στοιχεῖα τοῦ κόσμου in Galatians." *New Testament Studies* 53: 204–24.

2011. *Galatians: A Commentary*. Louisville, KY: Westminster John Knox Press.

2020. *Paul, Theologian of God's Apocalypse: Essays on Paul and Apocalyptic*. Eugene, OR: Cascade.

deSilva, David A. 2014. *Galatians: A Handbook on the Greek Text*. Waco, TX: Baylor University Press.

2018. *The Letter to the Galatians*. Grand Rapids, MI: Eerdmans.

Donaldson, Terence L. 1997. *Paul and the Gentiles: Remapping the Apostle's Convictional World*. Minneapolis, MN: Augsburg Fortress.

2007. *Judaism and the Gentiles: Jewish Patterns of Universalism (to 135 CE)*. Waco, TX: Baylor University Press.

Dörnyei, Zoltan. 2022. *The Psychology of the Fruit of the Spirit: The Biblical Portrayal of the Christ-Like Character and Its Development*. Grand Rapids, MI: Zondervan.

Downs, David J. 2016. *The Offering of the Gentiles: Paul's Collection for Jerusalem in Its Chronological, Cultural, and Cultic Contexts*. Grand Rapids, MI: Eerdmans. Originally Tübingen: Mohr Siebeck, 2008.

Downs, David J. and Benjamin Lappenga. 2019. *The Faithfulness of the Risen Christ: Pistis and the Exalted Lord in the Pauline Letters*. Waco, TX: Baylor University Press.

Dubbelman, Peter. 2020. "Augustine's View of Justification and the Faith That Heals." *Southeastern Theological Review* 11: 53–78.

Duff, Paul B. 2017. *Jesus Followers in the Roman Empire*. Grand Rapids, MI: Eerdmans.

Dunn, James D. G. 1990. *Jesus, Paul, and the Law: Studies in Mark and Galatians*. Louisville, KY: Westminster John Knox Press.

1993a. *The Epistle to the Galatians*. London: A & C Black.

1993b. *The Theology of Paul's Letter to the Galatians.* Cambridge: Cambridge University Press.

1994. *Christian Liberty: A New Testament Perspective.* Grand Rapids, MI: Eerdmans.

1998. *The Theology of Paul the Apostle.* Grand Rapids, MI: Eerdmans.

2005. "The New Perspective on Paul: Whence, What and Whither?" Pages 1–99 in *The New Perspective on Paul: Collected Essays.* Second edition. Tübingen: Mohr Siebeck.

2008. "ΕΚ ΠΙΣΤΕΩΣ: A Key to the Meaning of ΠΙΣΤΙΣ ΧΡΙΣΤΟΥ." Pages 351–66 in *The Word Leaps the Gap: Essays on Scripture and Theology in Honor of Richard B. Hays.* Edited by Ross Wagner, A. Katherine Grieb, and C. Kavin Rowe. Grand Rapids, MI: Eerdmans.

2009. *Beginning from Jerusalem: Christianity in the Making, Volume 2.* Grand Rapids, MI: Eerdmans.

2014. "What's Right about the Old Perspective on Paul." Pages 214–42 in *Studies in the Pauline Epistles: Essays in Honor of Douglas J. Moo.* Edited by Matthew S. Harmon and Jay E. Smith. Grand Rapids, MI: Zondervan.

Eastman, Susan G. 2010. "Israel and the Mercy of God: A Re-Reading of Galatians 6.16 and Romans 9–11." *New Testament Studies* 53: 367–95.

2017. *Paul and the Person: Reframing Paul's Anthropology.* Grand Rapids, MI: Eerdmans.

Eastman, Susan Grove. 2022. *Recovering Paul's Mother Tongue: Language and Theology in Galatians.* Second edition. Eugene, OR: Cascade.

Ehrensperger, Kathy. 2004. *That We May Be Mutually Encouraged: Feminism and the New Perspective in Pauline Studies.* New York: T&T Clark.

2009. *Paul and the Dynamics of Power: Communication and Interaction in the Early Christ-Movement.* New York: T&T Clark.

2019. *Searching Paul: Conversations with the Jewish Apostle to the Nations.* Tübingen: Mohr Siebeck.

2022. "Paul and Feminism." Pages 622–36 in *The Oxford Handbook of Pauline Studies.* Edited by Matthew V. Novenson and R. Barry Matlock. Oxford: Oxford University Press.

Eisenbaum, Pamela. 2001. "Is Paul the Father of Misogyny and Anti-Semitism?" *Crosscurrents* 50: 506–24.

2009. *Paul Was Not a Christian: The Original Message of a Misunderstood Apostle.* San Francisco, CA: HarperOne.

Elliott, Mark W., Scott J. Hafemann, N. T. Wright, and John Frederick, editors. 2014. *Galatians and Christian Theology: Justification, the Gospel, and Ethics in Paul's Letter.* Grand Rapids, MI: Baker Academic.

Engberg-Pedersen, Troels. 2010. *Cosmology and Self in the Apostle Paul: The Material Spirit.* Oxford: Oxford University Press.

Esler, Philip F. 1998. *Galatians.* London: Routledge.

2003. *Conflict and Identity in Romans: The Social Setting of Paul's Letter.* Minneapolis, MN: Fortress Press.

2022. "The Significance of Λογεία for the Meaning of Paul's Collection in 1 and 2 Corinthians." Pages 325–42 in *Greco-Roman Associations, Deities, and Early Christianity.* Edited by Bruce W. Longenecker. Waco, TX: Baylor University Press.

Foote, Julia A. J. 1879. *A Brand Plucked from the Fire: An Autobiographical Sketch.* New York: George Hughes & Co.

Fredriksen, Paula. 2010. "Judaizing the Nations: The Ritual Demands of Paul's Gospel." *New Testament Studies* 56: 232–52.

2017. *Paul: The Pagans' Apostle*. New Haven, CT: Yale University Press.
Gabrielle, Haley. 2023. "Re-remembering Hagar: Reading the Σάρξ in Galatians with Hortense Spillers." *Journal of Biblical Literature* 142: 305–24.
Gager, John G. 2000. *Reinventing Paul*. New York: Oxford University Press.
———. 2015. *Who Made Early Christianity? The Jewish Lives of the Apostle Paul*. New York: Columbia University Press.
Gaston, Lloyd. 1987. *Paul and the Torah*. Vancouver: University of British Columbia Press.
Gathercole, Simon. 2015. *Defending Substitution: An Essay on Atonement in Paul*. Grand Rapids, MI: Baker Academic.
———. 2018. "'Sins' in Paul." *New Testament Studies* 64: 143–61.
Gaventa, Beverly Roberts. 1986. "Galatians 1 and 2: Autobiography as Paradigm." *Novum Testamentum* 28: 306–26.
———. 2014. "The Singularity of the Gospel Revisited." Pages 187–99 in Elliott et al. 2014.
Goodman, Martin. 1998. "Jews, Greeks, and Romans." Pages 3–14 in *Jews in a Graeco-Roman World*. Edited by Martin Goodman. Oxford: Oxford University Press.
Gorman, Michael J. 2019. *Participating in Christ: Explorations in Paul's Theology and Spirituality*. Grand Rapids, MI: Baker Academic.
Grabbe, Lester L. 2021. *The Maccabaean Revolt, Hasmonaean Rule, and Herod the Great (175–4 BCE)*. Volume 3 of *A History of the Jews and Judaism in the Second Temple Period*. London: T&T Clark.
Greene-McCreight, Kathryn. 2020. "Figured In: Nonliteral Reading, the Rule of Faith, and Galatians 4." Pages 339–52

in *The Identity of Israel's God in Christian Scripture*. Edited by Don Collett, Mark Elliott, Mark Gignilliat, and Ephraim Radner. Atlanta, GA: Society of Biblical Literature.

Grindheim, Sigurd. 2013. "Not Salvation History, but Salvation Territory: The Main Subject Matter of Galatians." *New Testament Studies* 59: 91–108.

Gruen, Erich S. 2002. *Diaspora: Jews amidst Greeks and Romans*. Cambridge, MA: Harvard University Press.

Hafemann, Scott. 2014. "Yaein: Yes and No to Luther's Reading of Galatians 3:6–14." Pages 117–31 in Elliott *et al.* 2014.

Hagen, Kenneth. 1993. *Luther's Approach to Scripture as Seen in His "Commentaries" on Galatians, 1519–1538*. Tübingen: Mohr Siebeck.

Hagendoorn, Louk. 1993. "Ethnic Categorization and Outgroup Exclusion: Cultural Values and Social Stereotypes in the Construction of Ethnic Hierarchies." *Ethnic and Racial Studies* 16: 26–51.

Hall, Jonathan M. 1997. *Ethnic Identity in Greek Antiquity*. Cambridge: Cambridge University Press.

Harink, Douglas. 2017. "J. L. Martyn and Apocalyptic Discontinuity: The Trinitarian, Christological Ground of Galatians in Galatians 4:1–11." *Journal for the Study of Paul and His Letters* 7: 101–11.

Harker, Christina. 2018. *The Colonizers' Idols: Paul, Galatia and Empire in New Testament Studies*. Tübingen: Mohr Siebeck.

Harland, Philip A. 2019. "Climbing the Ethnic Ladder: Ethnic Hierarchies and Judean Responses." *Journal of Biblical Literature* 138: 665–86.

———. 2021. "'The Most Ignorant Peoples of All': Ancient Ethnic Hierarchies and Pontic Peoples." Pages 75–98 in *Ethnic Constructs, Royal Dynasties and Historical Geography around the Black Sea Littoral*. Edited by Altay Coşkun, Joanna Porucznik, and Germain Payen. Stuttgart: Franz Steiner Verlag.

2023. "Subject Peoples and Civilizational Priority: Competition among Babylonians, Egyptians, and Judeans in the Hellenistic Era." *Harvard Theological Review* 116: 317–39.

Harmon, Matthew S. 2010. *She Must and Shall Go Free: Paul's Isaianic Gospel in Galatians*. Berlin: de Gruyter.

Hays, Richard B. 2000. "The Letter to the Galatians: Introduction, Commentary, and Reflections." Pages 181–348 in *The New Interpreter's Bible 11*. Edited by Leander E. Keck. Nashville, TN: Abingdon.

2002. *The Faith of Jesus Christ: An Investigation of the Narrative Substructure of Galatians 3:1–4:11*. Second edition. Grand Rapids, MI: Eerdmans. Originally Chico, CA: Society of Biblical Literature, 1983.

2008. "What Is 'Real Participation in Christ'? A Dialogue with E. P. Sanders on Pauline Soteriology." Pages 336–51 in *Redefining First-Century Jewish and Christian Identities: Essays in Honor of Ed Parish Sanders*. Edited by Fabian E. Udoh et al. Notre Dame, IN: University of Notre Dame Press.

Heim, Erin M. 2017. *Adoption in Galatians and Romans: Contemporary Metaphor Theories and the Pauline Huiothesia Metaphors*. Leiden: Brill.

Hengel, Martin. 1987. "Der Jakobusbrief als antipaulinische Polemik." Pages 248–78 in *Tradition and Interpretation in the New Testament*. Edited by G. F. Hawthorne and O. Betz. Grand Rapids, MI: Eerdmans.

Hengel, Martin and Anna Marie Schwemer. 1997. *Paul between Damascus and Antioch: The Unknown Years*. London: SCM.

Holland, Tom. 2003. *Rubicon: The Last Years of the Roman Republic*. New York: Doubleday.
Hooker, Morna D. 1982. "Paul and 'Covenantal Nomism.'" Pages 47–56 in *Paul and Paulinism: Essays in Honour of C. K. Barrett*. Edited by Morna D. Hooker and Stephen G. Wilson. London: SPCK.
———. 1985. "Interchange in Christ and Ethics." *Journal for the Study of the New Testament* 25: 3–17.
———. 2016. "Another Look at πίστις Χριστοῦ." *Scottish Journal of Theology* 69: 46–62.
Horrell, David G. 2005. *Solidarity and Difference: A Contemporary Reading of Paul's Ethics*. London: T&T Clark.
Hubbard, Moyer V. 2002. *New Creation in Paul's Letters and Thought*. Cambridge: Cambridge University Press.
Hunn, Debbie. 2015. "Galatians 3:10–12: Assumptions and Argumentation." *Journal for the Study of the New Testament* 37: 253–66.
Hurd, John C. 2005. "Reflections concerning Paul's 'Opponents' in Galatia." Pages 129–48 in *Paul and His Opponents*. Edited by Stanley E. Porter. Leiden: Brill.
Hylen, Susan E. 2015. *A Modest Apostle: Thecla and the History of Women in the Early Church*. Oxford: Oxford University Press.
Ilan, Tal. 2002. *Lexicon of Jewish Names in Late Antiquity: Palestine 330 BCE–200 CE*. Tübingen: Mohr Siebeck.
Isaac, Benjamin. 2004. *The Invention of Racism in Classical Antiquity*. Princeton: Princeton University Press.
Jenkins, Richard. 1994. "Rethinking Ethnicity: Identity, Categorization and Power." *Ethnic and Racial Studies* 17: 197–223.

Jervis, L. Ann. 2023. *Paul and Time: Life in the Temporality of Christ*. Grand Rapids, MI: Baker Academic.

Jipp, Joshua W. 2023. *Pauline Theology as a Way of Life: A Vision of Human Flourishing in Christ*. Grand Rapids, MI: Baker Academic.

John, Felix. 2022. "Pauline Churches in South Galatia." Pages 293–322 in *Galatian Victories and Other Studies into the Agency and Identity of the Galatians in the Hellenistic and Early Roman Periods*. Edited by Altay Coşkun. Leuven: Peeters.

Johnson, Luke Timothy. 1989. "The New Testament's Anti-Jewish Slander and the Conventions of Ancient Polemic." *Journal of Biblical Literature* 108: 419–41.

Johnson Hodge, Caroline. 2007. *If Sons, Then Heirs: A Study of Kinship and Ethnicity in the Letters of Paul*. Oxford: Oxford University Press.

Kaalund, Jennifer T. 2020. "In Christ, but Not of Christ: Reading Identity Differences Differently in the Letter to the Galatians." Pages 23–43 in *Minoritized Women Reading Race and Ethnicity: Intersectional Approaches to Constructed Identity in Early Christian Texts*. Edited by Mitzi J. Smith and Jin Young Choi. Lanham, MD: Lexington Press.

⎯⎯⎯. 2021. "'You Can't See What I Can See': Reading Black Bodies in Galatians." Pages 324–38 in *Stony the Road We Trod: African American Biblical Interpretation*. Thirtieth anniversary expanded edition. Edited by Cain Hope Felder. Minneapolis, MN: Fortress Press.

Kahl, Brigitte. 2010. *Galatians Re-imagined: Reading with the Eyes of the Vanquished*. Minneapolis, MN: Fortress Press.

Kamell, Mariam J. 2014. "Life in the Spirit and Life in Wisdom: Reading Galatians and James as a Dialogue." Pages 353–63 in Elliott et al. 2014.

Keener, Craig S. 2018. *Galatians*. Cambridge: Cambridge University Press.

——— 2019. *Galatians: A Commentary*. Grand Rapids, MI: Baker Academic.

Kloppenborg, John S. 2019. *Christ's Associations: Connecting and Belonging in the Ancient City*. New Haven, CT: Yale University Press.

Kwon, Yon-Gyong. 2004. *Eschatology in Galatians: Rethinking Paul's Response to the Crisis in Galatia*. Tübingen: Mohr Siebeck.

Langton, Daniel R. 2005a. "Modern Jewish Identity and the Apostle Paul: Pauline Studies as an Intra-Jewish Ideological Battleground." *Journal for the Study of the New Testament* 29: 217–58.

——— 2005b. "The Myth of the 'Traditional View of Paul' and the Role of the Apostle in Modern Jewish-Christian Polemics." *Journal for the Study of the New Testament* 28: 69–104.

Law, Timothy Michael and Charles Halton, editors. 2014. *Jew and Judean: A Marginalia Forum on Politics and Historiography in the Translation of Ancient Texts*. Marginalia Review of Books. Ebook.

Levering, Matthew. 2013. *The Theology of Augustine: An Introductory Guide to His Most Important Works*. Grand Rapids, MI: Baker Academic.

Levine, Amy Jill. 2006. *The Misunderstood Jew: The Church and the Scandal of the Jewish Jesus*. San Francisco, CA: HarperCollins.

Levine, Lee I. 1998. *Judaism and Hellenism in Antiquity: Conflict or Confluence?* Seattle: University of Washington Press.

Levy, Ian Christopher. 2001. *The Letter to the Galatians*. Grand Rapids, MI: Eerdmans.

Linebaugh, Jonathan A. 2020. "'The Speech of the Dead': Identifying the No Longer and Now Living 'I' of Galatians 2:20." *New Testament Studies* 66: 87–105.

Longenecker, Bruce W. 1991. *Eschatology and the Covenant: A Comparison of 4 Ezra and Romans 1–11*. Sheffield: Sheffield Academic Press.

———. 1998. *The Triumph of Abraham's God: The Transformation of Identity in Galatians*. Edinburgh: T&T Clark; Nashville, TN: Abingdon.

———. 1999. "Until Christ Is Formed in You: Suprahuman Forces and Moral Character in Galatians." *Catholic Biblical Quarterly* 61: 92–108.

———. 2005. *Rhetoric at the Boundaries: The Art and Theology of New Testament Chain-Link Transitions*. Waco, TX: Baylor University Press.

———. 2010. *Remember the Poor: Paul, Poverty, and the Greco-Roman World*. Grand Rapids, MI: Eerdmans.

———. 2014. "The Love of God (Romans 5:5): Expansive Syntax and Theological Polyvalence." Pages 145–58 (and 246–48) in *Interpretation and the Claim of the Text: Resourcing New Testament Theology*. Edited by Jason Whitlark, Bruce Longenecker, Lidija Novakovich, and Mikeal Parsons. Waco, TX: Baylor University Press.

———. 2015. *The Cross before Constantine: The Early Life of a Christian Symbol*. Minneapolis, MN: Fortress Press.

———. 2016a. "Faith, Works, and Worship: Torah Observance in Paul's Theological Perspective." Pages 47–70 in *The Apostle Paul and the Christian Life: Ethical and Missional Implications of the New Perspective*. Edited by Scot

McKnight and Joe Modica. Grand Rapids, MI: Baker Academic.

2016b. "Philemon." Pages 151–96 in *Philippians and Philemon*. By James W. Thompson and Bruce W. Longenecker. Grand Rapids, MI: Baker Academic.

2018a. "Paul, Poverty and the Powers: The Eschatological Body of Christ in the Present Evil Age." Pages 363–87 in *One God, One People, One Future: Essays in Honour of N. T. Wright*. Edited by John Anthony Dunne and Eric Lewellen. London: SPCK.

2018b. "Slave and Free: Ideal Ideologies in Vesuvian Villas and in Galatians 3:28." Pages 85–102 in *A Temple Not Made with Hands: Essays in Honor of Naymond H. Keathley*. Edited by Mikeal C. Parsons and Richard Walsh. Eugene, OR: Wipf & Stock.

2020a. *In Stone and Story: Early Christianity in the Roman World*. Grand Rapids, MI: Baker Academic.

2020b. "Irenaeus, Jerusalem, and Remembering the Poor." Pages 245–53 in *Irenaeus and Paul*. Edited by David Wilhite and Todd Still. New York: T&T Clark.

2020c. "Sin and the Sovereignty of God in Romans." Pages 35–48 in *Sin and Its Remedy in Paul*. Edited by John K. Goodrich and Nijay K. Gupta. Eugene, OR: Wipf & Stock.

2020d. "What Did Paul Think Was Wrong in God's World?" Pages 171–86 in *The New Cambridge Companion to St. Paul*. Edited by Bruce W. Longenecker. Cambridge: Cambridge University Press.

2022. "Configuring Time in Roman Macedonia: Identity and Differentiation in Paul's Thessalonian Christ-Group." Pages 289–308 in *Greco-Roman Associations, Deities, and Early*

Christianity. Edited by Bruce W. Longenecker. Waco, TX: Baylor University Press.

2023. "Apocalyptic Interpretations of Galatians and the Faithfulness of God." *Zeitschrift für die neutestamentliche Wissenschaft* 114: 215–45.

2024a. "The Rupture of an Association: Social Conflict and Its Management in the Thessalonian Christ Assembly." *Journal of Biblical Literature* 143: 143–62.

2024b. "The Wrath of the Deities and the Privileged Deceased: Narrating Death in the Associational Rupture at Thessalonica." *New Testament Studies* 70: 88–98.

Longenecker, Richard N. 1964. *Paul, Apostle of Liberty*. New York: Harper & Row.

1982. "The Pedagogical Nature of the Law in Galatians 3:19–4:7." *JETS* 25: 53–61.

1990. *Galatians*. Nashville, TN: Thomas Nelson.

2015. *Paul, Apostle of Liberty*. Second edition. Grand Rapids, MI: Eerdmans.

Lopez, Davina C. 2008. *Apostle to the Conquered: Reimagining Paul's Mission*. Minneapolis, MN: Fortress Press.

Lull, David John. 1986. "'The Law Was Our Pedagogue': A Study in Galatians 3:19–25." *Journal of Biblical Literature* 105.3: 481–98.

Luther, Martin. 1953. *A Commentary on St. Paul's Epistle to the Galatians*. London: James Clarke.

Lyons, George. 1985. *Pauline Autobiography: Toward a New Understanding*. Atlanta, GA: Scholars Press.

Macaskill, Grant. 2013. *Union with Christ in the New Testament*. Oxford: Oxford University Press.

Maccoby, Hyam. 1998. *The Mythmaker: Paul and the Invention of Christianity*. New York: Barnes and Noble.

Marchal, Joseph A. 2020. *Appalling Bodies: Queer Figures before and after Paul's Letters*. Oxford: Oxford University Press.

Marcus, Joel. 2017. "Lou Martyn, Paul, and Judaism." *Journal for the Study of Paul and His Letters* 7: 112–18.

Martin, Neil. 2020. *Regression in Galatians: Paul and the Gentile Response to the Jewish Law*. Tübingen: Mohr Siebeck.

Martyn, J. Louis. 1982. "A Review of *Paul the Apostle: The Triumph of God in Life and Thought*, by J. Christiaan Beker." *Word & World* 2: 194–98. Reprinted in Martyn 1997b, pages 176–81.

———. 1991. "Events in Galatia: Modified Covenantal Nomism versus God's Invasion of the Cosmos in the Singular Gospel: A Response to J. D. G. Dunn and B. R. Gaventa." Pages 160–79 in *Pauline Theology, Volume 1: Thessalonians, Philippians, Galatians, Philemon*. Edited by Jouette M. Bassler. Minneapolis, MN: Fortress Press.

———. 1997a. *Galatians: A New Translation with Introduction and Commentary*. New York: Doubleday.

———. 1997b. *Theological Issues in the Letters of Paul*. Edinburgh: T&T Clark.

Mason, Steve. 2007. "Jews, Judaeans, Judaizing, Judaism: Problems of Categorization in Ancient History." *Journal for the Study of Judaism* 38: 457–512.

———. 2021. "Paul without Judaism: Historical Method over Perspective." Pages 9–39 in *Paul and Matthew among Jews and Gentiles*. Edited by Ronald Charles. New York: Bloomsbury.

Mason, Steve and Philip F. Esler. 2017. "Judean and Christ-Follower Identities: Grounds for a Distinction." *New Testament Studies* 63: 493–515.

Matlock, R. Barry. 2012. "'Jews by Nature': Paul, Ethnicity, and Galatians." Pages 304–15 in *Far from Minimal: Celebrating the Work and Influence of Philip R. Davies*. Edited by Duncan Burns and J. W. Rogerson. London: T&T Clark.

McCaulley, Esau. 2019. *Sharing in the Son's Inheritance: Davidic Messianism and Paul's Worldwide Interpretation of the Abrahamic Land Promise in Galatians*. New York: T&T Clark.

——— 2020. *Reading While Black: African American Biblical Interpretation as an Exercise in Hope*. Downers Grove, IL: InterVarsity Press.

Moo, Douglas J. 2013. *Galatians*. Grand Rapids, MI: Baker Academic.

Morgan, Teresa. 2015. *Roman Faith and Christian Faith: Pistis and Fides in the Early Roman Empire and Early Churches*. Oxford: Oxford University Press.

——— 2020. *Being "in Christ" in the Letters of Paul: Saved through Christ and in His Hands*. Tübingen: Mohr Siebeck.

Moses, Robert E. 2014. *Practices of Power: Revisiting the Principalities and Powers in the Pauline Letters*. Minneapolis, MN: Fortress Press.

Nanos, Mark D. 2002. *The Irony of Galatians: Paul's Letter in First-Century Context*. Minneapolis, MN: Fortress Press.

——— 2017. *Reading Paul within Judaism: The Collected Essays of Mark D. Nanos, Vol. 1*. Eugene, OR: Cascade.

Ngien, Dennis. 2023. *Grace and Law in Galatians: Justification in Luther and Calvin*. Eugene, OR: Cascade.

Niang, Aliou Cissé. 2009. *Faith and Freedom in Galatia and Senegal: The Apostle Paul, Colonists and Sending Gods*. Leiden and Boston: Brill.

Novak, David. 1983. *The Image of the Non-Jew in Judaism: An Historical and Constructive Study of the Noahide Laws.* Lewiston, NY: Edwin Mellen.

Novenson, Matthew V. 2012. *Christ among the Messiahs: Christ Language in Paul and Messiah Language in Ancient Judaism.* Oxford: Oxford University Press.

———. 2014. "Paul's Former Occupation in Ioudaismos." Pages 24–39 in Elliott *et al.* 2014.

———. 2022. *Paul, Then and Now.* Grand Rapids, MI: Eerdmans.

———. 2024. *Paul and Judaism at the End of History.* Cambridge: Cambridge University Press.

Oakes, Peter. 2015. *Galatians.* Grand Rapids, MI: Baker Academic.

Oakes, Peter and Andrew K. Boakye. 2021. *Rethinking Galatians: Paul's Vision of Oneness in the Living Christ.* New York: T&T Clark.

O'Donovan, Oliver. 2014. "Flesh and Spirit." Pages 271–84 in Elliott *et al.* 2014.

Oliver, Isaac and Gabriele Boccaccini, editors. 2018. *The Early Reception of Paul the Second Temple Jew: Text, Narrative, and Reception History.* New York: T&T Clark.

Osten-Sacken, Peter von der. 2019. *Der Brief an die Gemeinden in Galatien.* Stuttgart: Kohlhammer.

Pagels, Elaine Hiesey. 1975. *The Gnostic Paul: Gnostic Exegesis of the Pauline Letters.* Philadelphia, PA: Fortress Press.

Parker, Angela N. 2018. "One Womanist's View of Racial Reconciliation in Galatians." *Journal of Feminist Studies in Religion* 34: 23–40.

———. 2021. *If God Still Breathes, Why Can't I? Black Lives Matter and Biblical Authority.* Grand Rapids, MI: Eerdmans.

Perriman, Andrew. 2023. "When the Fullness of the Time Came: Apocalyptic and Narrative Context in Galatians." *Catholic Biblical Quarterly* 85: 315–32.

Pervo, Richard I. 2010. *The Making of Paul: Constructions of the Apostle in Early Christianity*. Minneapolis, MN: Fortress Press.

Phillips Wilson, Annalisa. 2022. *Paul and the Jewish Law: A Stoic Ethical Perspective on His Inconsistency*. Leiden: Brill.

———. 2023. "'One Thing': Stoic Discourse and Paul's Reevaluation of His Jewish Credentials in Phil. 3.1–21." *Journal for the Study of the New Testament* 45: 429–50.

Pollmann, Karla and Mark W. Elliott. 2014. "Galatians in the Early Church: Five Case Studies." Pages 40–61 in Elliott et al. 2014.

Prothro, James B. 2016a. "The Strange Case of Δικαιόω in the Septuagint and Paul: The Oddity and Origins of Paul's Talk of 'Justification.'" *Zeitschrift für die neutestamentliche Wissenschaft* 107: 48–69.

———. 2016b. "An Unhelpful Label: Reading the 'Lutheran' Reading of Paul." *Journal for the Study of the New Testament* 39: 119–40.

———. 2018. *Both Judge and Justifier: Biblical Legal Language and the Act of Justifying in Paul*. Tübingen: Mohr Siebeck.

———. 2023. *A Pauline Theology of Justification: Forgiveness, Friendship, and Life in Christ*. Eugene, OR: Cascade.

Rabens, Volker. 2014. "Indicative and Imperative as the Substructure of Paul's Theology-and-Ethics in Galatians?" Pages 285–305 in Elliott et al. 2014.

Riches, John. 2013. *Galatians through the Centuries*. Chichester: Wiley-Blackwell.

Riesner, Rainer. 1997. *Paul's Early Period: Chronology, Mission Strategy, Theology*. Grand Rapids, MI: Eerdmans.

Rosen-Zvi, Ishay. 2017. "Pauline Traditions and the Rabbis: Three Case Studies." *Harvard Theological Review* 110: 169–94.

Rowlandson, Jane. 2013. "Dissing the Egyptians: Legal, Ethnic, and Cultural Identities in Roman Egypt." Pages 213–47 in *Creating Ethnicities & Identities in the Roman World*. Edited by Andrew Gardner, Edward Herring, and Kathryn Lomas. London: University of London Press.

Sanders, Ed Parish. 1973. "Patterns of Religion in Paul and Rabbinic Judaism: A Holistic Method of Comparison." *Harvard Theological Review* 66: 455–78.

———. 1977. *Paul and Palestinian Judaism: A Comparison of Patterns of Religion*. Minneapolis, MN: Fortress Press.

———. 1983. *Paul, the Law, and the Jewish People*. Minneapolis, MN: Fortress Press.

———. 2015. *Paul: The Apostle's Life, Letters, and Thought*. Minneapolis, MN: Fortress Press.

Sänger, Dieter. 2006. "Das Gesetz ist unser παιδαγωγός geworden bis zu Christus (Gal 3,24)." Pages 236–60 in *Das Gesetz im frühen Judentum und im Neuen Testament: Festschrift für Christoph Burchard zum 75. Geburtstag*. Edited by Christoph Burchard, Dieter Sänger, and Matthias Konradt. Göttingen: Vandenhoeck & Ruprecht.

Schäfer, Peter. 2020. *Two Gods in Heaven: Jewish Concepts of God in Antiquity*. Princeton, NJ: Princeton University Press.

Schoeps, Hans-Joachim. 1959. *Paul: The Theology of the Apostle in the Light of Jewish Religious History*. Cambridge: Lutterworth Press.

Schreiner, Thomas R. 2010. *Galatians*. Grand Rapids, MI: Zondervan.

Schröter, Jens, Simon Butticaz, and Andreas Dettwiler, editors. 2018. *Receptions of Paul in Early Christianity: The Person of Paul and His Writings through the Eyes of His Early Interpreters.* Berlin: de Gruyter.

Schüssler Fiorenza, Elisabeth. 1983. *In Memory of Her: A Feminist Theological Reconstruction of Christian Origins.* New York: Crossroad.

Schweitzer, Albert. 1931. *The Mysticism of Paul the Apostle.* Translated by William Montgomery. London: Adam and Charles Black. Originally *Die Mystik des Apostels Paulus.* Tübingen: J. C. B. Mohr, 1930.

Segal, Alan F. 1977. *Two Powers in Heaven: Early Rabbinic Reports about Christianity and Gnosticism.* Leiden: Brill.

Smith, David. 2020. *The Epistles for All Christians: Epistolary Literature, Circulation, and the Gospels for All Christians.* Boston: Brill.

Smith, Mitzi J. 2020. "Hagar's Children Still Ain't Free: Paul's Counterterror Rhetoric, Constructed Identity, Enslavement, and Galatians 3:28." Pages 45–69 in *Minoritized Women Reading Race and Ethnicity: Intersectional Approaches to Constructed Identity and Early Christian Texts.* Edited by Mitzi J. Smith and Jin Young Choi. Lanham, MD: Lexington.

Snodgrass, Klyne R. 1988. "Spheres of Influence: A Possible Solution to the Problem of Paul and the Law." *Journal for the Study of the New Testament* 10: 93–113.

——— 2022. *You Need a Better Gospel: Reclaiming the Good News of Participation with Christ.* Grand Rapids, MI: Baker Academic.

Stanley, Christopher D. 1996. "'Neither Jew nor Greek': Ethnic Conflict in Graeco-Roman Society." *Journal for the Study of the New Testament* 64: 101–24.

Staples, Jason A. 2021. *The Idea of Israel in Second Temple Judaism: A New Theory of People, Exile, and Israelite Identity*. Cambridge: Cambridge University Press.

Stendahl, Krister. 1976. *Paul among Jews and Gentiles, and Other Essays*. Philadelphia, PA: Fortress Press.

Streete, Gail P. 2021. *Violated and Transcended Bodies: Gender, Martyrdom, and Asceticism in Early Christianity*. Cambridge: Cambridge University Press.

Stubbs, David L. 2008. "The Shape of Soteriology and the *Pistis Christou* Debate." *Scottish Journal of Theology* 61: 137–57.

Stuckenbruck, Loren T. 2017. "The Need for Protection from the Evil One and John's Gospel." Pages 187–215 in *The Myth of Rebellious Angels: Studies in Second Temple Judaism and New Testament Texts*. Grand Rapids, MI: Eerdmans.

Tedder, Samuel J. 2020. *Children of Laughter and the Re-creation of Humanity: The Theological Vision and Logic of Paul's Letter to the Galatians*. Eugene, OR: Wipf & Stock.

Thate, Michael J., Kevin J. Vanhoozer, and Constantine R. Campbell, editors. 2014. *"In Christ" in Paul: Explorations in Paul's Theology of Union and Participation*. Grand Rapids, MI: Eerdmans.

Thiessen, Matthew. 2016. *Paul and the Gentile Problem*. Oxford: Oxford University Press.

———. 2023. *A Jewish Paul: The Messiah's Herald to the Gentiles*. Grand Rapids, MI: Baker Academic.

Thomas, Matthew J. 2020. *Paul's "Works of the Law" in the Perspective of Second-Century Reception*. Downers Grove, IL: InterVarsity Press.

Torvend, Samuel. 2008. *Luther and the Hungry Poor: Gathered Fragments*. Minneapolis, MN: Fortress Press.

Trevett, Christine. 1996. *Montanism: Gender, Authority and the New Prophecy*. Cambridge: Cambridge University Press.

Vanhoye, Cardinal Albert and Peter S. Williamson. 2019. *Galatians*. Grand Rapids, MI: Baker Academic.
Walters, James C. 2003. "Paul, Adoption, and Inheritance." Pages 42–76 in *Paul in the Greco-Roman World: A Handbook*. Edited by J. Paul Sampley. Harrisburg, PA: Trinity Press International.
Wan, Sze-kar. 2023. "Mainstreaming the Minoritized: Galatians 3:28 as Ethnic Construction." Pages 68–87 in *Paul's Gospel, Empire, Race, and Ethnicity: Through the Lens of Minoritized Scholarship*. Edited by Yung Suk Kim. Eugene, OR: Pickwick Publications.
Wasserman, Emma. 2018. *Apocalypse as Holy War: Divine Politics and Polemics in the Letters of Paul*. New Haven, CT: Yale University Press.
Watson, Francis. 2004. *Paul and the Hermeneutics of Faith*. London: T&T Clark.
Wedderburn, Alexander J. M. 2004. *A History of the First Christians*. London: T&T Clark.
Wengert, Timothy. 2014. "Martin Luther on Galatians 3:6–14: Justification by Curses and Blessings." Pages 91–116 in Elliott *et al.* 2014.
Werline, Rodney. 1999. "The Transformation of Pauline Arguments in Justin Martyr's *Dialogue with Trypho*." *Harvard Theological Review* 92: 79–93.
Westerholm, Stephen. 2003. *Perspectives Old and New on Paul: The "Lutheran" Paul and His Critics*. Grand Rapids, MI: Eerdmans.
    2013. *Justification Reconsidered: Rethinking a Pauline Theme*. Grand Rapids, MI: Eerdmans.
White, Benjamin L. 2014. *Remembering Paul: Ancient and Modern Contests over the Image of the Apostle*. Oxford: Oxford University Press.

Wiley, Tatha. 2005. *Paul and the Gentile Women: Reframing Galatians*. New York: Continuum International.

Wilken, Robert Louis. 1984. *The Christians as the Romans Saw Them*. New Haven, CT: Yale University Press.

Williams, Logan. 2023. *Christology and Ethics in Galatians: Love and the Shared Self*. Cambridge: Cambridge University Press.

Williams, Sam K. 1997. *Galatians*. Nashville, TN: Abingdon.

Wink, Walter. 1984. *Naming the Powers: The Language of Power in the New Testament*. Philadelphia, PA: Fortress Press.

——— 1992. *Engaging the Powers: Discernment and Resistance in a World of Domination*. Minneapolis, MN: Augsburg Fortress.

Witherington, Ben. 1998. *Grace in Galatia: A Commentary on St Paul's Letter to the Galatians*. Edinburgh: T&T Clark.

Wright, N. T. 1978. "The Paul of History and the Apostle of Faith." *Tyndale Bulletin* 29: 61–88.

——— 2021. *Galatians*. Grand Rapids, MI: Eerdmans.

Yarbro Collins, Adela. 2023. "Ethics in Paul and Paul in Ethics." *Journal of Biblical Literature* 142: 6–21.

Young, Norman H. 1987. "*Paidagogos*: The Social Setting of a Pauline Metaphor." *Novum Testamentum* 29: 150–76.

Zetterholm, Magnus. 2016. "The Antioch Incident Revisited." *Journal for the Study of Paul and His Letters* 6: 249–59.

——— 2020. "From Jewish to Gentile 'Christianity': A Change of Perspective within the Radical New Perspective on Paul." Pages 194–204 in *Nordic Interpretations of the New Testament: Challenging Texts and Perspectives* (*Studia Aarhusiana Neotestamentica*, volume 5). Edited by Eve-Marie Becker, Ole Davidsen, Jan Dochhorn, Kasper Bro Larsen, and Nils Arne Pedersen. Göttingen: Vandenhoeck & Ruprecht.

Index of Ancient Literature

OLD TESTAMENT

Genesis, 8, 120
  12:3, 39, 147
  15, 174
  15:6, 39
  16–22, 54
  17:9–14, 9
  18:18, 39
  21:9–10, 55
  21:10, 55
  21:14–21, 55
  22, 174
  26:5, 9
Exodus, 120
  3:2, 86
Leviticus
  18:5, 9, 41–42, 144, 153, 164
  19:18, 59, 138
Deuteronomy
  6:4, 92, 168
  21:23, 42, 112
  25:1, 142
  27:26, 9, 40–42, 99
  29:20–21, 41, 99
  33:2, 86
Psalms
  7:8–9, 142
  9:4, 142
  9:7, 142
  11:7, 142
  17:1–7, 142
  17:15, 142
  18:20–24, 142
  68:17, 86
  143:2 (LXX 142:2), 34, 38, 142
Isaiah
  43:9, 142
  43:26, 142
  49:1, 28
  49:5–6, 28
  50:8, 142
  53:11, 142
  54:1, 54
Jeremiah
  1:4–5, 28
Micah
  7:9, 142
Habakkuk
  2:4, 42, 144

NEW TESTAMENT

Matthew
  5:3–10, 138
  5:18, 180
  5:46–47, 130
Mark
  12:29–30, 92
  14:36, 50, 109
John
  1:42, 30
  10:18, 106
Acts, 11, 173
  7:38, 86
  7:53, 86
  8:9–24, 180
  10:28, 121
  14:4, 173
  14:14, 173

Acts (cont.)
  14:19–20, 62
  16:20–21, 69
  17:6–8, 69
  20:35, 138
  21:18–26, 17
  21:21, 17
  21:23–26, 56
Romans, 163–66, 193, 209
  1:16, 119, 165
  1:25, 169
  2:9, 119, 165
  3:4–5, 146
  3:7–8, 34, 174
  3:8, 174
  3:9, 76, 169
  3:20, 164
  3:22, 110
  3:25, 110
  3:26, 110
  3:30, 168
  4, 119, 138
  4–5, 96
  4:6, 138
  4:9, 138
  4:9–12, 166
  4:15, 96, 164
  4:16, 166
  4:17, 105
  4:24–25, 105–6
  5, 170
  5:5, 167
  5:8, 137
  5:12–21, 110, 169
  5:13, 96, 164
  5:20, 95
  5:21, 76, 131
  6, 169
  6–7, 76, 131
  6:1, 34
  6:4, 106
  6:9, 106
  6:15, 34
  7, 82
  7:4, 106
  7:6, 167
  7:7, 96, 164
  7:7–25, 169
  7:12, 82, 164
  7:13, 164
  7:14, 82, 164, 169
  7:16, 164
  7:22, 164
  7:23, 82
  7:25, 164
  8, 131, 167
  8:1–3, 113
  8:2, 167
  8:3–13, 131
  8:4, 167
  8:6, 167
  8:6–13, 167
  8:9–11, 168
  8:11, 106
  8:14, 167
  8:14–15, 167
  8:15, 167
  8:23, 168
  8:26–27, 168
  8:34, 106
  9–11, 146, 150, 165
  9:5, 166, 169
  9:19–23, 165
  10:4, 165
  10:5, 164
  10:9, 106
  11, 19
  11:1, 152, 165
  11:1–6, 165
  11:7, 165
  11:7–25, 165
  11:11–14, 165
  11:13, 118
  11:13–22, 118
  11:13–24, 119
  11:17–24, 165
  11:18, 118
  11:19–22, 118
  11:20, 118
  11:25, 165
  11:26, 165
  11:26–29, 165
  11:28, 166
  11:28–29, 119
  12, 135
  12:8, 167
  12:13–16, 167
  12:20–21, 130
  13:11–12, 6
  14–15, 19
  14:1–15:6, 118, 166
  14:1–15:7, 119

15:7–13, 125, 146
15:8, 166
15:19, 5
15:26, 210
15:27, 119, 165
16:20, 170
1 Corinthians, 166, 193, 208, 210
1:9, 146
1:12, 30, 212
3:22, 30, 212
5:5, 170
6:12, 34, 174
6:14, 106
7:5, 170
7:17–20, 19
7:21, 108
7:21–24, 108
7:22, 108
7:29, 6
8:6, 168
9:5, 30, 212
9:19–23, 17, 205
9:23, 137
9:26–27, 132
10:1–7, 92
10:13, 146
10:23, 34, 174
10:24, 137
10:33, 137
11:1–16, 172
11:17–34, 167
12, 135
12:13, 172
13:5, 137
15, 169
15:4, 106
15:5, 30, 212
15:7, 212
15:12–17, 106
15:20, 106
15:26, 169
16:1, 208–10
16:1–4, 167
2 Corinthians, 166, 210
1:3, 169
1:8–9, 62
1:18, 146
2:11, 139
2:12, 170
4:14, 106
5:15, 106

5:17, 103
5:21, 112–13
6:3, 62
8–9, 167, 210
9:7, 138
9:13, 130, 167
11:14, 170
11:22, 152
11:22–33, 17
11:23–25, 27
11:23–27, 62
11:24, 17
11:31, 169
12:7, 170
Galatians, 166
1, 198
1–2, 52, 106, 179, 196
1:1, 25, 28, 37, 55, 104, 106, 147, 179, 181
1:1–5, 26
1:1–9, 13, 24–26
1:2, 25, 143
1:3, 25
1:4, 13, 25, 34, 37, 76, 86, 100–1, 113, 148, 196
1:6, 10
1:6–9, 26, 157
1:7, 8
1:8–9, 63
1:10, 9, 27
1:10–24, 13, 26–29
1:11, 64, 143
1:11–17, 27
1:12, 28, 179, 181
1:13–14, 22, 27, 198
1:14, 27, 56
1:15, 88
1:15–16, 29, 55
1:15–17, 181
1:15–20, 10
1:16, 28, 58, 102
1:17, 179
1:18, 28–30
1:23, 22, 28
1:40, 69
2:1, 29
2:1–10, 10, 14, 29–33, 145, 152, 181
2:1–14, 27, 29
2:2, 29, 179
2:3, 29, 31
2:4, 30
2:5, 30, 182

Galatians (cont.)
  2:6, 31
  2:6–9, 158
  2:7–8, 165
  2:9, 30–31
  2:10, 32, 167
  2:11, 30, 122, 182
  2:11–14, 10, 32–33, 145, 180, 194
  2:11–21, 14, 32–37
  2:12, 33
  2:14, 29–30, 32–33, 122
  2:15, 16, 32–33, 91, 99, 122, 152
  2:15–16, 32, 111, 152
  2:15–21, 29, 32–33, 38, 40, 144, 152
  2:16, 34, 41, 46, 58, 94, 99, 110, 142, 188
  2:16–17, 142, 144
  2:17, 20, 34–35, 74, 101, 104, 111, 122–23, 152, 170
  2:17–18, 36, 76
  2:18–19a, 35
  2:18–20, 35
  2:18–21, 35
  2:19, 20, 35, 102, 153
  2:19–20, 50, 131, 144, 184, 195, 197
  2:19a, 36
  2:19b, 36, 43
  2:19b–20, 36, 109
  2:20, 36–37, 58, 102, 109–11, 113, 131–32, 136–37, 142, 148
  2:20–21, 152
  2:21, 35, 44, 52, 56, 94, 105, 111, 143–44
  3, 43, 110
  3–4, 9, 32
  3:1, 38, 40, 134, 199
  3:1–5, 6, 32, 38, 43, 88, 134
  3:1–6, 39
  3:1–9, 14, 37–40
  3:2, 40, 188, 206
  3:3, 38, 58
  3:5, 6, 40, 50, 188, 206–7
  3:6, 39, 54, 142
  3:6–14, 50
  3:6–9, 39, 42
  3:7, 39
  3:7–9, 39
  3:8, 39, 142, 147
  3:9, 39, 96
  3:10, 21, 41–42, 98–99, 144, 188
  3:10–14, 14, 40–43, 99
  3:11, 42, 142, 144
  3:12, 41, 153, 164
  3:13, 42, 60, 99, 112, 136, 144
  3:14, 39, 42, 136, 144
  3:15, 43, 64, 143
  3:15–29, 14, 43–48
  3:16, 13, 43, 85, 177, 179
  3:17, 44, 85
  3:18, 44, 50
  3:19, 44–45, 76, 85, 87, 91, 95–96, 98, 102, 150, 179
  3:19–25, 45
  3:20, 44, 48, 88, 92, 96, 125, 168
  3:21, 21, 44, 94, 97, 142, 144, 177
  3:21–22, 184
  3:22, 16, 20, 34, 45–46, 49, 74, 76, 83, 95, 97, 100, 104, 110, 151, 154, 164, 170
  3:23, 47, 83, 90
  3:23–24, 47
  3:24, 47, 88, 142
  3:24–25, 46, 90, 150
  3:25, 98
  3:26, 48, 102
  3:26–29, 50
  3:27, 102
  3:28, 18, 48, 71, 125, 130, 151, 171, 194, 196, 198–99
  3:29, 43, 48, 55, 179
  4, 47
  4:1–2, 48
  4:1–7, 102
  4:1–11, 14, 48–52
  4:2, 49, 90
  4:3, 15, 20, 49, 74, 77, 83, 90, 197
  4:4, 49, 69, 93, 98, 112, 148–49
  4:4–5, 119, 148, 150–51, 166
  4:4–6, 168
  4:4–7, 50
  4:5, 50, 94, 148, 159, 165
  4:6, 44, 50, 88, 168
  4:7, 50–51
  4:8, 51, 92
  4:8–11, 51, 123
  4:9, 7, 15, 20, 49, 51, 74, 77, 80, 94, 107, 127, 197
  4:10, 10, 51
  4:11, 52
  4:12, 64, 143, 198
  4:12–20, 14, 52–53
  4:12b–15, 52, 133
  4:13, 134

INDEX OF ANCIENT LITERATURE 245

4:13-14, 58
4:14, 134
4:15, 134, 138
4:16, 53
4:16-17, 9
4:17, 53, 55
4:19, 53, 57-58, 64, 102, 127, 198-99
4:20, 53
4:21, 10, 21, 55
4:21-31, 10, 14, 53-56, 84, 90, 153, 177, 199, 210
4:21-5:1, 84
4:22, 54
4:23, 54, 58
4:24, 54
4:24-25, 54
4:25, 56, 63, 153
4:26, 54
4:27, 54
4:28, 55, 64, 143
4:29, 55, 58, 144
4:29-30, 54
4:30, 21, 54, 157, 209
4:31, 55, 64, 143
5, 57, 71, 130
5-6, 37-38, 110
5:1, 58, 179
5:1-12, 14, 56-58
5:2, 52, 56-57
5:2-3, 10
5:3, 56
5:4, 10, 56-57, 142
5:4-6, 141
5:5, 13, 15, 34, 57, 60, 127, 129, 141-42, 145
5:5-6, 57
5:6, 57-58, 63, 126-27, 135, 175, 184, 186, 203
5:7, 10
5:7-12, 57
5:10, 142
5:11, 64, 143
5:12, 10, 58, 198-99
5:13, 58, 61, 64, 131, 133, 135, 143, 206
5:13-6:10, 14, 58-63
5:14, 59-60, 137-38, 144, 195
5:15, 59, 72, 105
5:16, 59, 133
5:16-17, 131
5:17, 59, 131-32
5:18, 59, 133
5:19, 131
5:19-21, 59, 72, 83, 108
5:20, 92
5:20-21, 61
5:21, 13, 60, 129, 139, 144, 170
5:22, 62
5:22-23, 60, 135
5:23, 60, 132
5:24, 60, 102, 131
5:25, 61, 133
5:26, 59, 61, 72
6, 57, 130
6:1, 64, 131, 139, 143, 179
6:1-10, 61
6:2, 21, 61, 135
6:3, 61, 139
6:4, 136
6:4-5, 61
6:6, 62
6:7, 62
6:7-8, 127
6:7-10, 132
6:8, 62, 131, 133
6:9-10, 62
6:9-20, 167
6:10, 50, 130, 136, 195
6:11-18, 14, 62-64
6:12, 8, 10, 29, 63
6:12-13, 10, 63
6:12-14, 62
6:13, 58
6:14, 62, 102, 131, 179
6:15, 13, 37, 63, 103, 108, 126, 155-56, 158, 170, 179, 194
6:16, 63, 119, 141, 155-59, 165, 179
6:17, 27, 62, 194, 198
6:18, 26, 64, 143
Ephesians, 166
 1:20, 106
 2:14, 171
 2:14-16, 75
 3:6, 171
 3:10, 76, 171
 3:12, 110
 4:28, 167
 5:22-6:9, 108
 6:12, 75, 170

Philippians, 166, 173
  1:6, 146
  1:18, 17
  1:27, 64
  2:4, 137
  2:6–8, 110
  2:9–11, 28
  2:12, 132
  2:13, 132
  3:5, 152
  3:5–8, 124
  3:9, 110
  3:10, 132
  3:12–13, 132
  4:23, 64
Colossians, 166, 172
  1:15–20, 170
  2:8, 172
  2:12, 106
  2:20, 172
  3:18–4:1, 108
1 Thessalonians, 69, 166, 173, 193
  1:6, 68
  1:9–10, 4, 92
  1:10, 106
  2:2–4, 68
  2:7, 198
  2:13, 132
  2:14–16, 211
  2:18, 170
  3:7, 68
  3:12–13, 132
  4:14, 106
  4:17, 6
  5:3, 68
  5:14, 167
  5:15, 130
  5:24, 146
2 Thessalonians, 166, 173
  3:6–13, 167
1 Timothy, 166
  5:3–16, 167
2 Timothy, 166
  2:8, 106
Titus, 166
  3:13, 167
Philemon, 166, 173
  25, 64
Hebrews
  2:2, 86
  5:12, 79

James, 173–75
  2:14, 173
  2:17, 173, 184
  2:18, 174
  2:20, 174, 184
  2:21–22, 174
  2:24, 174
  2:24–26, 174
  2:26, 184
  3:13, 175
1 Peter
  2:24, 113
2 Peter
  3:16, 173, 175
Revelation, 83

EARLY JEWISH LITERATURE

Apocrypha and Pseudepigrapha

1 Maccabees, 116
2 Maccabees, 116
  2:21, 22, 27
  8:1, 22, 27
  14:38, 22, 27
3 Maccabees, 116
4 Maccabees, 116
Wisdom
  13:1–9, 79
Sirach
  44.19–20, 9
4 Ezra
  6:55–56, 121
2 Baruch
  57.1–3, 9
Apoc. Abr.
  1–8, 8
Jubilees, 153
  1.27–29, 86
  12.1–21, 8
  15.1–2, 14
  16.28, 9
  22.16, 120
  22.17–18, 120
Letter of Aristeas
  139, 120
  142, 120

Dead Sea Scrolls

4Q216
   5.1, 86

Josephus

Ant.
   1.155, 8
   15.136, 86

Philo

Contempl.
   3–5, 78
Her.
   190, 79
   197, 78
   209, 78
   226, 78
Mos.
   1.96, 78
On Dreams
   1.140–44, 86
Opif.
   131, 78
Spec.
   2.166, 47
Virt.
   219, 8

GRECO-ROMAN AUTHORS

Apuleius
   The Golden Ass
      11.23, 88
Aristotle
   Metaph.
      5.1014a–1014b, 79
      5.1014b, 79
      998.A26, 78
Cicero
   Amic.
      20.74, 89
Cleanthes
   Hymn to Zeus, 73

Diodorus Siculus
   Library of History
      5.49.5, 88
Juvenal
   Sat.
      14.97, 47
Libanius
   Or.
      58.7, 89
Lucretius
   On the Nature of Things
      2.11–13, 73
      2.14–16, 73
      6.14–16, 73
Martial
   Epigr.
      11.39, 89
Ovid
   Metamorphoses
      3.658–59, 88
Petronius
   Sat.
      44, 73
      94, 89
Plato
   Crat.
      422A, 78
   Laws
      7.790C, 79
Plautus
   Bacch.
      422–23, 89
Plutarch
   Alex.
      24.6, 89
   Mor.
      37D, 89
   Prim. frig.
      7, 79
Porphyry
   Christ., 181
Quintilian
   Inst.
      1.3.17, 89
Tacitus
   Hist.
      5.4, 116
      5.5, 116
      5.5.4, 47

EARLY CHRISTIAN
AUTHORS

Acts mart. Scillit.
  12, 177
Acts of Paul and Thecla,
  197
Books of Jeu
  1.3.5, 179
5 Ezra, 177
Ignatius
  Eph.
    12, 180
  Rom.
    4.3, 180
Irenaeus
  Haer.
    3.13.3, 182
Jerome

Epist.
  112.3.4–11, 182
Justin
  2 Apol.
    5:2, 79
  Dial., 178
Pseudo-Clementines
  Ep.Pet.
    2, 180
  Hom., 180
    2.17–18, 180
    17.13–19, 180
Tertullian
  Marc.
    5.2, 178
    5.3.3, 182
Theophilus
  Autol.
    2:35, 79

Index of Authors and Names

Aageson, James W., 177
Abasciano, Brian J., 9
Akhtar, Shabbir, 203
Andrews, William M., 197
Ascough, Richard W., 117

Bachmann, Michael, 9, 158, 213
Barclay, John M. G., 1, 16, 69-70, 106, 117, 119, 140, 153, 158, 187, 191-92, 213
Barrett, C. K., 213
Bauckham, Richard J., 116, 181
Bedford, Nancy Elizabeth, 198
BeDuhn, Jason D., 179
Beker, J. Christiaan, 193
Belleville, Linda L., 89
Bird, Michael F., 110, 177
Blackwell, Benjamin C., 1, 109, 144, 177
Boakye, Andrew K., 105, 213
Boccaccini, Gabriele, 151, 177
Bockmuehl, Markus, 17, 121
Bowens, Lisa M., 194, 197
Boyarin, Daniel, 16, 119, 202-3
Braxton, Brad Ronnell, 195-96
Brewer, Eric J., 40, 68
Bryant, Robert A., 105
Butticaz, Simon, 177
Byrne, Brendan, 153

Calvert-Koyzis, Nancy, 8
Calvin, John, 186
Campbell, Constantine R., 109
Campbell, Douglas A., 103, 186, 192
Carter, T. L., 76
Charlie, 195
Chester, Stephen J., 186
Collins, John J., 117

Congdon, David W., 213
Cosgrove, Charles H., 7, 114
Coşkun, Altay, 11

Das, A. Andrew, 99, 213
Davies, Jamie, 179, 192
de Boer, Martinus C., 8-9, 16, 79, 86, 91, 95, 131, 144, 192, 213
deSilva, David A., 9, 11, 23, 79, 213
Dettwiler, Andreas, 177
Dodson, Joseph R., 177
Donaldson, Terence L., 121, 126
Dörnyei, Zoltan, 135
Downs, David J., 110, 147, 208
Dubbelman, Peter, 184
Dunn, James D. G., 5, 16, 76, 85, 95, 109-10, 187-90, 213

Eastman, Susan G., 127, 153, 158, 192, 213
Ehrensperger, Kathy, 17, 200
Eisenbaum, Pamela, 197, 202
Elaw, Zilpha, 197
Elliott, Mark W., 176, 213
Engberg-Pedersen, Troels, 107
Erasmus of Rotterdam, 182
Esler, Philip F., 22, 114, 123, 210

Foote, Julia A. J., 197
Frederick, John, 213
Fredriksen, Paula, 9, 17, 153-54
Fuchs-Kreimer, Nancy, 201

Gabrielle, Haley, 199
Gager, John G., 151, 201, 203
Gaston, Lloyd, 151, 203
Gathercole, Simon, 76, 112

Gaventa, Beverly Roberts, 106, 109, 192
Goodman, Martin, 117
Gorman, Michael J., 139
Grabbe, Lester L., 117
Greene-McCreight, Kathryn, 84
Grindheim, Sigurd, 95
Gruen, Erich S., 117

Hafemann, Scott J., 186, 213
Hagen, Kenneth, 186
Hagendoorn, Louk, 114
Hall, Jonathan M., 115
Halton, Charles, 22
Harink, Douglas, 86
Harker, Christina, 198
Harland, Philip A., 114–15
Harmon, Matthew S., 84
Hays, Richard B., 109–10, 213
Heim, Erin M., 102
Hengel, Martin, 5, 174
Holland, Tom, 73
Hooker, Morna D., 103, 110, 188
Horrell, David G., 125
Hubbard, Jeff, 1
Hubbard, Moyer V., 103
Hunn, Debbie, 99
Hurd, John C., 9
Hylen, Susan E., 197

Ilan, Tal, 116
Isaac, Benjamin, 115

Jenkins, Richard, 115
Jervis, L. Ann, 93
Jipp, Joshua W., 136
John, Felix, 11
Johnson, Luke Timothy, 114
Johnson Hodge, Caroline, 107

Kaalund, Jennifer T., 199
Kahl, Brigitte, 198
Kamell, Mariam J., 174
Keener, Craig S., 11, 23, 90, 213
King, Martin Luther, Jr., 194
Kwon, Yon-Gyong, 142

Langton, Daniel R., 202
Lappenga, Benjamin, 110, 147
Law, Timothy Michael, 22
Levering, Matthew, 184
Levine, Amy Jill, 197

Levine, Lee I., 117
Levy, Ian Christopher, 176
Linebaugh, Jonathan A., 109
Longenecker, Bruce W., 16, 68, 70–71, 76, 81, 101, 108, 125, 134, 146, 158, 167, 169, 179, 190
Longenecker, Richard N., 17, 89, 95, 213
Lopez, Davina C., 198
Lull, David John, 89, 95
Luther, Martin, 17, 182–86, 188
Lyons, George, 106

Macaskill, Grant, 109
Maccoby, Hyam, 201
Marchal, Joseph A., 199
Marcus, Joel, 153
Martin, Neil, 123
Martyn, J. Louis, 9, 16, 86, 91, 95, 144, 153, 164, 192–94, 213
Mason, Charles Harrison, 194
Mason, Steve, 22
Matlock, R. Barry, 153
McCaulley, Esau, 196
Melanchthon, Philip, 186
Moo, Douglas J., 90, 157–58, 213
Morgan, Teresa, 22, 109
Moses, Robert E., 79

Nanos, Mark D., 17, 151
Ngien, Dennis, 186
Niang, Aliou Cissé, 198
Novak, David, 121
Novenson, Matthew V., 17, 23, 154, 158

Oakes, Peter, 134, 144, 213
O'Donovan, Oliver, 140
Oliver, Isaac, 177
Osten-Sacken, Peter von der, 158

Pagels, Elaine Hiesey, 179
Parker, Angela N., 199
Perriman, Andrew, 170
Pervo, Richard I., 177
Phillips Wilson, Annalisa, 124–25
Pollmann, Karla, 176
Prothro, James B., 15, 142, 144

Rabens, Volker, 140
Ransom, Reverdy Cassius, 194
Riches, John, 176
Riesner, Rainer, 5

INDEX OF AUTHORS AND NAMES

Rosen-Zvi, Ishay, 177
Rowlandson, Jane, 115
Rubenstein, Richard, 201

Sanders, Ed Parish, 11, 103, 186–88
Sänger, Dieter, 89
Schäfer, Peter, 16
Schoeps, Hans-Joachim, 187, 201
Schreiner, Thomas R., 95, 213
Schröter, Jens, 177
Schüssler Fiorenza, Elisabeth, 196
Schweitzer, Albert, 103
Schwemer, Anna Marie, 5
Segal, Alan F., 16
Seymour, William J., 194
Smith, David, 164
Smith, Mitzi J., 199
Snodgrass, Klyne R., 78, 109
Sprinkle, Preston M., 110
Stanley, Christopher D., 114
Staples, Jason A., 159
Stendahl, Krister, 16, 189
Streete, Gail P., 197
Stubbs, David L., 110

Taubes, Jacob, 201
Tedder, Samuel J., 84
Thate, Michael J., 109
Thiessen, Matthew, 17, 107, 122, 151, 153

Thomas, Matthew J., 188
Torvend, Samuel, 185
Trevett, Christine, 197

Vanhoozer, Kevin J., 109
Vanhoye, Cardinal Albert, 213

Walters, James C., 102
Wan, Sze-kar, 196
Wasserman, Emma, 79
Watson, Francis, 92
Wedderburn, Alexander J. M., 5
Wengert, Timothy, 186
Werline, Rodney, 178
Westerholm, Stephen, 15, 186–87
White, Benjamin L., 177
Wiley, Tatha, 197
Wilken, Robert Louis, 181
Williams, Logan, 140
Williams, Sam K., 213
Williamson, Peter S., 213
Wink, Walter, 79, 82
Witherington, Ben, 213
Wright, N. T., 16, 91, 158, 190–91, 213

Yarbro Collins, Adela, 199
Young, Norman H., 89

Zetterholm, Magnus, 17

Subject Index

Abraham, 8–9, 12–13, 38–40, 42–44, 48, 50, 53–56, 71, 91, 120, 125, 142, 144, 147, 166

circumcision, 30–31, 56–57, 64, 155, 158
collective worship of God, 124–26, 142, 145, 149

ethnic hierarchies, 114–24

faithfulness of God, 39–40, 109–11, 146–50
to ethnic Israel, 148–50, 157–59, 166
intra-divine faithfulness, 147–48
financial generosity, 62, 166–67
remember the poor, 30–31, 167

Galatians
and non-Pauline NT texts, 172–75
outline of, 13–14
and the Pauline corpus, 166–72
and Romans, 163–66
Galatians in reception history
apocalyptic, 191–94
early church, 176–82
Early Judaism, 186–91
gender and power, 200
Jewish and Muslim interpreters, 200–3
Luther and the medieval church, 182–86
racial justice, 194–96

historical context, 4–11, 92, 117–18, 130

idolatry, 4, 7–8, 12–13, 47, 49, 51, 59, 91–94, 96, 98, 109, 120–21, 125–26, 140, 149

interpretative approaches
apocalyptic, 15–16
new perspective, 16
radical new perspective, 16–18
traditional, 14–15
two ways, 150–55
Israel of God, 64, 155–59

Jerusalem, 9–10, 28–31, 54, 63
Jesus Christ
being in, 12–13, 43, 48, 50, 102–4, 125, 140, 145
born under the Torah, 148–49
comes alive, 28, 36–37, 50–51, 61, 64, 109–11, 123, 140
the death of, 35–36, 42, 62–63, 98, 100–9, 111–13
dying with, 12–13, 36–37, 102–9, 111–13, 123
and monotheism, 44–45, 125, 168–69
and mystery deities, 28, 87–88
the nonexistence of, 105–9, 123, 147–48
and relational abundance, 135–39
resurrected by God, 25, 28, 37, 88, 98, 102, 105–9, 145, 147–48
and the Roman imperial order, 72–74
sent by God, 50, 69, 94, 143, 148–49
and the sovereignty of God, 12–13, 102, 105–9, 145, 170–71
trust in, 12–13, 34, 39, 41–42, 50, 53, 56–57, 61, 145–46, 151, 165
the trust of, 109–11

macro-identity, 12–13, 48, 114, 123–26, 153
micro-identity, 12–13, 19–20, 48, 114, 123–26, 155

SUBJECT INDEX

new creation, 37, 63-64, 103, 108, 126, 155, 170
new teachers, 8-10, 32-33, 38, 40, 52-56, 62-63, 93, 157

Paul
  the authority of, 24-27
  and the Galatians, 52-53, 133-35
  life "in Judaism," 27

righteous/righteousness, 12-13, 33-35, 39, 41, 56-57, 60, 94, 111, 123, 129, 135, 141-47, 152, 155, 159

sarx, 38, 58, 152
  as the propensity for self-centered living, 58-60, 63, 72, 74, 76, 131-33
Sin, the power of, 12-13, 15-16, 20, 34-36, 45-46, 49-50, 69, 71, 74-78, 81-85, 92, 94-98, 100-3, 105-8, 111-12, 114, 116, 122-23, 126, 129-30, 145, 151, 154, 169-70
  and the power of Death, 170

sins, 12-13, 25, 34-35, 45-46, 76, 95, 100
  and forgiveness, 101-4
social Darwinism, 67, 71-74, 114, 139
Spirit of God, 6-8, 12-13, 38, 42-44, 50-51, 53, 55, 57, 59-61, 72, 78, 88, 104, 107-9, 124, 128-40, 144-47, 167-69
  the fruit of, 60-61, 135-36
stoicheia, 15-16, 20, 49, 51, 71, 74, 77-85, 123-24, 169, 172

Torah, 7-9, 12-13, 18-21, 35-36, 39-48, 51, 55, 60, 85-87, 95-98, 101, 109, 111-13, 118, 120, 125, 143, 151-53, 164-65
  the curse articulated by the, 99, 111-13
  the fulfillment of, 59
  as pedagogue, 46-48, 70, 88-94, 98, 120, 126, 147-50, 164
  as taxonomy, 49-50, 96-98, 164
trust works in enslaving love, 127-30

For EU product safety concerns, contact us at Calle de José Abascal, 56–1º,
28003 Madrid, Spain or eugpsr@cambridge.org.

www.ingramcontent.com/pod-product-compliance
Lightning Source LLC
LaVergne TN
LVHW020343260326
834688LV00045B/1506